# Bioethics in Historical Perspective

*by*
**Sarah Ferber**

palgrave
macmillan

© Sarah Ferber 2013

First published 2013 by
PALGRAVE MACMILLAN

Palgrave Macmillan in the UK is an imprint of Macmillan Publishers Limited, registered in England, company number 785998, of Houndmills, Basingstoke, Hampshire RG21 6XS.

Palgrave Macmillan in the US is a division of St Martin's Press LLC, 175 Fifth Avenue, New York, NY 10010.

Palgrave Macmillan is the global academic imprint of the above companies and has companies and representatives throughout the world.

Palgrave® and Macmillan® are registered trademarks in the United States, the United Kingdom, Europe and other countries

ISBN: 978-1-4039-8723-5 hardback
ISBN: 978-1-4039-8724-2 paperback

This book is printed on paper suitable for recycling and made from fully managed and sustained forest sources. Logging, pulping and manufacturing processes are expected to conform to the environmental regulations of the country of origin.

A catalogue record for this book is available from the British Library.

A catalog record for this book is available from the Library of Congress.

Printed in China

# Contents

For Leigh Dale

# Preface and acknowledgements

In modern 'culture wars', bioethics is a political minefield. Reading into bioethics culture, one becomes increasingly attuned to the personal or political starting points of authors. Routinely one wonders: Are they in the pay of a drug company? Is religion a motive? Are they afraid to seem radical/reactionary because of their professional position/the political climate? What exactly do they intend when they use the word 'life'? Why did they leave out this or that piece of seemingly relevant information? Are they making a tacit case for/against abortion rights? Because bioethics by its very nature leaps across cultural divides – from legislature into the clinic, from the seminary into the courtroom, from the lecture theatre into the late news bulletin, from the deathbed onto the web – the starting points of academics involved in bioethics commentary are possibly more than usually exposed to public view. Mindful of the potential for wariness in readers, bioethics authors quite often make their own position clear. If the reading of texts should not be affected by the knowledge of the author's racial, religious, gender or ethnic identity, or indeed their academic training, the growing politicization of knowledge and far-reaching debates about 'speaking position' and the meaning of authorship have made it increasingly difficult to claim such a thing as methodological objectivity in academic writing. And bioethics particularly seems to invite questions as to why people say what they say. Where, then, to separate one's own background and experience from one's professional work?

Those reading between the lines of this book might well automatically look for 'where I am coming from', so perhaps it is some help to say a little about my interest in this field. I came to bioethics from a position of 'concerned junior citizen', in the 1970s. As a 17-year-old I went to work over the summer in a Catholic psychiatric hospital. This was a period when the Scottish psychiatrist R. D. Laing was still taken seriously among those interested in mental health: anti-psychiatry was deeply bound up with cultural critique and to read Laing was as radical as reading Marx and also more fashionable. My job as it turned out – and as I had half hoped – brought me close to the medical treatment of electroconvulsive therapy (ECT or 'shock treatment'). My specific task was to hold anaesthetized patients in a stable position while they underwent the treatment and then monitor them afterwards: I lasted a full thirty minutes. The kindly mother-superior asked me to pause with her in the chapel on the way out so she could 'put a bit of religion' into me. This appears not to have worked.

Bioethics in Australia in the 1980s revolved around two major areas: psychiatry and reproductive technology. Psychiatry and psychiatric institutions were reform priorities and there was a series of government investigations into the practices of state and private psychiatric hospitals, including, most dramatically, the exposure of some terrible experiments in 'deep sleep' therapy, conducted by Dr Harry Bailey. Australia was also the second country to develop human *in vitro* fertilization (IVF) and the first in which a jurisdiction introduced laws limiting aspects of its clinical and laboratory practice. The then-new reproductive technologies were front-page news over several years and as a feminist I became concerned about the relative silences around the effects of IVF on women and on children born through anonymous donor gamete programmes. In the years I was writing a PhD on early modern French religious history, I also kept up with the medical literature, writing in the student press about problematic aspects of IVF research. Later with a group called FINRRAGE (Feminist International Network for Resistance to Reproductive and Genetic Engineering), I worked on media releases and submissions to government enquiries and set up community meetings about infertility, IVF, surrogacy and potential long-term issues for children. Little or none of this work helped make any difference to policy or regulation in Australia or elsewhere. It seems to have been simply too hard for regulators to accommodate discussions of the risks of IVF into a debate which seemed perennially split between those who seek to defend the human embryo and those who oppose the regulation of medical research. The concerns of children born through anonymous donation programmes are only beginning to surface as the children now reach adulthood, finding a voice in news reports, documentaries or a film like 'The Kids Are All Right', as well as through the work of grassroots groups.

Some of the analyses put forward by members of FINRRAGE have been referred to as 'radical feminist'. This term does not mean just radical and feminist: it refers to a political stance that holds that male–female relations are the primary axis through which power more generally is created and understood. My own views are more traditional feminist social democrat, but I was and remain wary of how readily so-called 'liberal feminism' has adapted the language of choice to accept more or less uncritically medical technologies the physical and social consequences of which seem to demand more concerted investigation.

In the end, I think the liberal view of the woman's 'right to choose' must trump other arguments, but this must stand alongside an awareness of the commercial and ideological forces which qualify and might even serve to undermine the idea of the liberal free agent. I try not to be over-confident about the rightness of my own views on this matter, and the experience of infertility has reinforced the difficulty of arguing against access even to problematic technologies.

The danger of the game of detecting the background or prejudice of the author was brought home to me sharply in the latter stages of the writing of this book. I learned through my mother's genealogical research that a cousin of my German great-grandfather was the psychiatrist and writer Alfred Hoche. In 1920, Hoche and the lawyer Karl Binding wrote a book with a title to make one shudder: *Die Freigabe der Vernichtung lebensunwerten Lebens* (*Authorization for the Destruction of Life Unworthy of Life*) which directly influenced Nazi euthanasia policy in relation to people in mental hospitals and similar institutions. Many of these people were killed under medical auspices in what has been seen as a preliminary to wider genocidal policies. As an Australian, I am accustomed to people referring with some pride to their distant convict ancestors, seeing the fame or quaint notoriety of forebears as somehow relevant to them. I do not know what to do with the thought that I can be connected with someone such as Alfred Hoche. Hoche himself is said to have repudiated his views and he was also married to a Jew, but repudiation of such repugnant ideas is less than too little too late. As someone of Jewish ethnicity myself, on my father's side, blessed with having had a very special brother who suffered from major disabilities, the 'family connection' seems ironic at best.

Since it has also become almost *de rigueur* for bioethics authors who offer a critique of modern medicine to reassure readers that they are nonetheless its beneficiaries, I gladly do the same, on my own behalf and that of many people close to me. Taking a political stand on bioethics questions can often lead to a sense of division between concerns about the global effects of practices and local, individual choices. For example, I have concerns about inter-country adoption as a response to infertility, but I cannot fault people who adopt HIV-infected children from Haiti, in full knowledge they might attend their funerals; I am concerned about organ donation, but cannot say a relative 'should not' have received a donor's heart, nor a friend a donor's lung. I don't know if I want to be an organ donor myself and I wonder how it would affect my partner if I chose to be one. Concerned about the effects of the drugs used in IVF on women, I still could not counsel a friend undergoing donor insemination not to take any drugs, only to be informed. Personal motives can be 'pure' but wider implications problematic in the same moment. The world of bioethics is a complex epistemological terrain: subject and object come in and out of focus in kaleidoscopic and unpredictable ways.

Like many authors who write about social aspects of medicine, I, too, must aver that I am not a medical sceptic, or rather, not a medical cynic. There is too much evidence of genuinely benign emotional investment on the part of health-care professionals to be able to reduce scepticism about the industrial and ideological aspects of medicine to a formula impugning legions of dedicated and overworked colleagues. Nonetheless, as I explore in Chapter 1, it is the role of the historian as a social scientist to adopt a stance of exploratory scepticism, the scepticism which insists on reading against the grain, on reading outside of the self-determined framework of other people's texts. The scientific stance requires a procedural scepticism but it also requires authors ultimately to seek out and challenge their own assumptions, to know that they might not know why they write what they write. This is very hard to do. One can only try to see one's own assumptions, and to be willing to change or modify views, for we are all participant–observers in modern medical culture.

In 1996, the University of Queensland invited me to develop an undergraduate course on bioethics history and the further fourteen years of research that accompanied the teaching of that course has led to this book. This project began more with an eye to the medical policy issues with which I was familiar than to the debates in bioethics culture of the USA. I realized quite late that without understanding something of the hothouse bioethics culture of the USA, it was not possible to put medical ethics more generally in perspective. In particular, I slowly realized that bioethics wasn't what I thought it was, or rather, that the world of medical ethics with which I was familiar intersected with the world of academic philosophical ethics in complex ways and that in this area of intersection lay one of the battle grounds of medical ethics/bioethics itself. As a historian working in a more traditional field, the kind of controversy and even antipathy that seemed regularly to arise in bioethics forums was at times unsettling. I realized I was somewhat naïve about the academic politics of bioethics, and was in particular unaware of the divide between philosophers and social scientists over how best to understand and address medical ethics. For that reason, Chapter 1 attempts to describe that particular methodological and political landscape. The remainder of the book is intended as both an introduction to some aspects of bioethics history and debate, and as a meditation on the relationship of history to ethics.

Over the long process of research and writing, I have accumulated many debts, which I can only begin to honour now. Many people and institutions have contributed to the development of this book. I acknowledge the Australian Research Council which provided a two-year Discovery Grant, and the UQ Foundation at the University of Queensland which provided funds from a Research Excellence Award. Latter stages benefited from research funding from my current employer, the University of Wollongong and its Institute for Social Transformation Research (ISTR). This work does not to my knowledge reflect any conflicts of interest.

The Wellcome Library has been an invaluable source for medical history materials. Inter-library loans staff at the University of Queensland Library provided help over many years, as more recently have library staff at the University of Wollongong. At the University of Melbourne Brownless Medical Library, Patrick Condron helped me find key references; Christopher Lyons at the Osler Medical Library at McGill University gave generously of his time and knowledge; Martina Darragh at the Kennedy Institute of Ethics library and Chris McKee at the Hastings Center library each provided friendly and invaluable advice and references.

My thanks are due to the Hastings Center for the privilege of spending five weeks there as a Visiting Scholar in 2005. In the shared apartment at the centre, I had as resident colleagues a young Dutch physician, a young English philosopher and a Lutheran Pastor. The mealtimes we shared have become for me emblematic of the first principle of bioethics as a social conversation: it is best done face to face with the full humanity of interlocutors given a chance to be revealed. The centre's own shared lunch hours and visiting speakers added to the sense of the possibilities and value of 'ecumenism'. The University of Queensland Medical Humanities Reading Group ('The Moggies') read two chapter drafts. Alison Bashford kindly offered comments on a draft of the chapter on eugenics.

Several distinguished scholars graciously replied to my 'cold-call' email contact: I thank Sylvia Cruess, Richard Cruess, Arthur Frank, Charles Rosenberg, Margaret Somerville, as well as Roger Cooter, who in addition very kindly offered key advice on a draft of the introduction. Other one-off respondents are thanked in endnotes. Friends, students past and present, and colleagues have also contributed materially to the completion of this project. Some did paid research on the project;

others gave me materials as they came across them in the course of their own research. All have shared their thoughts in conversation. I thank Helen Bode, Jodie Brown, Benjamin Capps, Frances Cruickshank, Marion Diamond, Janice Dowell, Carolyn Ells, Helen Gilbert, Wayne Hall, Vera Mackie, Robert Mason, Susie O'Brien, Jo Robertson, David Sobel, Elli Storey, Ingeborg van Teeseling, Sally Wilde, Emily Wilson, Heather Wolffram, Sarah Yeates and Chris Tiffin, who also prepared the index. Megan Brayshaw, Kerry Ross and Yorick Smaal have been particularly generous in their assistance and I thank them sincerely. Nicola Marks kindly gave her expert views on Chapters 3 and 4 and corrected several errors. Any remaining errors in the book are my own.

For their support I thank: Adrian Howe, Carmel Bird, Lynne Hillier, Felicity Nottingham, Alison Sayers, Sandy Jeffs, Robyn Adams, Diane Simmons, Helen Ferber, Jenny Ferber, Ken Orr, Francis Goodfellow, Johanna Hough, Brian White, Katie McConnel, Nick Eckstein, Kate Eckstein, Helen Pausacker, Stasia Zika, Charles Zika and Sue Hardisty. I thank most of all my partner, Leigh Dale, who has gone over the book too many times and to whom it is dedicated.

I wish to thank the Bioethics Research Library at Georgetown University, Kennedy Institute of Ethics, Georgetown University, Washington, DC, USA, for permission to reprint the Bioethics Research Library Classification Scheme (http://bioethics. georgetown.edu).

# Introduction

Bioethics can be understood as the most recent expression of the social exchanges entailed in weighing up and assigning value in the world of medicine. The word 'bioethics' dates from the twentieth century: in 1927, the German Protestant theologian Fritz Jahr coined 'Bio-Ethik' to encapsulate his view that ethical reflection should not be limited to behaviour among human beings but should extend to the entire living world.[1] Apparently not widely taken up, 'Bio-Ethik' appears to have faded from use well before 1970, when the US research oncologist Van Rensselaer Potter II devised a similar English word, 'bioethics', to promote his vision for a 'new field devoted to human survival and an improved quality of life'. Potter's bioethics had the goal of linking the biological sciences with the study of ethics.[2] Around the same time, and possibly independently again, R. Sargent Shriver, a philosopher, and André Hellegers, a foetal physiologist, both of whom were associated with the Catholic Georgetown University, used the word 'bioethics' to denote a form of applied philosophical ethics which addressed developments in the biomedical sciences.[3] While much bioethics literature still addresses issues pertaining to the biosphere, in Jahr's and Potter's sense, the narrower, biomedical understanding of the term has probably become the most recognized and influential, and is the subject of this book.[4]

The rapid uptake of the term 'bioethics' in Anglophone cultures and elsewhere marked a historically important moment of 'branding'. Bioethics gave a name to a diverse collection of public policy concerns about medicine and science which had been increasingly on the agenda in many Western countries since the Second World War (1939–1945). Atomic power and the horrific effects of the bombs released on Hiroshima and Nagasaki prompted sustained reflection about the capacities of science, as did the emerging potentialities of modern genetics. Revelations about unethical medical experimentation and the conditions for research on human subjects preoccupied commentators inside and outside of the medical professions. Fertility control, reproductive rights and new birth technologies were on the policy agenda. Medical interventions in behaviour and thought elicited concerns about the limits of psychiatry and clinical psychology. Transplant surgery and mechanical life support pointed to new questions about the line between life and death. And the sometimes tragic consequences of the mid-twentieth-century pharmaceutical revolution influenced regulation to slow the pace of the transition from laboratory to market.[5] Thus by the 1970s the scene was set for a new term like 'bioethics' to make cultural sense.[6]

The emergence of bioethics coincides with a dramatic expansion in the number of ways in which medicine helps to shape modern individual, social and political worlds. Historian George Weisz claims:

> Medicine has assumed a cultural importance in modern societies that goes far beyond its ability to make people feel better. Understanding its role has become fundamental to understanding our culture. The development and international diffusion of bioethics is itself a social phenomenon of considerable importance with consequences for our understanding of the entire medical enterprise.[7]

Bioethics represents the socially interpretative dimension of modern medicine. However, bioethics is not merely outsiders' commentary on the ethics of medical matters as they unfold in their 'natural habitat' of clinics, labs or hospitals. Medicine has become a powerful medium for all human relations and bioethics, too, now holds a place in these relationships. It has both clarified and altered the meaning of medicine. Institutional forms of bioethics – academic bioethics, institutional ethics review, legal reforms, clinical ethics consultations – position non-medical individuals and institutions at the very core of medical practice, on such issues as clinical conduct, research and funding priorities, and health policy. Physician and philosopher Jonathan Moreno argues that bioethics not only evaluates change but has become part of the process of change itself. He adds: 'since bioethics has in practice attached itself to a particular set of themes in social reform, including but not limited to the reform of medical education, it can be called a social reform movement'.[8]

Before the emergence of bioethics, the term 'medical ethics' generally referred to the medical profession's internal codes, particularly concerning intra-professional conduct in relation to such areas as advertising and competition.[9] In the 1960s and 70s era of political activism, critics who perceived medical authority as a form of social control or who were wary of medicine's links with industry challenged traditions of peer regulation in the medical profession and the culture of medical-commercial *laissez faire*. The activism of the new 'bioethics' both reflected and redirected these critiques. Medical decision-making, once understood as the treatment choices of individual doctors, ideally in discussion with their patients, has increasingly become a community, state and global concern. Many medical decisions now occupy not only physicians and patients, but medical scientists, non-clinical healthcare and paramedical providers, lawyers and legislators, philosophers, historians of science and medicine, theologians and the churches, social scientists, health bureaucrats, medical consumers, as well as activists in areas of identity politics, such as women's rights, sexuality, race, disability and ethnicity, to name only some. All of these groups or constituencies now contribute to debate on current medical practice and policy.[10] And, crucially, many commentators undertake to speak on behalf of others: experimental animals, socially marginalized people, the incapacitated, the unborn, the newborn, the ill and terminally ill, the comatose, the brain-dead, and the dead.[11]

Bioethics is a wide range of social conversations which now feed into any given clinical action, a development which has led traditional doctor-patient 'medical ethics' to be subsumed under 'bioethics'.[12] The forums for these ethical conversations are not only those of immediate medical decision-making in clinical treatment and research, but mainstream and specialist media, the Internet, academic conferences and centres, policy think-tanks, courts and legislatures, ethics committees, and even, on occasion, the streets.[13] Seen as a part of the social history of medicine, this modern 'bioethical enterprise' makes visible and expands the ongoing historical dialogue between medicine and social morality, a dialogue which pre-existed both the word and the institutions of bioethics. Not only is it 'a cliché to emphasize that all medicine is social medicine', but moreover, 'every medical encounter has an ethical component'.[14]

## Social history of medicine

Since the 1960s, too, researchers in social history of medicine have investigated the effects of social and political developments on medical culture, as well as the influence of the medical profession and medical paradigms on social policy. Writers in this field of history have sought to understand, for example, the ways in which medical authority and the cultural agendas of medicine have developed, notably in relation to issues such as the categorization of physical and mental disease, medical experimentation in its social dimensions, and the role of the medical profession in the history of social policy initiatives. They have also recovered the histories of public health, nursing and hospitals, medicine in war, medicine's professionalization, and its corporate advance-ment.[15] More recently, they have begun to write new histories of bioethics, challenging some of the earlier more purely celebratory histo-ries to show that among other things that there is no single history of bioethics. To write 'the' history of bioethics is therefore an increasingly imposing task and not the aim of this book. Its aim is to provide insights into both the history of bioethics as a social practice, and into the wider history of medicine in its social context.

Bioethics can be seen in historical perspective in three ways: in the history of bioethics debates; in the historical examples referred to within those debates; and through an understanding of the history of medicine in society, which provides the conditions for many of the questions asked in bioethics. All of the issues considered in this book reflect in some way on these three aspects of bioethics in historical perspective.

An increasing number of historians are showing the ways in which it is possible, in the words of Ruth Schwarz Cowan, to 'resolve bioethical puzzles with historians' tools': that is, they have shown that both the empirical knowledge and the interpretative skills of historical research can play a part in appraising the political and moral dimensions of medicine, and in mediating medical change.[16] They have evaluated knowledge of sometimes forgotten or misremembered events in order to forge a deeper understanding of modern medicine. Sociologist Aviad Raz urges the value of seeing ethical issues not as universals but as the products of distinct historical moments. He asks of ethical debates, 'Why are these issues defined as ethical concerns by these people in these times and these places?'[17] A sense of the need for historical reflec-tion is affecting bioethics in other disciplines: physician and philoso-pher Howard Brody has recently urged that history needs to be taken into account in the evolution of informed ethics, while the philosopher authors of the major work on genetics policy, *From Chance to Choice*, acknowledge their debt to the archival work of a colleague who is a historian.[18]

This book aims, then, to use the contributions of recent historical work and the wider literature of bioethics to develop the case for think-ing about history in relation to medical ethics. It proposes that bioethics can be as much about our relationship to the past as it is about medical innovation in the present and that knowledge of history – of ideas, events and institutions which still have bearing on the conduct of medi-cine – can be used to contribute to effective medical policy and practice. In elucidating and building on the work of historians and other commentators, the book is intended to make a contribution to academic bioethics, broadly construed, as well as to the book's 'home discipline' of history. The book draws upon and, where possible, develops the insights of prior research, to test the limits to which historical comparisons and examples can be applied to contemporary practice. It will explore some of the ways in which attitudes to the past, and attitudes *from* the past, affect bioethical thinking today.

The book is intended for both college and graduate student readers, providing basic information about some key issues in bioethics, as well as a guide to different ethical standpoints. It is not meant to be an introduction to all topics in bioethics, nor to the current 'hot-button' items: some issues are considered in passing, others not at all.[19] Rather, it is meant to provide conceptual tools, derived from the discipline of history, to enable students to think critically about what is happening in the present. With some new twists added to well-known stories, it is also intended to be of interest to those more familiar with bioethics. In practical terms, it seeks to give newcomers to the field of bioethics knowledge to recognize the context and underlying values that inform commentary in mainstream and specialist media. It also aims to give professionals in fields such as medicine and para-medicine, law, journalism, sociology of medicine and public policy some of the historical knowledge required to make sense of contemporary cultures of medical bioethics. Additionally the book should make it possible for all readers, as medical 'consumers', to better understand the medical world(s) in which they live and even the choices they themselves might face, as participants in medical cultures.

## Definitions of bioethics

Defining what bioethics is (or are), and who has the authority to contribute to bioethical debate, is itself far from settled.[20] Academics, activists and others have disputed 'ownership' of bioethics for many years, and commentators regularly differ in their views as to what belongs within the bioethical sightline. Some of these debates will be addressed in detail in Chapter 1. For now, it is enough to state that the bioethics to be considered in this book is not the branch of applied ethics of academic philosophy, but reflects a wider understanding of bioethics in its social and institutional contexts. For readers familiar with bioethics debate in academia, this claim signals a position within those debates: they will guess that the goals of the book can only be accomplished by giving priority to a particular way of seeing bioethics, which has been called 'cultural' bioethics. Daniel Callahan, philosopher and co-founder of the influential Hastings Center in New York State, defined this form in the 'Bioethics' entry of the 2004 *Encyclopaedia of Bioethics*. His working model of the main categories of the field identifies four related species of bioethics. The first, theoretical bioethics, 'deals with the intellectual foundations of the field'. The second, clinical ethics, 'refers to the day-to-day moral decision making of those caring for patients'. The third, regulatory and policy bioethics, aims 'to fashion legal or clinical rules and procedures designed to apply to types of cases or general practices'. The fourth form, 'cultural bioethics',

> refers to the effort systematically to relate bioethics to the historical, ideological, cultural, and social context in which it is expressed. How do the trends within bioethics reflect the larger culture of which they are a part? What ideological leanings do the moral theories undergirding bioethics openly or implicitly manifest?[21]

'Cultural bioethics', then, acknowledges the intensely felt and politically charged nature of much bioethics debate; it is informed by an awareness of the essentially social encounters which make up modern medicine. In this perspective, questions such as 'Whose views shape debate?', 'Whose are left out?', and 'How do some issues come to be seen as more pressing than others?' play important roles in shaping the ethical landscape. Seen in this way, cultural bioethics seeks to understand the historical and present questions of medical choices and outcomes of individuals and groups, and the clinical and experimental cultures in which these are shaped.[22] In the words of historian Charles Rosenberg '[W]e cannot understand the structure of medical choice without an understanding of the specific histories of medicine and society that have created those choices'.[23]

For philosophers, in particular, this book might present some frustrations when a word with a technical meaning in the discipline of philosophy is used here in the vernacular. Indeed, 'ethics' itself is such a word, which can refer to the systematic examination of ethics in philosophy scholarship, the localized ethos or code of a professional group such as physicians, or the broader, less readily measured, circumstantial ethics at work in any given situation.[24] For historians, too, it is important to note that the book is not a history of medical ethics codes in Western medicine, nor a history of 'bioethics before bioethics', that is, of early social debates about medical accountability. Nor indeed is it a history of modern bioethics in its institutional forms.[25] The book is also not the product of traditional archival history (involving the excavation of a single seam of evidence): by and large, the research of others, historians as well as other bioethics commentators, complemented by some original research, forms the basis for its empirical content. It explores several examples from modern bioethics history to suggest that the practice of bioethics – whether expressed in academic, legal, biomedical or public policy forums – can best be undertaken with awareness not only of important historical facts, but of the role of history in our thinking. The book does not shrug in the face of moral absolutes, but assumes even absolute claims to be primarily the products of culture.

## What use is history to bioethics?

The study of history is often caricatured as the accumulation of facts, notably in the form of dates. Something generally enters the category of 'historical' when it is seen either as forgettable (because done with) or memorable (because influential or innovative). Perhaps as a result of the common-sense belief that history writing traffics in essentially moribund data, historical thinking has played a relatively minor role in bioethics. Thinking about history and historical method in a more reflective mode, however, can help us to understand the ways in which attitudes to the past affect perceptions of the present; the past is continually dwelt upon, invoked, reinterpreted, mobilized, politicized, condescended to and held up to scrutiny. Daily, people make conscious and unconscious choices about the past and how to relate to it, manifested in decisions about whether to forget or to remember; regret or repudiate. Such choices bear a broadly 'ethical' imprint, reflecting attitudes about wrong and right, and relative value.

Crucially, then, the relationship of the modern world to its antecedents is never static. Just as modern wars can reignite hostilities of centuries' standing, choices to represent particular events in a certain way, or to teach them to school or university students, rehearse and redefine the meaning and place of the past in the present. The ways in which the past is invoked, as a precedent or as a lesson learned, and choices made about whether the past is best honoured or forgotten, have all had a bearing on recent bioethics. Thinking about the past can facilitate an understanding of the present, for example, by testing claims to novelty and to improvement, to continuity or change. Deciphering both continuities and ruptures with the past is the work of the historian. And as trained readers, historians look for silences and omissions as much as they look for declarations and achievements.

From a common-sense view, the academic discipline of history might seem quite removed from the complex policy world of bioethics. As Rosenberg observes: 'We feel that historians should look backward, while the essence of policy is to look forward – as though the past is not in the present and the present not in the future.'[26] Yet as he rightly suggests, history and policy are not mutually exclusive. From this standpoint, historical method is not an alternative to ethical debate, but a key part of it, affecting such fundamentals as 'the choice of questions discussed in healthcare ethics and politics'.[27] Historical reflection on medical ethics can be concerned not only with finding answers to immediate policy issues, therefore, but asking how questions are posed about medical practice and policy in the first instance.[28] English historian of medicine John Pickstone develops the point:

> One could, in the manner of bioethics courses, simply debate the pros and cons of present positions, but history offers more … As well as using an analytical framework to clarify debates, it serves to link attitudes to traditions and social projects. It allows one to ask about the origins and pertinence of questions (as well as about answers).[29]

Similarly, the editors of the collection *Bioethics in Cultural Contexts* argue: 'Moral answers, as well as the methods used to produce them, are rooted in cultural traditions that are themselves diverse and dynamic.'[30] And Claudia Wiesemann, in the same collection, suggests that the past infuses the present with ethical traces: '[T]hrough historical narratives', she argues, 'medical history is always a force in today's ethical debates. These narratives do not just explain the past; more importantly, they also interpret the future. Thus they structure ethical debates and help legitimise ethical policies.'[31] In this view, only historical knowledge can make fully decipherable the reasons why different parties align in particular ways on specific issues.

An understanding of the uneven and inherently socially framed character of medical ethics is reinforced and expanded in an evocative formulation by Rosenberg. He sums up the place of history in a policy world which is both chaotic and structured. 'The real world', he argues,

> is not a very orderly place. Policies on the ground seem less a coherent package of ideas and logically related practices than a layered conglomerate of stalemated battles, ad hoc alliances, and ideological gradients, more a cumulative sediment of negotiated cease-fires among powerful stakeholders than a self-conscious commitment to

data-sanctioned goals. ... Thus, the familiar dismissal of the historical community's potential contribution to policy seems ... paradoxical. Structured contention and contingency are history and so is contemporary policy – even if historians and historical data seem tangential to the ... task of anticipating the consequences of particular present actions.[32]

Daniel Callahan reinforces this sense of the seemingly chaotic real-world dimensions of bioethics policy, arguing for awareness of the unexpected and contingent as well as the use of reason in the realm of policy. He says: 'The contribution of the imagination is not just to see what logically might follow from a clinical or policy decision, in a chain of cause-effect relationships, but what might, in the hurly burly of real life, actually happen, logically or not.'[33]

One implication of adopting such an interpretative stance is to recognize that bioethics debates need to be understood as not just 'arising' naturally from changes in medical practices, but as having been actively propelled into the public domain. How policy is formed and how questions are framed in media debates depend on the capacity of stakeholders to present their perceptions and values as the given or 'natural' terms of debate. Contention is interest-driven: campaigns are launched, media releases drafted and sound bites conceived, placement and timing attended to, all to create the sense of the newsworthiness not just of a particular issue, but the rightness of a particular point of view.

Bioethics, in short, is political in its essence. As instinctive as it might seem to be to envisage that the dramatic medical innovations of the mid-to-late twentieth century of themselves present ethical questions, new technology does not of itself 'prefabricate' the questions which are asked of it. New products and techniques as a result of their particular forms and capacities, do, of course, provide specific openings for consideration and can therefore give shape to the ways in which they can be seen, but their social meanings and ethical significance are the result of choices.[34] Responses always arise as a result of perceptions and it is inevitably activism of some kind which takes questions into a different cultural arena, for example, when a particular clinical scenario transits into the courtroom, or when public funding is sought for a particular type of research.

Finding a place for history in the world of medical ethics is also about insisting on the need for continuous debate, alongside the daily and policy resolution of ethical questions. This can entail something as simple as finding time to read and reflect. Canadian sociologist Arthur Frank has linked the ethical process very simply to a need to 'slow down ... and create a space to deliberate'.[35] The tertiary education environment can be one of the few places where deliberation and the relatively unpressured evaluation of ideas can occur, where incomplete reflections and unresolved emotions can be explored. The question of who has time to read the vast quantity of material produced in medical, paramedical, policy and academic spheres is both a political and institutional one. Human labour hours are costly: the capacity to deliberate is part of the political economy of modern medicine. The job of humanities research and writing is to distil evidence and arguments, and point to new analyses. In this light the book aims to show that thinking about the past can contribute to a broader 'bioethical literacy'.

## Chapter outline

In the course of writing this book, I became aware that going straight to medical narratives would bypass the important 'institutional history' of bioethics itself. Bioethics is part of modern medicine but it also has a distinct history and profile in academia. Readers coming to bioethics for the first time might not be aware of the kind of debates which regularly characterize the academic world, nor of the particularly heartfelt contestations within bioethics. Chapter 1 therefore considers some key debates within bioethics scholarship and explores tensions between the diverse disciplines in the humanities and social sciences which claim authority to interpret emerging medical policy issues. Understanding the history of these debates will help make more intelligible the sometimes subtle references (and indeed occasional silences) found in scholarly bioethics and wider public debate. Chapter 2 develops this argument in relation to the significance of language and rhetoric in analyses of medical and ethical debate.

The remaining chapters are designed to provide a point of entry into several major topics of contemporary bioethics debate: euthanasia; reproductive gene technology; medical experimentation; and pharmaceuticals policy. Chapter 3 considers the use of the so-called 'Nazi analogy' in contemporary debate about euthanasia. When critics raise the spectre of Nazism in a bioethics debate, they point to the role of medicine in one of the most terrible political regimes of modern history to draw attention to what they see as the potential risks of contemporary medicine. The use of the Nazi analogy is perhaps the most pervasive source of emotional impact in bioethics debates. Nazi 'euthanasia' was a policy of extermination of people with disability, which began at the start of the Second World War.[36] Modern opponents of euthanasia law reform and end-of-life health care funding frequently claim that any legal concession to pro-euthanasia activism will begin a slide down an inevitable 'slippery slope' into Nazi-like social policy. How valid is this argument, both as a form of historical argument and in light of recent legal developments? To address this question, Chapter 3 considers the recent history of two jurisdictions which introduced laws to allow for euthanasia and physician-assisted suicide: Australia's Northern Territory in 1995 and the Netherlands in 2000. Did enabling legislation permitting euthanasia and physician-assisted suicide follow this predicted trajectory of the slippery slope in either case? If not, are the Nazi analogy or the slippery slope model useful or distracting bases for argument?

Chapter 4 considers a question related to that posed by the use of the Nazi analogy: are the extreme and now repudiated eugenics of the past and the capacities or directions of modern human reproductive genetics in any way analogous? Eugenics was a major international social movement in the late nineteenth to mid-twentieth centuries, attracting reformers from all points on the political spectrum. In different ways, all eugenicists imagined and campaigned for what they saw as social betterment through the control of human heredity, often linking their goals to the ideal of 'health' for a race or nation, or both. Eugenics not only provided the rationales for such extremes as so-called 'euthanasia', but for government-mandated involuntary sterilization, in many jurisdictions but most notably Germany and many states in the USA. Some critics, concerned about the potentialities of recent genetic science, have invoked the extremes of eugenics as a point of comparison with present-day practices, suggesting that assisted reproductive technologies which used genetic probes, for example, might lead *de facto* to eugenic outcomes. Yet how valid is it to argue that modern scientific and social interest in heredity are either directly continuous with eugenics or analogous to it? After decades of debate both in favour of, and against, the 'eugenic analogy', increasingly nuanced arguments have proven to be a fruitful source of comparison with modern developments, even when the analogy has not been sustained systematically.

Chapter 5 investigates the cultural conditions which have facilitated medical experiments widely regarded as unethical, and the kind of aspirations and inducements which have led individuals and institutions to undertake them. It also looks at the historical background to the modern institutional review of human experimentation. Codes to guide or bind the ethics of those who conduct medical research have evolved in the light of both revelations about abuses and the ongoing need for experimental data to serve humane therapeutic purposes. For educators, a major challenge is to cultivate an awareness of the history of ethical problems in medical research, while striking a balance between anachronistic alarmism on the one hand and 'presentist' complacency on the other. ('Presentism' is the idea that the present provides a unique perceptual and moral vantage point, as an automatic consequence of being the most recent moment in history.) In the present day, the range of effective medical interventions is widening at the same time as the gaps which allow breaches and abuses are narrowing. There exists now an enormous array of institutional review boards, hospital ethics committees, laws, protocols, state-level ethics panels, as well as globally oriented pronouncements intended to protect human research subjects. Why, then, recall events that occurred in times when such an array of monitoring and braking mechanisms did not exist? In setting out an answer to this question, Chapter 5 will explore the view that present practice is best served by qualified recollection.

The final chapter (Chapter 6) considers the 'rehabilitation' of the multivalent drug thalidomide. The history of modern pharmaceuticals is indelibly affected by the tragic story of thalidomide, a drug introduced in 1957 as a sedative and for the treatment of morning sickness, which ultimately left 8,000–12,000 children with only partially formed limbs, as well as other major health problems. Many thousands more affected babies died at birth, and many women pregnant with thalidomide-affected foetuses spontaneously aborted. This trail of destruction contributed to drug licensing becoming one of the most vigilantly policed areas of the medical industry. Increasingly, however, researchers have identified potential new uses for thalidomide and have sought special permission to use it. How industry and government have accommodated producers', patients' and survivors' concerns is a study in negotiating a profound historical burden imposed by the drug, in the light of new laboratory research and expanding clinical trials.

A few caveats apply in relation to the selection of the material for the book. Given global inequities of health and medical treatment, the focus of the book on predominantly rich countries, and among them, on predominantly Anglophone ones, might seem indefensible. There have been many valid critiques of bioethics as culturally insular and particularly US- and Anglophone-oriented, and this book itself could be seen as an unreconstructed primer for a Western-centred 'Bioethics 101'. It can be argued, however, that medicine has played and continues to play a considerable part in the redistribution of privilege even within privileged countries, and that this issue remains a legitimate focus of enquiry. In privileged countries, those who are disadvantaged socially and economically – such as women, the poor, people of colour, indigenous and non-dominant ethnic groups, children, the disabled, the mentally ill and intellectually impaired – can also be the most vulnerable in terms of health care. Having said this, the fact remains that even in wealthy systems, the greatest risks to most healthcare clients do not come from the events in the established canon of bioethical themes: they lie in much more mundane areas such as mistaken procedures, mal-administered drugs, unsanitary hospital environments or lack of access to health care.[37] In defence of the choices reflected in this book, I maintain that writing which considers some of the 'standard issues' of mainline bioethics from a different angle can contribute to an understanding of the field of bioethics itself and to the several spheres of medicine which – notwithstanding that they are widely and frequently canvassed – affect the lives of so many.

## Further reading

Andre, J. (2002) *Bioethics as Practice* (Chapel Hill and London: University of North Carolina Press).

Beauchamp, T., L. Walters, J. Kahn and A. Mastroianni (eds) (2008) *Contemporary Issues in Bioethics*, 7th edn (Belmont, CA: Thomson/Wadsworth).

Bynum, W. F. and R. Porter (eds) (1997) *Companion Encyclopedia of the History of Medicine*, 2 vols (London and New York: Routledge).

Cooter, R. and J. Pickstone (eds) (2000) *Medicine in the Twentieth Century* (Amsterdam: Harwood Academic).

Cooter, R. and C. Stein (2013) *Writing History in the Age of Biomedicine* (New Haven, CT: Yale University Press).

Fox, R. C. and J. P. Swazey (2008) *Observing Bioethics* (Oxford and New York: Oxford University Press).

Hoffmaster, B. (2001) *Bioethics in Social Context* (Philadelphia: Temple University Press).

Jonsen, A. R. (1998) *The Birth of Bioethics* (New York and Oxford: Oxford University Press).

Koch, T. (2012) *Thieves of Virtue: When Bioethics Stole Medicine* (Cambridge, MA: MIT Press).

Lupton, D. (1994) *Medicine as Culture: Illness, Disease and the Body in Western Societies* (London: Sage Publications).

Mann, S. (2010) *Bioethics in Perspective: Corporate Power, Public Health and Political Economy* (Cambridge: Cambridge University Press).

McGee, G. (2012) *Bioethics for Beginners: 60 Cases and Cautions from the Moral Frontier of Healthcare* (Chichester: John Wiley and Sons).

Pickstone, J. V. (2000) *Ways of Knowing: A New History of Science, Technology and Medicine* (Manchester: Manchester University Press).

Post, S. G. (ed.) (2004) *Encyclopedia of Bioethics*, 3rd edn (Farmington Hills, MI: Thomson Gale).

Rosenberg C. E. (1999) 'Meanings, Policies, and Medicine: On the Bioethical Enterprise and History', *Daedalus*, 128.4, 27–46.

Squier, S. M. (2004) *Liminal Lives: Imagining the Human at the Frontiers of Biomedicine* (Durham, NC: Duke University Press).

Stevens, M. L. T. (2000) *Bioethics in America: Origins and Cultural Politics* (Baltimore, MD: Johns Hopkins University Press).

Stevens, R. A., C. E. Rosenberg and L. R. Burns (eds) (2006) *History and Health Policy in the United States: Putting the Past Back In* (New Brunswick, NJ: Rutgers University Press).

## Journals

*American Journal of Bioethics*
*Bioethics*
*BioSocieties*
*Daedalus* (Bioethics Special Issue (1999) 128.4)
*Hastings Center Report*
*Health and History*
*International Journal of Feminist Approaches to Bioethics*
*Journal of Bioethical Inquiry*
*Journal of Medical Ethics*
*Journal of Medical Humanities*
*Kennedy Institute of Ethics Journal*
*Medical History*
*Medical Humanities*
*Medicine Studies*
*Monash Bioethics Review*
*New Genetics and Society*
*New Review of Bioethics*
*Perspectives in Biology and Medicine*
*Science in Context*
*Social History of Medicine*
*Social Science and Medicine*
*Theoretical Medicine and Bioethics*

# 1
# Bioethics as Scholarship

The present chapter outlines some of the history and politics of scholarly writing in bioethics. To be able to identify arguments and tendencies which are already familiar to bioethics 'insiders' can have practical implications. Students undertaking a course in a philosophy school, a science and technology studies (STS) programme, a medical school, a law school, an English literature department, or a church-funded college or a secular institution, will probably come across very different ways of looking at the same issues. Specific agendas and protocols can be masked in the sophisticated world of bioethics politics, and the questions asked and expected answers often reflect the disciplinary training and assumptions of the professor concerned. Teachers and the books and articles they ask a student to read can differ not only in their interpretations, but on basic questions about what makes for a valid academic activity. Knowing how to identify narrative approaches and buzzwords, for example, can affect questions such as: Which bodies of literature should be used to research an assignment? To which journal should a graduate student send her or his first academic paper? Who should assess a dissertation? Student journalists, too, acclimatizing to the world of sound bites and media releases, need to be able to recognize readily the distinctive terms which identify particular mindsets within bioethics. The US sociologist Charles Bosk has underscored these broadly political dimensions of bioethics when discussing specialist bioethics education programmes:

> The pedagogic choices that programs make as they establish themselves in intellectual space ... have political consequences. ... They define who is and who is not a bioethicist. They define what is and what is not a legitimate subject for inquiry. They define what does and what does not count as reliable knowledge. They establish who has a place at the table and is taken seriously and who is not.[1]

By the end of the chapter, it will also be apparent that this kind of statement is typical of the approach taken by a social scientist.

15

To be considered here are how and why authors constitute their version of authoritative bioethical knowledge and analysis in the way they do. The chapter will look at the role of religion in bioethics, as a way of building a context for the development of scholarly bioethics. This will be followed by an examination of the academic disciplines within the interdisciplinary field of bioethics, with specific reference to the diverse historical reasons for scholarly activism in relation to medicine. It will consider in this context the innovation of applied philosophy in bioethics; tensions between the different schools of philosophy, and between philosophy and the social sciences (such as sociology, anthropology and ethnography). The chapter will end with a consideration of the 'ethics of bioethics', a source of ongoing concern in light of the success of professionalization in bioethics.

## The importance of religion, then and now

Religion is perhaps an unexpected place to begin an account of scholarly bioethics. It is just one thread to pull out of the web of recent bioethics history, but the historical importance of religion for bioethics is so profound that it might sometimes, paradoxically, be overlooked, particularly in nominally secular societies. Even when religion is not mentioned, rarely is it more than one step removed from the history of bioethics conversations. Religion provides a starting point for understanding both the history of modern medicine itself and the form of many debates which have arisen in scholarly bioethics. Recognizing its significance can also provide insight into the depth of feeling expressed by religionists and their adversaries in bioethics.[2]

### *The cleric and the physician*

Much modern bioethics debate can be seen as part of a standoff between two competing notions of the sacred: the sacred calling to heal, and a theologically informed perception of the sacredness of human life. These two positions are evident in debates such as those concerning abortion, foetal tissue and embryo research, and euthanasia. From the European Middle Ages until as late as the nineteenth century, physicians and the clergy (particularly Catholic priests) were in many ways rival or complementary 'health service providers'. In the nineteenth century, medicine became both more professionalized and secularist, and the right to heal became increasingly contested.[3] Medical practitioners during this period came to assume something of a sacred aura, an aura harnessed to the powerful, uplifting Enlightenment ideal of scientific knowledge as possessed of an inherent moral authority to rival that of religion.[4] Modern medical practitioners thus bear some of the mantle of the traditional healing clerical class, an identity which, it could be suggested, at once ennobles and potentially inflates a sense of the medical mission. The relatively new capacity of medicine genuinely to heal a wide variety of conditions has rightly enhanced this image. Clinicians and their industrial and research counterparts are held to be producing something, that is, in theory at least, an unalloyed good.[5]

This distinctive medical status is what Rosenberg refers to when he suggests 'there remains something special about the physician's vocation, about the profession's peculiar configuration of ethical and knowledge-based claims'.[6] He argues that critiques of medicine must move beyond a simple materialist view of what motivates the medical professions:

> Individuals crave moral legitimacy – and in medicine, legitimacy has traditionally implied mastery of a particular body of knowledge; that possession of such knowledge implies or might bring with it economic advantage (or social status) does not mean that the motivation for acquiring it can be understood in exclusively economic terms.[7]

The widespread practice of clinicians performing *pro bono* work typifies this. Medicine is nonetheless highly commercial: much medical employment, whether government or private, is today tied to outcomes in the form of marketable procedures and products. In this light, Western medical clinicians and researchers generally work in the gaps they can find between what might be called 'medicine as ministry' and 'medicine as industry'.

## Religion and politics

Religion is deeply implicated in many areas of Western cultural politics, not only in the world of medicine. Emphatically, its presence is evident in relation to gay and women's rights issues, and in bitter debates about the teaching of evolution versus creationism in school biology. Commentary on religion and medicine needs therefore in many cases to be read off a larger script about religious activism as a force which encroaches increasingly on both knowledge creation and knowledge transmission. Religiously based views within and outside the academy provide an explanation for what seems at times to be an equally militant 'hyper-rationalism' among some philosophically trained bioethics commentators. Read in this way, many modern bioethics debates are re-enactments of Enlightenment-era controversies over the role of the clergy.

Overall, bioethics would have been unlikely to develop as a field of public interest or as an academic pursuit, on the scale or in the way it has, without the presence of strong religious currents. In recent decades, religious lobbies have emerged among the most insistent purveyors of a sense of urgency about medical ethics on the public sphere, in several Anglophone countries, especially the USA, and to some extent in Western Europe. There are differences within and between different religious groups, but medical research and clinical practice have in general been among the chief forums in which diverse elements within modern Western Christianity, in particular, have fought their battles.[8] Religion has both contributed to bioethics debate and itself has found new meanings and footholds in its promotion. Probably the most significant legal changes in medicine were the liberalization of abortion laws (e.g. 1967 in the UK; 1969 in Canada; 1973 in the USA; 1977 in New Zealand) under different circumstances, together with the widespread legitimation of the criteria of 'brain death' (from the late 1960s). These developments have provided arguably two of the most enduring talking points of bioethics and in each case religious sensibilities or attitudes to religion have helped shape debate.[9]

Religion is so crucial a presence in bioethics that it has even become an exigency for academic conflict-of-interest disclosure, something historically reserved for financial or family links.[10] One example from the literature is telling: alert to such defining undercurrents of debate, the editors of the *Journal of Bioethical Inquiry* include an 'Author's Disclosure Statement' which, alongside the request to declare financial conflict of interest, asks contributors whether they have a 'deep personal or religious conviction that may have affected what you wrote'.[11] Such innovation is a useful indicator of the widespread significance of religion in bioethics debate, as well as being an implicit acknowledgement that the influence of religious beliefs in scholarly and research contexts can be difficult to discern.

What are the some of the underlying religious views in bioethics? An unvarnished version of the Judaeo-Christian tradition (the most influential in Western bioethics) has as its foundation the belief that the sovereign authority of God will be undermined if human beings make decisions about the nature and limits of life and death.[12] In this tradition, God has (and is) the first and last word. This core belief provides a context for the cliché of 'scientists playing God'. Even when religionists in these traditions couch their claims in different terms, including often very humane and considered terms, for most there is a core concern of honour to the deity, and secondarily, service to humanity in the deity's name. Such a belief has implications for the meaning of Christian altruism, in particular, for altruism can pertain to the fate of the eternal soul of *any* human, however construed, not just (for example) the sentient adult. At the policy level, in all the major Christian churches, this understanding of one's 'neighbour', as an entity possessed of a human soul, provides a deep moral logic for the expression of equivalent concern – sometimes incomprehensible to non-believers – for the fate of the human embryo or foetus as for a fully grown human being.

As noted above, religion in the era of the new bioethics and 'bio-politics' has been one of the mediums through which the traditional political landscape itself has been remoulded. In the USA, for example, the peculiar situation has arisen that the Republican Party, traditionally an uncritical ally of industry, has adopted the views of the religious right on bioethics issues, seeking to limit certain elements of the medical industry. In particular, it has been hostile to federal funding of human embryonic stem cell research. Under President George W. Bush (r. 2000–2008), too, the President's Commission on Bioethics attracted hostile critique from the liberal left, who were sceptical of its members' perceived stalling tactics on such scientific developments. The Democrats, by contrast, have historically been somewhat more open to regulatory initiatives which potentially slow the expansion of industry. It was Democrats, for example, who urged tighter regulation of new drugs in the 1960s, and who in the late 1960s and early 1970s proposed the control of medical research on human subjects, ultimately mandating of institutional ethics review boards (IRBs).[13] Yet one of President Barack Obama's earliest policy moves was to legalize federal funding for human embryonic stem cell research. This policy change stamped the liberal-democratic identity of Obama's early incumbency.[14] Obama also disbanded Bush's Commission and moved to establish a group less given to what the White House referred to as 'arcane philosophical' ruminations, their debates perceived as slowing research and by implication, commercialization and patient access to treatments.[15]

## Bioethics scholarship and activism

Scholars writing on bioethics face two ways: they gesture at once towards the public policy and clinical arenas of bioethics, and they participate in scholarly debates. All bioethics writing is, therefore, perhaps more than other fields, strategic writing. Early US bioethics created a generation of scholars who claimed a specialist skill in interpreting the relationship of medical science to wider society. By bringing their philosophically (and, in some cases, theologically) shaped views to the discussion of complex and potentially conflictual social issues, bioethicists assumed prominent places as trained moral mediators for government, medical industries and their clients.

Many of the developments in the early years of the new 'bioethical enterprise' in the USA were the result of energetic work by several philosophers who were either directly aligned to the Catholic church, or who found themselves increasingly at variance with it, having once been so aligned. Daniel Callahan, who in 1969 co-founded (with the psychiatrist Willard Gaylin) the Institute of Society, Ethics and the Life Sciences (later Hastings Center) in upstate New York, had edited a Catholic magazine while studying philosophy at Harvard. Around the same time, according to Albert Jonsen – a historian of US bioethics, casuist philosopher and former Jesuit – the Catholic Democrat Kennedy family funded a centre and a library at Georgetown University which he says 'fostered the theological aspects of bioethics'.[16]

The Hastings Center and the Kennedy Institute of Ethics (KIE) were not the only places of bioethics' early institutionalization but, in the long view, they have been the most influential in the USA.[17] The activism that led to their creation was to some extent in keeping with the outward-looking attitudes of the social justice Catholicism of the period. Dramatic reform in the church in this period, often identified by the term 'Vatican II', the modernizing general council of the Catholic Church (1962–1965), both reflected and encouraged the many Catholic intellectuals dedicated to addressing social justice issues. (The right-to-life movement, which responded to increasing legalization of abortion, has intersected with but is by no means coextensive with, the religiously informed views of much scholarly bioethics.) This background provides a context for understanding some of the key academic debates in bioethics. To identify early institutional forms of the new US bioethics as being to some extent either a Catholic thing or a philosophical thing – or some combination of these – would only be a slight exaggeration. What philosophers and theologians had in common was a sense of the need for social relevance for their fields, if at times they held contrary views.

Philanthropy, government and public interest helped to make bioethics a major academic industry in a relatively short time.[18] By

1998, when Albert Jonsen (who was originally connected to Georgetown) wrote a landmark celebratory history of modern bioethics, he was able to identify 'almost 200 centers, departments, and programs'.[19] This new professional field, for philosophers and other scholars, spread widely and deeply within the tertiary and professional education sector, including in an array of new scholarly publications. The *Hastings Center Report* was the first major academic journal devoted to bioethics: it first appeared in 1971 and continues to the present day, now with a companion journal *IRB* (which studies Institutional Review Boards). Scholars launched other new journals or revamped older ones through the 1970s and 1980s. Reference works out of the Kennedy Institute of Ethics have attested to and nourished the expansion of bioethics: the institute sponsored the first annual *Bibliography of Bioethics* in 1975: its 1996 edition listed 3,620 'books, essays, and articles on bioethics' and the figure for c. 2006–2009 is 8,195 new citations.[20] The Institute similarly supported the philosopher Warren Reich's *Encyclopedia of Bioethics* which first appeared in 1978 and was last updated in 2004. Perhaps the most successful publication in the history of modern bioethics is the textbook *Principles of Biomedical Ethics*, by Tom L. Beauchamp and James F. Childress, both of whom were associated with the KIE in 1979, when the book first appeared. In 2008 it went into its sixth edition.[21]

Significant legal and regulatory change also followed from bioethics advice. For example, a task force on death and dying, at the Hastings Center, endorsed the Ad Hoc Committee of the Harvard Medical School on its Definition of Brain Death, a definition that later came widely into law.[22] As a medical journal article on the legal acceptance of brain death noted in 1977, 'six of the last seven laws have used one or two models proposed by the American Bar Association (ABA) and the Institute of Society, Ethics and Life Sciences, Hastings-on-Hudson, N. Y.'.[23] Two early bioethics philosophers, Albert R. Jonsen, then Associate Professor of Bioethics at University of California San Francisco, and Karen Lebacqz, Associate Professor of Christian Ethics at the Pacific School of Religion, were members of the commission which developed the influential 1979 Belmont Report (discussed below).[24] In the UK, a philosopher, Mary Warnock (now Baroness Warnock) brokered the introduction of an ambitious regulatory system for the new reproductive technologies (1984–1990), resulting in the foundation of the Human Fertility and Embryo Authority.[25] In these ways scholarly authority and skill were turned to account, to create regulatory forms of authority which directly affect clients' and practitioners' access to and experience of medical procedures and practices. Many lawyers, too, have also been influential in the history of bioethics, their own traditions crossing boundaries between legal commentary and the already existent world of case law and statutory law reform.[26]

## Feminism and bioethics

A simple linear narrative of what has been called the 'birth of bioethics', however, lacks a wider context for diverse forms of secular activism present across Western society in the 1960s and 1970s. Critiques of medicine came from both within and outside the relevant professions. Medical reflections tended to take shape within the confines of professional associations (such as the World Medical Association), while as a sphere of public policy engagement bioethics had some of its many roots in the patients' rights and women's rights movements of the 1960s and 1970s. Of these, the one to have had the greatest impact at an interdisciplinary level was the women's movement and its direction into feminist bioethics. When there is a risk that the reproductive issues in bioethics are recast as merely 'beginning of life' questions,[27] or when a general text on bioethics explicitly sets the perspectives of feminist bioethics aside, for proponents to voice,[28] it is important to underscore here the historical significance for women and feminism of the politics of medicine.

In an era when collectivism and communal self-help in many forms were celebrated, feminists articulated a critique of traditional gynaecology as a profession which had tended to overlook the woman as a whole person, reducing her to (the problems of) her reproductive anatomy. A new women's health movement drew attention to instances of mistreatment and exploitation of women by abortionists, pharmaceutical companies, doctors and producers of medical devices. In response to perceived paternalism among doctors, government and industry, grassroots women's health centres grew up in many jurisdictions. The feature of these centres was an emphasis on collective self-help underpinned by a sense of women 'identifying with' women (in the newly expressed term), and commensurately, confidence that this identification was the most beneficial means to physical and emotional health. Perhaps no single cultural product better expressed this sense that women's physical beings and their experience were inseparable than the publication of the bestselling book by the Boston Women's Health Collective, *Our Bodies Our Selves*, the feminist pillow book of the 1970s (which is still in print). Its goal was 'to assert that, in an age of professionals, we are the

best experts on ourselves and our feelings, to begin the collective struggle for adequate health care'.[29] The gay liberation movement of the
1970s came to develop strong medical-activist tendencies, in the wake
of the toll from the 1980s of HIV/AIDS on gay men, on issues of drug
access as well as euthanasia.

From the 1960s, campaigns for abortion law reform took place across
much of the world. In some places extremely liberal abortion laws came
into being: in many jurisdictions, however, limits were imposed not
only on the point during pregnancy after which abortion would
become illegal, but on the terms under which it was permissible at all.[30]
The United States has in some senses been a barometer of the status of
abortion. In 1973, when the Supreme Court case *Roe v. Wade* ruled that
to prevent a woman procuring an abortion was unconstitutional on the
grounds of the citizen's right to privacy, many state laws against abortion became unenforceable. A number of states in the USA have gradually pressed back the influence of the decision, with the possibility that
a return to the Supreme Court may ensue.

Feminist bioethics represents a major international forum for debate
about the place of women in the context of different health cultures
generally, and about the implications and effects of assisted reproductive technology for women in particular. Founded in 1992, the
International Network on Feminist Approaches to Bioethics, which also
publishes a journal, *International Journal of Feminist Approaches to
Bioethics*, had 900 members worldwide in 2006, from a range of backgrounds. In contemporary terms, 900 could be said to amount to a
movement. The entry for 'Feminist bioethics' in the *Stanford
Encyclopedia of Philosophy* positions academic feminist bioethics:

> Since the early 1970s feminist scholars have been complementing
> the agendas of activists. Some straddle both scholarly and activist
> communities. ... By the early 1990s feminist bioethics had come to
> be recognized as a distinctive academic concentration offering a
> sustained critique of mainstream bioethics.[31]

The term 'feminist bioethics' poses an ironic challenge to the procedural neutrality sometimes imagined in mainstream bioethics: 'feminist
bioethics' admits a political view as its starting point. Underlying questions of feminist bioethics are questions such as 'What are the implications of this for women?' and 'What would a "gender-sensitive" reading
of this mean?' Feminists participating in bioethics, however, do not all
share the same views by any means and like women's studies and

gender studies feminist academic input into bioethics is also multidisci-plinary, including scientists, historians, social scientists, philosophers and scholars of literature, STS and history of science, expressing a wide range of views. Like most radical movements, feminism has been char-acterized by significant but not unproductive dispersion and fragmen-tation, including within the world of scholarship.

Up to this point, we have considered: background issues of the historically 'sacred' role adhering to medicine since the nineteenth century; some core beliefs of Christian and Jewish religionists in bioethics; the importance of the 1960s and 1970s for emerging forms of bioethics activism and their impact; and some of the political dimen-sions of bioethics. We shall turn now to a more detailed consideration of the role of the academic disciplines of philosophy and the social sciences in bioethics.

## From moral philosophy to applied ethics

Up until the 1950s, very few philosophers of ethics considered medical ethics.[32] When medical people, government and philanthropists turned to philosophers to contemplate the ethics of medicine, they were asking philosophers to reinvent themselves.[33] Philosophers who began in the late 1960s to contribute to debate on medical issues were moving outside the confines of their formal training. In the USA and the UK, in particular, training in philosophical ethics took the form of philosoph-ical modelling, a branch of so-called meta-ethics, rather than a practice connected to the changeable worlds of clinical decision-making or public policy. Many newly trained philosophers, however, influenced by the climate of political activism of the 1960s, saw this tradition as focusing unduly on rarefied argumentation to the exclusion of real-world referents.[34] According to Stephen Toulmin, in an important 1982 historical essay entitled 'How Medicine Saved the Life of Ethics', US philosophers in the first 60 years of the twentieth century saw their role as not to take sides, issuing so-called normative judgements – but 'to consider in a more formal way what *kinds* of issues and judgments are properly classified as moral in the first place'.[35] Mary Warnock, England's most influential bioethics policy philosopher, writing in 1960, similarly decried the 'refusal of philosophers in England to commit themselves to any moral opinions'.[36]

Toulmin's often-cited article does not argue, as is sometimes assumed, that medicine gave philosophers jobs, though it did so for some. Toulmin argues that active engagement with real-world issues gave life to a discipline which he saw as becoming moribund from two sides: moral philosophy's exclusive contemplation of abstractions on the one hand, and the threat to philosophy from relativism (which asserts that one morality is as valid as another) and emotivism (which sees values as the product of emotions).[37] Neither of these admits of decisive action. Thus not only did Toulmin celebrate the worldly engagement of philosophy as a means to escape arid intellectualism in the mid-twentieth century's teaching programmes, he also saw the call for ethics to provide answers to actual social dilemmas as a way to step back from the perils of relativism. In response, philosophers began to practise what they referred to as 'applied ethics': ethics applied not only to medicine, but also for some to real-world fields such as journalism, law and business.

For trainee philosophers to contemplate a career in a field of applied ethics such as bioethics was in the mid-1960s culturally innovative, institutionally subversive and intellectually controversial. Recognizing this, Daniel Callahan in a 1973 article attempted to position bioethics as a new academic discipline, arguing that bioethics should be practical, and aimed a glancing shot at the then-dominant priorities of academic philosophy when he wrote: 'The discipline of bioethics should be so designed and its practitioners so trained, that it will directly – at whatever cost to disciplinary elegance – serve those physicians and biologists whose positions demand that they make the practical decisions.'[38] The reference to 'disciplinary elegance' refers to skill at philosophical debating, a theme to which Callahan returned in later years. Within the analytic philosophy fraternity, applied ethics was a suspect disciplinary novelty. Many 'rejected the applied philosophy of bioethics as an illegitimate form of philosophy' and saw the applied ethics scholars as interlopers in a field characterized previously by refined abstraction on moral questions: applied ethics, tarred with the brush of real-world referents (empiricism), seemed to embody at best a contradiction in terms.[39]

Philosophers in bioethics thus developed something of a hybrid form of their discipline, retaining some of the formal philosophical technique of analytic philosophy, while directly addressing policy debates. As empirical philosophers Borry and colleagues observe: 'Mainstream bioethics was patterned after the field of philosophy (with the aim of logical reasoning, conceptual clarity, coherence, and rational justification), to produce a rational and decontextualised discourse.'[40] That 'rational and decontextualised discourse' took the form of firm advice, normative statements about the morality of particular choices in medical practice and policy. Philosophically trained commentators attuned to the times offered to governments and other administrative bodies a vital combination of readiness and reasoning power. They had an adaptable disciplinary tradition which could function intellectually in the absence of data, and were thus positioned to see each new event as amenable to a universal reasoning style. Borry et al. explain:

> The concept of applied ethics is based on a top-down rationalistic and deductive model, and can be used for all kinds of ethical problems (i.e., suicide, abortion, animal rights, nuclear arms, euthanasia, etc.). By applying ethical theories and principles, professional ethicists can proffer practical recommendations and prescriptions on ethical problems supplied mainly by nonethicists.[41]

Time and timing mattered: as Callahan emphasized, part of the self-proclaimed charter of the new bioethics was that it had to be able to participate in making 'practical decisions'.[42] Whereas academic approaches to problems tend to be open-ended, in the public sphere, debate seeks closure. Media attention only lasts so long and governments need to be seen to act. Bioethics advisory roles might be understood, then, as being set against the ticking of three different clocks: the 'clock' of mortality within the human body, which can summon the moral imperative to act; the second, related, clock against which clinicians and medical researchers race to save lives or to become the provider or discoverer of medical innovation; and third, the political clock, which measures time against such things as the schedule of elections, the passing of legislation, and responses to activism.[43] Whether bioethics is a political activity carried out by scholars or a scholarly activity which feeds into politics and thence the clinical and experimental sphere is the unanswerable question. It is the willingness as much as the capacity to offer normative advice that sets applied ethicists apart from scholars in other fields in philosophy.

## Principles and 'principlism'

Beauchamp and Childress's successful 1979 *Principles of Biomedical Ethics* built on a model for the protection of research participants which had been prefigured at government level in the US National Research Act of 1974. The Act created a National Commission for the Protection of Human Subjects of Biomedical and Behavioral Research, whose job was to 'identify the basic ethical principles that should underlie the conduct of biomedical and behavioral research involving human subjects and to develop guidelines which should be followed to assure that such research is conducted in accordance with those principles'. The report was a set of bioethics principles 'at a level of generalization that should assist scientists, subjects, reviewers and interested citizens to understand the ethical issues inherent in research involving human subjects' to 'assist in resolving the ethical problems that surround the conduct of research with human subjects'.[44] The commission set down three principles on the basis of which human subject research in medicine could be undertaken: (1) Respect for Persons; (2) Beneficence; and (3) Justice.[45] Such principles are intended to frame a commonality, but in so doing, they speak implicitly of difference and the likelihood of disagreement. Stephen Toulmin, himself associated with the work of the National Commission, argued in his essay 'The Tyranny of Principles' (1981) that a principles-based approach was little more than a means of masking and squaring opposing views in the new era of committee-driven medical ethics.[46] Tom Beauchamp, who had been involved in some of the deliberations of the commission, developed with James Childress a model to encompass four slightly different principles to guide ethical reasoning: justice, autonomy, beneficence and non-maleficence. Beauchamp and Childress envisaged that these could provide a foundation for all biomedical ethics decision-making, not only decisions in relation to human experimentation. *Principles* itself reflects a compromise, if of a slightly different kind from that noted by Toulmin. In the interests of devising its four working principles, Beauchamp and Childress put aside their respective allegiances to each of the two dominant philosophical schools in bioethics debate: utilitarianism and deontology. Beauchamp is identified as favouring utilitarianism, a form of philosophical 'consequentialism'. James Childress, by contrast, is a proponent of the school known as deontology, or duty-based ethical theory.[47]

'Utilitarianism' refers to the notion that the ethical value of an act can be measured only according to its utility. It is an implicitly secular view developed by Jeremy Bentham (1748–1832) and John Stuart Mill (1806–1873), sometimes over-simplified in the term 'greatest happiness principle'. Utilitarianism in practice maintains that decisions about the right and wrong way to proceed in any given situation can only be arrived at by reference to their effects on those involved in the outcome (the consequences in 'consequentialism').[48] In its least subtle form utilitarianism can be rehearsed as 'cost-benefit' argumentation, where the interests of all parties to a debate are weighed up and value allotted to them according to where the greatest amount of human happiness (crudely understood) can be generated. Utilitarianism has been the most accommodating mode of reasoning in bioethics, as it is aligned to a market liberalism, which holds that government intervention should only be permitted to prevent manifest harm and that the individual has the right to make his or her own choice about what medical services to enlist in order to fulfil their own idea of happiness.

A deontological view of morality is based on the notion that moral duties can be identified and should be followed, a view most often associated with the philosopher Immanuel Kant (1724–1804). As a view that holds there is a single morally right position which lies somewhere outside the realm of particular interests, deontology can readily accommodate the laws of revealed religion (and indeed James Childress is also a Protestant theologian). Thus, the argumentation arising from deontological philosophy presumes the existence of a correct answer to ethical dilemmas according to a moral duty, for example the duty implied by a term such as 'life is sacred'.

In *Principles*, the authors show a three-step link between their philosophical theories and practical decisions in the medical sphere. Theories are their starting point; principles are derived from them; and rules, which are more numerous and specific, are developed from principles and point finally to 'particular judgments and actions'.[49] The book is divided into sections which outline the particular application of the principles of justice, autonomy, beneficence, non-maleficence (sometimes referred to by critics as the 'Georgetown mantra', a reference to Georgetown University as the home of the KIE, where Beauchamp and Childress were based when they wrote the book). Implicitly the path from theories to actions mirrors the cooperation manifested in the authorship of the book itself. If two philosophical theories cannot be reconciled in the language of philosophy, they might still find common ground in a looser set of lay imperatives, in the form of principles. These become the stabilizing structure intended to support practical decisions.

Widely cited in training for medical and allied clinical professions, the very success of *Principles of Biomedical Ethics* was a source of controversy. Its intention to assist the increasingly diverse range of people involved in medical decisions exposed the authors to criticism that a universalized principles-based ethics can have the effect, however unintended, of over-simplifying the decision-making process. Some philosophers felt that this approach bleached from bioethics many of the difficulties they saw as intrinsic to the contested medical cultures with which they, as bioethics commentators, were dealing. Toulmin identified the problems he saw in the use of principles as the starting point for bioethics judgements: '[w]e ... need to recognize that a morality based entirely on general rules and principles is tyrannical and dispro-portioned, and that only those who make equitable allowances for subtle individual differences have a proper feeling for the deeper demands of ethics'.[50] Toulmin represents here a casuist philosophical approach. The essence of the practice of casuistry is that the extensive knowledge of the details of the ethical matter at hand are seen as crucial to finding a suitable ethical response.[51] (Although Toulmin's article was published two years after the appearance of the Beauchamp and Childress text, it nonetheless discreetly does not cite *Principles*.)

Expressing similar concerns to those of Toulmin the philosophers Clouser and Gert coined the pejorative term 'principlism' (in 1990) to urge their view that the use of principles as the dominant mode of ethi-cal reasoning was contrary to the goals of dealing with ethical and cultural complexity.[52] They provide an extensive critique of Beauchamp and Childress's text, contending that 'so-called "principles" function neither as adequate surrogates for moral theories nor as directives or guides for determining the morally correct action'.[53] They argue for the necessarily time-bound nature of moral theory, which is 'an ongoing attempt to explain and justify our common moral intuitions', adding that 'morality is a very complex phenomenon, and we can hardly expect a theory that explains it to be statable in one sentence slogans'.[54] A 1994 collection, *Matter of Principles: Ferment in US Bioethics*, under-scored this critique. The editors posit that 'principlism' simplifies complex cultural and political questions and has implicitly if inadver-tently pointed to resolutions that favour a liberal individualist free market approach to medicine, suited to the medical *status quo* in the USA. (They also note the submerged but still salient role of religion: '[e]ven religious ethicists working in the area more often than not ... speak the language of principles rather than their own religious language, especially when engaged in public discourse'.[55])

The reception of *Principles of Biomedical Ethics* can stand as an index of two of the key debates which have characterized scholarly bioethics: those involving philosophical critiques of the principles-based biomed-ical ethics and those involving social science's (and to a lesser extent other disciplines') critiques of both a principles-based approach and of philosophical bioethics more widely. The nub of the problem (from the point of view of critics) is that the search to find agreed-upon grounds for debate must confront the realities of what brings people to the table in the first place. Daniel Callahan pinpointed this concern in 2003, harking back to his early resistance to the arid intellectualism of traditional moral philosophy. He expressed frustration at the *modus operandi* of those philosophers whom he saw as being wedded to the reductionist aspects of a principles-based approach, with its reliance on pure reason as the basis of judgements. He argues:

> None of us ... can rationally defend our ultimate premise and starting point; there is always some beginning leap to be made. Reason can not judge reasoning without finally begging the question. Nor should reason be sharply separated from emotion. Our reasons ordinarily embody and express some emotions just as our emotions embody some cognitive judgements. ... Rationality is important, but it is never enough. The worst possible mistake on the part of philosophers, all too common, is to think that good ethics comes down to good arguments.[56]

Callahan is a communitarian philosopher, following a branch of reasoning characterized by 'methodological claims about the importance of tradition and social context for moral and political reasoning, ontological or metaphysical claims about the social nature of the self, and normative claims about the value of community'.[57] He focuses on the wider social domain, with implications that set his view apart from bioethics utilitarians.[58] Callahan is known as a friend to the social sciences and in some ways his view overlaps with the views of social scientists, who when they write about bioethics factor in complex social realities and questions of power.

It should now be starting to become clear, therefore, why a social scientist, C. L. Bosk, the scholar quoted at the beginning of this chapter, should urge that bioethics pay attention to the social contexts of specific debates, as well as to the power embodied in the institutionalized forms of bioethics itself. Those themes are pursued here.

## Between philosophers and social scientists

Applied philosophy brought to bioethics an institutional history which set trained philosophers to some extent on a methodological collision course with commentators from within the social sciences. The place of the social sciences in public and scholarly conversations about bioethics has therefore been a subject of sometimes heated debate since at least 1981.[59] Bioethics in the early years since the word was coined represented several academic disciplines: according to one study, by a group of sympathetic philosophers, 'Initially, people from many different disciplines, such as medicine, law, theology, biological sciences, social sciences, philosophy, humanities, etc. entered the dialogue. However, in a process of professionalisation and institutionalisation, the bioethical discussions quickly became anchored in the fields of theology and philosophy.'[60] Contributors in the social sciences were active throughout this period, notably in the field of medical sociology, but according to these philosophers, 'Their presence ... was minimal, and certainly not wished for by most [philosophical] bioethicists.'[61]

In 1984, however, US sociologist Renée C. Fox (an early member of the Hastings Center) and her historian colleague Judith P. Swazey identified what they saw as both the nationalist and disciplinary short-sightedness of US bioethics in an article entitled 'Medical Morality Is Not Bioethics: Medical Ethics in China and the United States'. They claimed: 'Bioethics, particularly its philosophical aspects, is viewed as largely *a*cultural and *trans*cultural in nature.'[62] Recently the two authors have reflected on the response to their article among bioethics philosophers which they experienced as largely negative and in one instance caustic. [63] Similarly to Fox and Swazey, George Weisz introduced a collection on social science approaches to bioethics with a critique of philosophical bioethics: 'In their analyses of complex situations, ethicists often appear grandly oblivious to the social and cultural context in which these occur, and indeed to empirical referents of any sort.'[64]

As two writers in the new field of 'sociology of bioethics' observe: 'Scholars tend to be reductionist, to see the world through the lenses of the disciplines to which they have devoted their lives. This tendency is aggravated in bioethics where members of the different disciplines vie for the last word on what is *morally* right and wrong.'[65] And when there are historical reasons for different views of the moral issues, this can compound matters. For philosophers, a lengthy historical dialogue with theology since at least the Enlightenment era has been in turn imprinted by the potent role of religion in modern medical 'street activism'. For social scientists (but sociologists in particular) their history is grounded in strongly secularist assumptions and focuses on systems of human interaction and power relations. Thus their vision of ethics is a social one.

A group of 'empirical philosophers' – for which, read: philosophers sympathetic to the social sciences – has provided some of the cultural background to philosophers' resistance to the scholarly practice of the social sciences. Their account can be summed up briefly: for philosophers to derive a normative statement from empirical evidence confuses two central categories, the category of what *is* (which is the province of the social scientist) and the category of what *ought to be* (the province of the philosopher).[66] If scholars in the social sciences, with their commitment to creating data, participate in an argument about ethical matters, it offers an implicit challenge to this received wisdom. Furthermore, for philosophers, a related factor is that social sciences are prepared to acknowledge the complexities of applying global morality to local issues. If social sciences are contributing to bioethics conversations at the level of normative statements (e.g. giving policy advice), such a cultural stance can logically on this view entail a slide from cultural relativism to the perceived hazard of moral relativism. At the extreme, so-called 'emotivism' – a view that morality is individual and no different from a matter of taste – lies at the end of this relativistic route.

Crossfire in the world of learning is usually something which occurs within disciplines: for one discipline to critique another requires a certain degree of audacity, for if one does not belong in the field, how can one claim to know it? Indeed Fox and Swazey referred to their 1984 critique of philosophical bioethics as 'mischievous'.[67] Fox and Swazey's article was a call for reorientation of perspective, in a critique of what they saw as the philosophical bioethics' uncritical absorption of the cultural imperatives of aspects of US culture. In particular they critiqued the idea that individuals are ethically identical because truly autonomous, standing free of any social constraints and without social obligations.[68] Mindful of tensions emerging between the disciplines, philosopher Mary Mahowald cautioned in an early collection which sought to bridge the divide (the 1986 *New Directions in Ethics: The Challenge of Applied Ethics*) that '*genuine* interdisciplinarity is difficult to achieve, since it entails admission of limitation on the part of the inter-disciplinary contributors',[69] while in the same book, a social scientist, Bruce Jennings, declared that social science had destroyed the credibility of philosophy, making it impossible to sustain the view that there could be a strict demarcation between normative and empirical.[70] He conceded, though, that 'At its best applied ethics can help us explore the human significance of abstract, universal moral rules when those rules are embodied in concrete relationships'.[71] In 1990, George Weisz saw promise in a 'growing tendency in some circles to retreat from the notion of universally applicable norms and to embrace, with more or less enthusiasm, the cultural embeddedness of ethical values'.[72]

If at times in the history of modern bioethics scholars have regarded each other warily across seemingly impassable disciplinary differences, there is also evidence of mutual respect: indeed it has been suggested that without disciplinary differences and the specific problems posed in bioethics, 'the generative tensions of the field are lost'.[73] Debate around modern medicine itself has become a transformative and often unifying force. Scholars have challenged each other to think through issues in new ways, leading to collaborative ventures which embrace diverse interpretative approaches. Many multidisciplinary essay collections, for example, have bridged this divide in a productive, practical way, rather than through attempts at theoretical resolution. Mainline philosophical bioethics, too, has more recently expanded its own terms of reference: it has, for example, internationalized its ethical frame and addressed the multiplicity of faith-based ethics beyond the Judaeo-Christian model. Philosophers have also expressed impatience with the narrow medical focus of bioethics and argued for the use of philosophical analysis to advance bioethical discussion on important matters of public health. And bioethics scholars from continental Europe have started to form alliances with colleagues from the UK and USA, shifting the centre of gravity in geo-political as well as ethical terms.[74]

In the end, conversation between philosophers and social scientists and other humanities scholars has probably arisen more as a result of shared social justice sensibilities or shared professional obligations (such as committee work). Influential early bioethics philosophers Stephen Toulmin and Albert Jonsen, for example, said they found committee work both ethically satisfactory and intellectually satisfying, because it allowed for the exposure of divergent perceptions and worked for consensus. At each end of the spectrum, there are still commentators holding the disciplinary line, but beyond these disciplinary tensions lies the question of the ethical standing of the field itself.[75]

The very success of bioethics has invited scrutiny not only as an academic field but as an 'enterprise'. Historians of medicine Charles Rosenberg and Roger Cooter have strongly critiqued bioethics, depicting it as having taken up residence inside the 'belly of the whale' of the vast modern medical enterprise, rendering doubtful the ideal of the independent viewpoint integral to the work of the scholar.[76] Gerontologist Tom Koch has echoed this sentiment, explicitly aligning utilitarian bioethics with a wider 'triage' mentality in health-care funding.[77] Thus the 'ethics of bioethics' (the subject of an eponymous 2007 collection to which several philosophers contributed), considers such ethically contentious areas of bioethics discourse as funded ethics consultation, bioethics roles on corporate ethics committees and industry subsidies for academic commentary.[78] These debates reflect a wider ideological discussion about the relationship of medical science to individuals, communities and governments. At the level of health policy, the scholarly politics of bioethics is not only rarely far from view, it is a defining feature of the field.

## Discussion

The purpose of this chapter has been to consider the antecedents of different forms of scholarly writing in bioethics literature. To see religious input, active or implied, one can look to see what is being defended and why. For example, absolute refusal to countenance the destruction of life in any form (from the human embryo and its stem cells, to the foetus, to the person seeking active euthanasia) generally reflects a Judaeo-Christian view in mainstream bioethics. Not everyone who holds such views is necessarily Jewish or Christian and other creeds hold a diverse range of views in relation to clinical and experimental medicine. The most influential schools of philosophy have been the deontological (or Kantian) and utilitarian (or consequentialist). While the deontological approach allows for duties to be derived from theological precepts, and the consequentialist view is secular in orientation, these two have in common that they each use a deductive reasoning method, starting with general rules which are used to analyse specific cases. Because each can reflect to some extent one or other side in the 'right to life' versus 'medical free market' debate, they have tended to be highly visible at policy level. Some very notable bioethics philosophers, however, have represented other schools, such as the communitarian and casuist approaches. While a deontological view might point to theocracy and a consequentialist view might point to a contract-based society with small government, the communitarian view holds that there is such a thing as the public good and that it can be furthered and determined through the diverse instrumentalities constituting the public domain. The casuist approach treats each case on its merits: the moral choice is the choice best suited to a scenario about which the most pertinent detail available is known and all parties' views are understood and accounted for. Such a view also approximates a new 'empirical' philosophy, which appears to have been taken up recently among some Catholic and Catholic-influenced philosophers. The 'empirical turn' in philosophy can be understood as related to increasing confluences between philosophers and social scientists, after many decades of tensions. Social science is in theory intended to be descriptive, as it creates data, while prescriptive or so-called normative advice is meant to be the province of applied philosophy. In fact, this distinction has not held up other than in the abstract. The new 'applied philosophy' paved the way for real-world scenarios to be an essential element in the work of philosophy in its activist, public mode. And social scientists have urged that true ethical understanding requires deep insight into the interactions of those involved, for example in a clinical scenario. Implicit in this view is that resorting to rules or principles screens out precisely the kind of knowledge that can further the human good. On this basis, social scientists have felt legitimated in playing an active role beyond that of mere providers of data.

Scholarly bioethics maps onto a complex cultural and political terrain, interacting with social forces such as law, industry, church politics, traditional party politics and non-party activism. Discussion on methodological grounds of one school of thought in scholarly bioethics can rarely be separated wholly from the social alignments of which the language of scholarship sometimes tacitly speaks. What writers say – and how they say it – can reflect both the internal histories of their disciplines and the history of attitudes to other disciplines. The aim of this chapter has been to provide some basic tools for recognizing the constituent debates of scholarly bioethics as it has evolved, with an emphasis on questions of politics and manner of scholarly enquiry. The term 'scholarly bioethics' was generally preferred over 'academic' bioethics because much important bioethics work is done by scholars who are acting in consulting or commentary roles outside university confines. If not all academically trained commentators speak as they would to scholarly audiences, their approach generally displays the traces of the system in which they originally studied and on the basis of which they maintain, at least in part, the authority to analyse bioethics.

Every academic discipline has its own internally agreed methods for reaching conclusions. The goals of each form of truth- or judgement-seeking differ, and what constitutes a true or useful answer to a question posed in one field is rarely adequate to the expectations of another. All scholars are trained into their own more or less agreed ways of obtaining and narrating information and of interpreting key texts. This is in essence what the academic disciplines of the humanities and social science are: rules of engagement with a particular kind of subject matter which govern in turn the process of building a relationship of relative authority for one's own work to that of perceived peers living and historical. This cumulative building of intellectual authority adds a historical dimension to academic conversations, some of which have been going on for decades, even centuries.

Modern bioethics is, among other things, a story of the ways in which members of different forms and forums for truth- or judgement-seeking have interacted with each other to stake out discursive territory in medical and health policy. Differences in academic discipline and training have played a part in shaping modern bioethics commentary and such differences have often been to some extent shaped and over-laid by the diverse motivations which brought academics into the realm of modern bioethics in the first place. Questions of politics have shaded into questions of methodology and in turn into questions of whose authority carries weight in wider bioethics debate.

## Further reading

DeMarco, J. P. and R. M. Fox (eds) (1986) *New Directions in Ethics: The Challenge of Applied Ethics* (New York: Routledge and Kegan Paul).

De Vries, R., L. Turner, K. Orfali and C. Bosk (2007) *The View from Here: Bioethics and the Social Sciences* (Malden, MA: Blackwell).

DuBose, E. R., R. P. Hamel and L. J. O'Connell (1994) *A Matter of Principles? Ferment in US Bioethics* (Valley Forge, PA: Trinity Press International).

Fox, R.C. and J. P. Swazey (2008) *Observing Bioethics* (Oxford and New York: Oxford University Press).

Hedgecoe, A. M. (2004) 'Critical Bioethics: Beyond the Social Science Critique of Applied Ethics', *Bioethics*, 18, 2, 120–143.

Jonsen, A. R. (2005) *Bioethics Beyond the Headlines: Who Lives? Who Dies? Who Decides?* (Lanham, MD: Rowman and Littlefield).

Kuhse, H. and P. Singer (eds) (1999) *Bioethics: An Anthology*, 1st edn (Malden, MA: Blackwell).

Latour, B. and S. Woolgar (1986) *Laboratory Life: The Construction of Scientific Facts* (Princeton, NJ: Princeton University Press).

Orfali, K. and R. G. DeVries (2009) 'A Sociological Gaze on Bioethics' in William C. Cockerham (ed.), *The New Blackwell Companion to Medical Sociology* (Hoboken, NJ: Wiley-Blackwell), 487–510.

Scully, J. L., L. Baldwin-Ragaven and P. Fitzpatrick (eds) (2010) *Feminist Bioethics: At the Center, on the Margins* (Baltimore, MD: Johns Hopkins University Press).

Walter, J. K. and E. P. Klein (2003) *The Story of Bioethics: From Seminal Works to Contemporary Explorations* (Washington: Georgetown University Press).

Weisz, G. (ed.) (1990) *Social Science Perspectives on Medical Ethics* (Dordrecht: Kluwer Academic).

# 2
# Language, Narrative and Rhetoric in Bioethics

As bioethics became more multidisciplinary in the 1990s, scholars from a range of academic fields began to pay greater heed to the role of language, narrative and rhetoric in the presentation and understanding of medical ethics issues. The collection *Stories and their Limits*, from 1997, for example, investigated the impact of this new trend and included works by 'physicians, literary critics, religious studies scholars, philosophers, sociologists [and] a comparatist' (i.e. scholar of comparative language, literature or culture).[1] The editor Hilde Lindeman Nelson is a philosopher who has worked with social science and literary scholars in the field of bioethics. Apparently writing to engage other philosophers, she explains where the work of those who study narrative and language belongs in the wider scheme of interdisciplinary bioethics:

> If 'doing ethics' means developing and defending formal ethical systems, then they are not doing ethics. But if it means reflecting on the moral aspects of particular encounters within a powerful social institution where what is said and done reveals a great deal about who we are and what matters in our lives, then they are indeed ethicists, in at least a loose sense of the word.[2]

To understand judgements about what should or should not be done, hearing the choice of words by those arguing for a particular view is one way of hearing their priorities. Rhetorical analysis considers the assumptions behind the linguistic habits of medical science, and can be the beginning of a sustained process of ethical understanding. Scholars using tools associated with literary analysis have begun to argue that all texts can be read 'against the grain', with a view to gaining insight into the particular cultural agendas which inform these professional spheres. And the so-called 'narrative turn' in social science

37

has generated readings of medical scenarios that focus on the narrative understanding of the experience of patients.[3]

This mode of analysis sees ethics as socially grounded and time-bound: social scientist Naomi Sunderland claims that 'Ethics, like language itself, finds its expression, production, and reproduction only *through the social medium*, the social round of shared experience, shared understanding, and shared access to meaningful social spaces.'[4] Similarly, Susan Squier follows cultural studies theorist Tony Bennett in arguing 'we need to explore how the text [for example a medical article] consists of a set of social relations' not only at the level of material production, 'but ... as the product of social negotiations'.[5] Historian of medicine Christian Bonah, paraphrasing the Polish bacteriologist Ludvik Fleck (1935), accentuates the conditions in which new scientific knowledge circulates, observing: 'information is partial and biased by the very essence of its existence and its exchange'.[6] In this light, even scientific meaning is both changeable and essentially social: 'Meanings are constantly subject to negotiation, even within a collective. Accordingly, the extent of meaning-stability and consensus in all phases of science must be regarded as an empirical matter.'[7]

These radical assertions about the contingent nature of ethical discourse and scientific knowledge underline both the power and the vulnerability of language in medicine. Attention to language prompts questions about how medical issues are framed: through the choice of descriptors; through grammatical constructions; and through devices such as metaphor. How do these ways of perceiving and describing shape or limit the language of medicine and of medical ethics?[8] Every choice about the language to be employed in medical culture has a political and ethical dimension, broadly speaking, as every statement explicitly or tacitly expresses a preference about *what should be* and about the shape that decisions *should* take. Historical analysis of the rhetoric of science explores the reasons why some statements carry more weight than others in a given social context; how social groups and individuals use language, and to what effect. This chapter looks at the importance of word choice in medicine, the rhetorical reading of 'real science'; the related question of the 'medical imaginary'; the use of the passive voice; the power of metaphor in medicine; and finally, the rhetorical strategies of bioethics itself.

It is important to stress that 'rhetoric', as it is used here, needs to be understood in its classical literary sense, meaning the art of persuasion effected in such things as phrasing, and the use of literary tropes, rather than 'rhetoric' in the lay sense (empty statements). Indeed, in the works of authors such as Bruno Latour, understanding of rhetoric underpins the conditions of all social analysis. For him, even the notion that there is such a thing as 'society' stakes a rhetorical claim, rather than describing an actuality. To speak of rhetoric, therefore, is to speak of the ways in which all statements arise within some kind of social matrix, and serve particular ends. Language does not merely describe the world as if through clear glass, but from within institutional contexts, from within traditions, and with particular ways of seeing already 'framed' by established knowledge.[9] To read writings in medical science as rhetorical is not to suggest in any sense that scientists might write in a misleading or polemical way; rather, seeing all science in rhetorical terms suggests that it is equally the *unconscious* use of routine scientific modes of analysis and perception that yield most fruitfully to reading as rhetoric.

## Word choice

While a generation accustomed to the idea of 'spin' – the deliberate use of language to convey a selective view of events – should have no difficulty acclimatizing to the idea that language is powerful, accepting this in relation to the 'hard' realities of medical science is possibly less easy.[10] Indeed, analysing the role of language in creating medical truths appears to be a paradox: it goes against at least a lay understanding of science as trafficking in physical constants, the truths of which are gradually unfolded as time goes by and techniques improve. While it might seem to make sense to think about the capacity to create meaning in advertising, or politics, for example, there is something which at base does not make 'emotional sense' about seeing science in a rhetorical light. This is perhaps particularly so for those trained in disciplines which see themselves as 'scientific': a claim to describe the world as it is is the *sine qua non* of modern scientific practice.[11] Medical science takes the form it does in different societies as a result not only of the physical realities of the body or its interactions with the environment, but because of the role of individuals and institutions in representing these entities and processes in language itself.[12]

New words come along all the time: not only 'bioethics', as discussed earlier, but terms now in everyday use were at one time actively invented (many in the past two hundred years) and became to a greater or lesser degree absorbed into the realm of the taken-for-granted: genes; genetics; eugenics; stem-cell; euthanasia; pro-life/pro-choice; superovulation; sperm donor; clone; brain-dead. Equally, former medical categories which were once givens can become redundant: the diagnostic category of hysteria, for example, or the one-time science of phrenology. And how medicine is described or read can potentially affect personal and medical decision-making: is organ transplantation 'the gift of life', for example, or 'trade' in 'spare parts' for human beings?[13]

New technology and new ideology can be reflected and furthered through the coining of new words. In the late 1980s, for example, the meaning and scientific legitimacy of a new medical descriptor, 'pre-embryo', became the focus of hard-fought political campaigns in the UK when the question of *in vitro* fertilization (IVF) embryo experimentation was on the agenda. As 'pre-embryo' enjoyed a degree of scientific status, as well as becoming subject to political debate, it serves as a good example of the political nature of the process of semantic innovation in developing science and bioethics. Christine Crowe describes the political context in which the word was first used. In July 1982, the UK Parliament established a consultative committee chaired by the eminent philosopher Mary Warnock to assess the extent to which the then new reproductive technologies (including IVF, embryo experimentation, IVF surrogacy and other interventions) could or should be subject to government regulation. The most controversial element of the committee's 1984 report was its recommendation to Parliament that experimentation on embryos created through the new technique of IVF should be permissible up to 14 days after the embryo's creation in the laboratory. After considerable discussion over the biological and ethical bases of a cut-off time for experimentation, the committee determined that day 14 was ethically significant, as the fusion of sperm and egg cells had taken place by then but the embryo cells had yet to differentiate from those cells which make the placenta.[14] The committee's advice was that this end point would permit early stage experimentation which destroyed the embryonic cell cluster. Parliament initially rejected this recommendation in 1984, but the next year it also rejected the 'right to life' view, when MP Enoch Powell unsuccessfully introduced the *Unborn Children Protection Bill* to ban all embryo experimentation on the grounds that the human embryo was not legally different from a human being.

Late in 1985, the British scientific lobby founded a group called Progress (now Progress Educational Trust[15]) to campaign for the legalization of embryo experimentation; in 1986 the Medical Research Council and the Royal Society of Obstetricians and Gynaecologists founded a Voluntary Licensing Authority (VLA) to embody the case for peer regulation (one might say, rather than regulation by the peerage) of embryo research.[16] The VLA used in its first annual report a term, 'pre-embryo', that had been coined a few months before by Progress, to mean an embryo less than 14 days into its development. They viewed the collection of cells up to that point as 'not an embryo, but a pre-embryo: a precursor of the embryo just as the separate sperm and egg were its precursors'.[17] The term met with considerable scepticism, even among some scientists; however, its gradual uptake in the public sphere and then in Parliament suggests that the credibility scientists were able to establish for 'pre-embryo' facilitated the move towards acceptance of embryo experimentation by Parliament, in 1990.[18]

The bioethical moment was the moment of intersection between a time in political history and a time in the development of the early human embryo which was interpreted and positioned as ethically meaningful. As Crowe argues, 'Concepts do not present themselves to the researcher already packaged and ready to be employed in scientific explanation. Particular knowledge … can be understood as the expression of one particular interpretation of a phenomenon taking place "in nature", rather than as merely a description of such events.'[19] The nature of the *object* does not change in the laboratory, but once it is surveyed through scientific, legal or moral eyes, a heavy discursive and fundamentally evaluative traffic passes through it. Perception and the attribution of meaning and value cannot readily be separated. Philosopher Kenneth Richman has noted of medicine in general that 'every medical encounter has an ethical component'; the story of the pre-embryo shows how language can install an ethics at the heart of meaning, scientific or otherwise.[20]

Another example, also from the world of gynaecology, is the history of the term 'hormone replacement therapy' (HRT). HRT is the name given to the prescription of hormones to women who are experiencing unwanted symptoms of menopause. R.A. Aronowitz describes a 'semantic sleight of hand' which naturalized use of the term 'hormone replacement therapy'. The term implied that the process of menopause was a morbidity, rather than a natural part of the female life cycle. The term 'replacement' implies something is missing which should be present, requiring replacement through HRT.[21] In the face of criticisms of the assumption underlying this term, the US National Institutes of Health (NIH) changed its documents in 2002 to use instead 'menopausal hormone therapy'.[22] These two examples, the pre-embryo and HRT, are simple cases in which word choice in medical research and nosology (disease categorization) have either exposed or focused political and ethical dimensions of scientific knowledge. Medical writing, too, has been the subject of analysis, notably in discussions of the use of the passive voice.

## The passive voice

The passive voice is a grammatical term used to describe a sentence in which the person or thing performing an action is not the subject of the verb in the sentence. George Orwell in his essay 'Politics and the English Language' referred to the passive voice as one of the constituent features of ideological language devised (in his argument, consciously) to remove a sense of agency.[23] Judith Segal explains: 'Using the active voice, a writer might say, "I selected the seven subjects", using the passive, he or she might say, "seven subjects were selected".[24] She further notes, instructively, that 'When the passive is employed, the verb is made complex, the object of the action is placed in the primary position and the agent, or doer of the action, may be suppressed. In the previous sentence, the passive appears four times.'[25] There are good reasons, of course, for medical scientists to write in the passive voice: it is intended to disavow bias and to express openness to the unexpected. But it can work to induce in readers a false sense of passivity on the part of scientists or clinicians, in that it insufficiently acknowledges the presence or the will of the person who performs the action (such as in an experiment or a treatment). It disavows, too, the fact that the author has any investment in the outcome: it takes the scientist out of the science. Thus it reinforces the sense that good science simply describes a world that is already there, rather than the cultures of science themselves shaping research and conventions of analysis.[26]

## Metaphor

Medical discourse has long been suffused with metaphor. Nancy Stepan has argued that metaphoric systems have helped construct differences and meanings within scientific paradigms and that a reason for 'uncovering or exposing metaphor in science is to prevent ourselves from being used or victimised or captured by metaphors'.[27] She cites Max Black, who observes that metaphor 'selects, emphasises, suppresses and organizes features' of reality.[28] Because ideas about what is natural change over time, metaphors and their significance always seem more apparent in hindsight. In the nineteenth century, metaphor was one way in which the capacities of new techniques became incorporated into ostensibly scientific readings of the way society already worked. In their 1889 book *The Evolution of Sex*, biologists Patrick Geddes and J. Arthur Thompson provided an unselfconscious reading of the way in which sperm and ovum contribute to procreation, assuming both the nature of differences between men and women and that their readers shared these assumptions. They wrote: 'At the very threshold of sex-difference, we find that a little active cell or spore [a sperm], unable to develop of itself, unites in fatigue with a larger more quiescent individual. Here, at the very first, is the contrast between male and female.'[29] The idea of males as small, active and failed is not an especially macho stereotype, but clearly for the authors there was a fit between the social world and the newly revealed microscopic world of reproduction. What would seem to most people now a metaphor was not strictly such: it is more readily seen as the use of a narrative, the story of a character on a journey. What Geddes and Thompson were in this way able to 'find' relied on an acceptance that an anthropomorphized reproductive cell is capable of behaving in a gendered way, and thereby stands for a social group.

Shifting from the microscopic to the macro, natural scientists in the nineteenth century held that human society, no less than any other form of life, was organic, the literal and the metaphorical blending in powerful ways.[30] Historian of biology Mark Lubinsky has demonstrated that for scientists and social commentators in this period, 'degenerations of organs, tissues, individuals, nations, and races were all considered part of one basic phenomenon'.[31] Medical scientists represented the moral and physical state of the individual human body as the vital forces which were both a metaphor of, and what literally held together, the social body (the so-called 'organicist metaphor').[32] Thus criminality, mental retardation, and perceived aberrant sexual behaviours, for example, were seen as destructive of the social body, affecting human progress in general and posing a particular threat to values such as nationhood, as well as the organic unity and strength of the nation itself.[33]

Medical writers supplied metaphors which reinforced social anxieties and hinted darkly at the urgent need for a medical response to perceived social problems such as poverty, criminality and sexual diversity, as well as medical conditions such as disease, disability and addiction. In the late nineteenth and increasingly in the early twentieth century, the so-called 'feeble-minded', for example, were typically referred to as 'festering sores', 'parasites' and 'cancers'. An American researcher in 1935 wrote: 'Crime and [social] dependency keep on increasing because new defectives are born, just as new cancer cells remorselessly penetrate into sound tissues.'[34] Here, the new science of microscopic cancer research provided a metaphor which traded on the fear of cancer and imputed anti-social agency to relatively powerless individuals. One German physician who applauded the new Nazi sterilization laws of 1935 under-scored this link, saying the laws were the 'most important public health measure since the discovery of bacteria by another German [Koch] which enabled humanity to rid itself of all plagues'.[35]

Metaphor has also been used to convey a sense of intrinsic moral worth in scientific endeavour.[36] Dr John Warbasse, writing at the height of then-new research into vitamins in the 1930s, claimed:

> One does not have to be a great scientist to have his character affected by the scientific mode of thought. The student, as he toils upward on the slopes of learning, enters the atmosphere of truth, and his habits and character develop ethical vitamins out of the actinic rays of science that play on his mind.[37]

In modern medical reportage many regular metaphors reside at the more upbeat end of medical innovation: the language of 'miracles', 'wonder drugs' and 'magic bullets' is pervasive. In 1997, *Time* magazine ran a cover story about Bobbi and Kenny McCaughey, following the birth of their septuplets. The cover read: 'Miracle in Iowa: Bobbi and Kenny McCaughey's Septuplets; The Brave New Science of Making Babies'.[38] Coming as it did in December, the miracle reference recalls Christianity's story of a 'miraculous birth'. Certainly it was joyous as well as overwhelming for the McCaugheys. And their children continue to thrive, believed to be the only septuplets in history to have all survived infancy. But it is hard to see what was miraculous about this event.[39] Why would journalists, or scientists, or doctors refer to the use of fertility drugs (without IVF) to bring about a dangerous multiple birth as a miracle? And little was new about the experience of the McCaugheys: fertility drugs had been in use since long before the first test-tube birth and several high-profile multiple births occurred in the 1960s and 1970s.[40]

The use of such a metaphor, however, serves to anticipate and defuse a focus on ethics.[41] Interestingly, *Time* hedged its bets about the ethics of the fertility treatment used to bring about the multiple birth. It gave its cover headline to the miracle analogy, with a nod to the overused double literary reference of the 'brave new world', but the full report itself was quite different. It dwelt on the pressure on hospital systems; the drugs whose uncontrolled effects in treating her conception prob-lems left Bobbi McCaughey the choice of undergoing selective termina-tion of some of her developing embryos, or risking her own and her children's health with a multiple birth; and the question of how the couple would cope financially. In this example, then, there are layers of rhetoric, each of which points in a different ethical direction – one would be that good things happen as a result of these interventions; another is that notwithstanding these good things, there are concerns about the effect on mother and children and secondarily on a hospital system which deployed extensive resources for the family's treatment. In this way, each readership is accounted for, if none is satisfied.

## 'Real science' as rhetoric and the medical imaginary

A term such as 'miracle' is instantly identifiable as a metaphor, but in scientific language at least, metaphors are perhaps most effective when they are presented and experienced as the 'natural' way of understanding perceived realities.[42] Recent research by historians of modern medical science has argued that the real challenge is to understand how deeply implicated in social priorities the presumed objectivity of medical science – the 'window on nature' – actually is. Lily E. Kay's *Who Wrote the Book of Life?* is a study of the dominant metaphors which have shaped the history of genetic science. Kay points out that the idea of genome as a Book of Life has been 'scientifically productive and culturally compelling', and that although the informational 'representations of genetic phenomena' were sometimes imprecise they served to help scientists imaginatively in the 'process of meaning making in and beyond the laboratory'.[43] Kay argues that each model used by scientists in their research into genetics has been governed by metaphors which not only resonate in particular imaginative ways, but are also ineradicably embedded in the real science of genetics. The upside of metaphors – such as the claim that genes have lock and key; are a cryptographic code; are a book of life, and that molecules have or are a language – is that they have 'aided the scientific imagination in the process of meaning making'.[44] Still, she notes that such metaphors render invisible other possible interpretations.[45]

The role Kay assigns to language is therefore central, as language not only represents the dialogue between medical science and other aspects of culture, but *creates* the realities that science seems merely to describe. Kay's central observation in relation to science policy is that the language which has been used to characterize genetics has inflated its scope, projecting the time-bound, partisan and local concerns of its practitioners onto what is represented as a timeless unitary and cosmic canvas. The gap she identifies is not so much between an accurate and inaccurate reading of genetic 'scripts'; rather she is concerned by the use of language which encourages those who use it – scientists, the media, the general public – to see scientists as having deciphered the language of the gods.

Literary scholar Susan Squier argues, too, that the imagination plays a role in conceiving of real scientific change, showing that it is impossible to draw a line between the fiction of speculation about what might come to pass, and the fictions which are identified in science *as* fiction. 'Fiction gives us access to the biomedical imaginary: the zone in which experiments are carried out in narrative, and the psychic investments of biomedicine are articulated.'[46] Unlike many medical humanities scholars who use 'high literature' to give insight into medical ethics decision-making, Squier raises the broader question of the use of literary images in all types of fiction and their relationship to developments in medical science.

Alex Preda in *Aids, Rhetoric, and Medical Knowledge* shows that the directions of new medical science can be shaped in the use of language and creation of meaning categories within the scientific literature itself.[47] Examining the medical literature of HIV/AIDS, Preda finds that 'scientific persuasion adopts, integrates, and adapts elements of rhetoric that are employed by the lay public in everyday life'.[48] In particular he shows that the medical literature conflated 'risk categories' of person (for example, gay men) with particular behaviours (unprotected male-male sex), in effect reading 'risk' back through the identity of sufferers, rather than through the way in which they came to be infected with the HIV virus. This, he argues, materially affected not only ways in which further knowledge about HIV was sought, but also helped to shape public education policies and the ways in which members of the 'general population' saw themselves as 'other than' the identified 'risk' groups.[49] In sum, it permitted non-male-gays, non-Haitian people and non-IV drug users to see themselves as outside the risk profile for HIV/AIDS, even though they might have been engaging in practices which meant that they could be infected by the virus. Thus this seemingly transparent scientific and epidemiological descriptor of 'risk categories' bore with it a set of assumptions which revealed as much about the world view of the scientists as it did about transmission of the illness.

## Rhetorical strategies of bioethics itself

Finally, but possibly most influentially, Tod Chambers has used 'narratological' analysis to study the role and power of narratives in bioethical literature itself. Narratology in this context refers to the investigation of narrative strategies identifiable in work that does not identify itself as fictive. In his challenging 1999 book *The Fiction of Bioethics*, Chambers offers a methodologically radical critique of the narrative strategies of established bioethics case studies, the kind of accounts given as the basis on which moral discussions in bioethics are carried out. He argues: 'the usefulness of narrative theory is primarily the manner in which it permits us to be critical of the evidence used to test moral theories. Such literary knowledge permits us to see the contingent nature of ethics and to be aware of how we cannot easily create a boundary between form and content.'[50] He takes his keynotes from Kenneth Burke who wrote: 'Every way of seeing is also a way of not seeing'[51] and Susan Sontag: 'Every style is a means of insisting on something'.[52] Literary devices as much as facts themselves serve to convey objectivity and sufficiency, and are intended to lead to the endorsement of the points of view of the authors.[53] While Chambers makes no judgement as to the validity of particular ethical claims, he identifies case-history accounts of ethical scenarios with an implicit ethics and, inescapably, broadly ideological elements. He argues that 'Bioethicists need to acknowledge that their selection of relevant facts is itself guided by their philosophical perspectives.'[54]

Chambers does not argue that bioethics case studies should be abandoned as a way of talking about ethics, but urges that readers need to be aware that 'when ethicists write cases, they are rhetorically imposing a world upon us, a world that excludes as well as includes those particularities that allow us to make the best possible moral decisions'.[55] Thus, 'the inclusion and exclusion of particularities can follow from prior philosophical ideas of what constitutes moral problems and how to resolve them'.[56] In particular, he targets the important role of narrative selection for the purpose of philosophical ethics in relation to the crucial shift from an empirical real world (or 'is') piece of information to the consideration of the 'ought'. This transition is sometimes referred to as *phronesis* (a Greek term) which refers to the application of moral philosophical principles to specific cases. He asks: 'How is the reader to evaluate the ethicist's *phronesis* if the ethicist is the one judging which particularities are relevant to the case?'[57] And he cautions in particular that a narrow principlism can be served by insufficient regard for the narrative strategies of bioethics cases: 'The conventions of the bioethics case can exclude from the narrative discourse features of essential value to those advocating approaches to ethics that attempt to broaden the scope of principlism.'[58] In pointing to the role of narrative in principlism (discussed in Chapter 1), Chambers alerts us to the centrality of language and rhetoric as the essential instruments of conversations about ethics, at the political and clinical levels, as well as in the humanities and social sciences which speak of bioethics.

## Discussion

The aim of this chapter has been to build on the discipline-related discussion in Chapter 1 to show that clinical and research cultures, as well as political and ethical conversations, can be understood in greater depth through a consideration of the use of language. Thus reading on bioethics, whether on issues in mainstream media, the medical press, or academic humanities and social science commentary can all benefit from being attuned to the nuances and usages of language. Attention to the passive voice, word choice, metaphor and the historical power of the medical imaginary, for example, can alert readers to rhetorical strategies and sensibilities that might otherwise go unnoticed. All bioethical reading therefore ideally occurs twice: once in line with the writing of an author and then against the grain, with attention to context, rhetoric and what lies between the lines.

## Further reading

Chambers, T. (1999) *The Fiction of Bioethics: Cases as Literary Texts* (New York: Routledge).

Frank, A. W. (1995) *The Wounded Storyteller: Body, Illness and Ethics* (Chicago: University of Chicago Press).

Kay, L. E. (2000) *Who Wrote the Book of Life? A History of the Genetic Code* (Stanford, CA: Stanford University Press).

Nelson, H. L. (ed.) (1997) *Stories and their Limits: Narrative Approaches to Bioethics* (New York: Routledge).

Preda, A. (2005) *AIDS, Rhetoric, and Medical Knowledge* (Cambridge: Cambridge University Press).

# 3
# Euthanasia, the Nazi Analogy and the Slippery Slope

In July 2009, the United States Democratic Party fulfilled a major policy objective of President Barack Obama, introducing to Congress a health-care funding bill, America's Affordable Health Choices Act of 2009. The bill's section 1233 made several references to 'end of life' health care: it proposed that government funding would be available for people to access physicians' advice pertaining, for example, to advanced medical directives in the event of grave illness; and it provided for medical proxies (nominated people who could speak for the patient).[1] That such a plan would provide an opening for opponents to invoke the history of so-called euthanasia policies under the German National Socialist (Nazi) regime (1933–1945) had been in evidence within days of the new president's election: in November 2008, anti-Obama commentators claimed to see in his plans for a national health scheme echoes of the Nazis' 'Aktion T4' programme in which doctors killed over 70,000 mentally and physically disabled children and adults.[2] The *Washington Times* predicted that under Obama the US would have its own 'T4 program [entailing] trivialization of abortion, acceptance of euthanasia, and the normalization of physician assisted suicide'.[3] Once the bill was tabled, opponents alleged, for example (in the words of Sarah Palin, 2008 Republican vice-presidential candidate and key figure of the new ultra-right Tea Party Patriots), that the national health scheme would create 'death panels' with control over the fate of the sick, the elderly and the disabled, based on their 'level of productivity in society'.[4] Other opponents claimed the new health insurance Act would lead to 'a revival of Hitler's euthanasia killing programme'.[5]

Opposition to a national health care scheme was to that point the most vigorous front against Obama's presidency and the invocation of the Nazi analogy only the latest in a long history of the use of this analogy in health-care debates.[6] The final version of the bill in March 2010 saw the policies and the trigger term 'end of life' removed.[7] (Language has played an important part in discussions of euthanasia. There are recognized euphemisms and trigger words for both sides. The very presence in the bill of the term 'end of life', for example, would have told opponents of legalized euthanasia all they wanted to know: that there were liberal secularists involved in the programme who were potential supporters of euthanasia legalization. Conversely, an accent on 'palliative care', which refers to the provision of as much comfort as possible for people whose lives are ending, tends to reflect an anti-euthanasia view.) Perhaps the bill was too ambitious in the scope of reform it envisaged, seeming to aim to educate health-care practitioners and consumers into thinking about 'the unthinkable', medical planning as death approaches; and perhaps physicians did not need a detailed list of matters such as advanced directives and 'orders regarding life sustaining treatment', which the bill outlined, to know what to discuss with their patients. (At no point did the bill mention physician-assisted suicide or euthanasia. Moreover, the relevant laws in the US on those matters are determined state by state.) Perhaps above all, inclusion of a section about end-of-life in an insurance bill was naïve. To be funded, the nature of the advice had to be a listed item in the scheme, but insurance is often seen as being about cost-avoidance. Thus the section left open the possibility that it invited citizens not to drain the scheme by lengthy or extensive clinical treatments covered in the same bill. Almost certainly, the section was intended to ensure that tragic scenarios such as those involving the late Terri Schiavo in 2005 did not occur again. (For those unfamiliar with the case, Ms Schiavo spent many years in a coma, while a protracted and high-profile series of court cases led in the end to a Supreme Court decision that her feeding tubes could be removed. The politicizing of this medical case was an unseemly intrusion in the private suffering of a woman and her family, made a *cause célèbre* of the religious right.) Provision for end-of-life care in the new scheme might have also reflected an assumption that because the use of the Nazi analogy in the bioethics press had been largely argued out of credence, it would not be entertained seriously in the upbeat days of the early Obama incumbency. The Nazi analogy, misused and overused as it often is, nonetheless continues to have high impact, and as this recent example shows, health care reformers ignore it at their peril.

Invocation of the Nazi analogy raises a wider question: is there any value in seeing history as a key to understanding, defining, even shaping contemporary debates? Or does the uniqueness of every historical moment render comparison useless? Historian William La Fleur speaks in favour of a qualified use of historical analogy as a moral and interpretative guide. He argues that even though 'events and processes do not make clones of themselves' nonetheless 'we scrutinize the past because, in spite of ... particulars, some features, sequences, or reasoning processes tend to reappear'.[8] With specific regard to euthanasia, however, Michael Burleigh, a leading historian of Nazi 'euthanasia', is vehement in his rejection of the Nazi analogy for contemporary euthanasia debates. He argues that the issues of modern euthanasia policy can be debated effectively without reference to the Nazi era.[9] In his own research Burleigh uses inverted commas around the word 'euthanasia', in order to signal from the outset his desire to separate Nazi medical killing carried out under the banner of 'euthanasia' from the modern euthanasia, with its strongly rights-based, individualist argumentation.[10] Modern euthanasia, he claims, has not been proposed under a murderous dictatorship. In whimsically stating a similar view against using the Nazi analogy, *Vanity Fair* columnist Fran Lebowitz writes: 'Things are very rarely exactly like other things. ... Nothing is like the Holocaust. Not that there haven't been other tragedies, other genocides. But simply that they were peculiarly, specifically, intrinsically, like themselves.'[11] And Arthur Caplan has claimed that comparisons between contemporary health-care debates and the war-driven 'medicine' of the Nazi era can trivialize the realities of Hitler's brutal regime.[12] Purely practically, it could be argued that the Nazi analogy has become void from both overuse and misuse, and more conducive to stifling debate than to promoting it. The aim of this chapter is to explore some of the recent history of euthanasia politics in the context of an evaluation of the Nazi analogy.

The chapter will begin with a brief definition of some key terms, followed by an account of Nazi 'euthanasia'. Next it will outline an idea closely linked with the Nazi analogy, the so-called 'slippery slope' argument. The idea of a slippery slope in relation to euthanasia draws on the case that US neurologist Leo Alexander posited after the end of the Second World War to the effect that government rationalization of health care points logically to forced 'euthanasia'. Together with the Nazi analogy, this influential concept will be considered in relation to a range of modern legal discussions of euthanasia. Moving to the contemporary scene, the first case study will be a brief period of legal euthanasia under enabling legislation in Australia's Northern Territory (Rights of the Terminally Ill Act 1995), the world's first enacted law allowing euthanasia, which came into force in 1996. The country's federal government overruled the Act in 1997, following the deaths of four people under its provisions. The second account will consider Dutch laws and legal decisions which since the early 1970s have evolved to facilitate certain forms of euthanasia in the Netherlands, culminating in the Termination of Life on Request and Assisted Suicide (Review Procedures) Act 2000, which came into force in 2002. It also considers the more recent and arguably more controversial move in the Netherlands to permit physicians to end the lives of severely afflicted newborns, with their parents' assent. It asks: is either the Nazi analogy or the 'slippery slope' argument useful in relation to these cases?

## Defining terms

'Euthanasia' is a broad term used to cover a wide range of debates with different clinical, ethical and legal significance. The 'euthanasia' to be considered here is exclusively that which involves the active participation of medical personnel in causing or providing the means for a person to cause their own death (euthanasia or physician-assisted suicide, respectively). For convenience, I will use 'euthanasia' as the cover term for the debate itself. The chapter does not concern the withdrawing or withholding of medical treatment, such as life support, in a way which might hasten an inevitable death (the kind of action considered in the initial Obama health-care bill). Included are both death sought by the patient (active and voluntary) as well as the troubling instances of so-called 'non-voluntary' euthanasia (counterpoised to 'involuntary' which indicates resistance) performed without the person's explicit request.

Euthanasia is a 'personal choice', but by definition it cannot be a private one: the moment a second party enters the scene, euthanasia becomes a matter of public policy.[13] The proposed introduction of legal euthanasia almost always relates to the involvement of physicians: the many cases of 'mercy killing' which arise as a result, for example, of partners' suicide pacts, are dealt with in the courts and under the traditional charges of either murder or manslaughter. Such cases might qualify as mercy killing (or 'good death', to literalise the word 'euthanasia') but these are not the subject of this chapter. When advocates of euthanasia argue for the enactment of new laws, they are in general devising the terms under which the laws which apply to lay people can be abrogated for the medical profession. Most governments which have, in broad terms 'legalized euthanasia' have created special laws which effectively provide a degree of protection for medical practitioners, to separate medical from other forms of mercy killing.

The laws at issue in euthanasia policy debates are statutes, that is, government legisalation which (in this case) defines crimes that can be prosecuted in the court system. By distinction, case law is the implementation of statute law, which takes place in the court system after someone is charged with a crime. Outcomes at case law rely not only on the letter of the statute law, but upon precedent and interpretation, which can at times reflect social attitudes and affect the implementation of statute law, either in findings or sentences. Thus it is the limits of the interpretation of statute law through case law which a physician might test when s/he kills a patient at the patient's request, to await the judgement of a court as to whether or not s/he is guilty of a statutory offence. Case law can serve as a testing mechanism for levels of social tolerance, or at least legal tolerance, of physician interventions in end-of-life choices. The most notable case of a physician testing the laws in this way was the American Dr Jack Kevorkian (one of several euthanasia advocates known in the popular press as 'Dr Death'), who claimed to have performed euthanasia in over 130 cases across several states, before he was finally convicted of second-degree murder in Michigan.[14]

At the time of writing (2013), the jurisdictions (national, state or territorial) which have enabling laws are the US states of Oregon, Washington and Montana (where assisted suicide is permitted); Switzerland (assisted suicide is permitted, not necessarily involving a physician); and Luxembourg, the Netherlands and Belgium, all of which allow a doctor to perform euthanasia.[15] Euthanasia has been or remains debated in several other jurisdictions, including Australia at both state and federal levels, France, Columbia and the United Kingdom.[16] 'Suicide tourism' (notably in Switzerland) and importation of lethal drugs, made easier by the Internet, are among the avenues outside the laws in their own countries through which people are seeking to procure for themselves the means of a non-violent death.[17]

## Nazi 'euthanasia'

In the 1930s, German psychiatry both envisaged and apparently practised the medical killing of the mentally ill for some time before the Nazi party formalized a policy of mass eradication of disabled children, then shortly after, asylum inmates, as it prepared for war in 1939. As early as 1920, a German psychiatrist Alfred Hoche and a lawyer Karl Binding published an influential book entitled *Die Freigabe der Vernichtunglebensunwerten Lebens* (*Authorization for the Destruction of Life*

*Unworthy of Life*), a carefully argued medicalized rationale for such killing. It reflected the then-current eugenicist mindset, asserting that there were some human lives 'unworthy of life' and, further, that there were professionals qualified to assess whose life was worthy. The book claimed that to keep some people alive was too costly for the state, particularly in government institutions and also in times of extreme exigency, such as war.[18] This was an early professional rationale for a programme of mass killing which was later reinforced by the extreme nationalist and productivity-oriented propaganda of the rising National Socialist (Nazi) movement, under the leadership of Adolf Hitler.

The Nazis came to power in 1933 and by the mid-1930s school students were learning of the so-called burden of 'mental defectives' on the German nation, through their mathematics textbooks. One problem to solve: calculate the cost of caring for 'the crippled, the criminal and the insane' against what could be spent providing housing and loans to newly married couples; another: 'The construction of an insane asylum requires 6 million RMs. How many housing settlements, at 15,000 RMs each, could be built for the same sum?'[19] The Nazis also commissioned feature films which debated the question of euthanasia of the disabled and concluded it was justified.[20]

In the winter of 1938–1939, as Hitler prepared for war, he signed an order permitting the 'euthanasia' of babies with disability, to be carried out in secret. A new 'Reich Committee for the Scientific Registration of Serious Hereditarily and Congenitally-based Diseases', comprised of medical and other professionals, required that parents register their disabled children. Then, on the basis of inspection of documents only, a panel of three doctors decided whether or not a child should be killed. Authorities reassured the parents that they were relinquishing their children to obtain treatment. 'Euthanasia' of these first victims meant either starvation or lethal injection. The bureaucrats who set up the programme found doctors sympathetic to its aims to kill 5,200 children between its inception and the end of the war in 1945.[21] Hitler soon extended 'euthanasia' to include adult inmates of state institutions for the mentally ill, intellectually impaired, disabled and chronically ill.

The start of war in September 1939 and a need for hospital beds provided Hitler with a further rationale. Under the name 'Aktion T4' (in reference to a villa at Tiergartenstrasse 4 in Berlin which served as a base) the expanded programme killed over 70,000 people in six centres. These centres were equipped with fake showers, fitted out to gas unwitting victims, who had been told to take a shower. In the case of most of the victims' deaths, staff from the institutions simply told their families that their relatives had died, but news began to spread about the true nature of events.[22] Hitler wound up Aktion T4 in 1941 because it was becoming harder to keep secret.[23] However, the regime extended these practices in an *ad hoc* way into the whole asylum system as well as into concentration camps and in captured territories under a new name (Aktion 14f13), resulting in the killing of tens of thousands more people by the end of the war.

'Euthanasia' practices ultimately provided the model, some of the personnel, and new technical means for the extermination of political enemies, Jews and other groups.[24] Execution of the 'unproductive' in the 'euthanasia' programme began with people with disabilities, but eventually included even wounded German citizens and mentally ill German soldiers. Nazi 'euthanasia' was thus no more than a euphemism for the systematic, state-sponsored murder of people of all ages, who were deemed to be mentally, psychologically or physically impaired. There was nothing merciful about it and there were no 'good deaths'. This abuse of the word 'euthanasia', however, provided later genera-tions with an avenue for protest at euthanasia law reform. In 1949, US neurologist Dr Leo Alexander took a first step in this direction when he underscored what he saw as a nexus between a quest for economic savings in a totalitarian order and mass extermination of those costly to the state.

## Leo Alexander: the slippery slope

Leo Alexander was one of the physicians involved in the prosecution of German doctors in 1947 at the Nuremberg war crimes trials and he helped to draft the Nuremberg Code for prevention of medical experi-mental abuses. In a wide-ranging 1949 article in the *New England Journal of Medicine*, entitled 'Medical Science under Dictatorship', Alexander recapitulated the history of Nazi 'euthanasia' to formulate what is often referred to as the 'slippery slope' argument in relation to euthanasia. He maintained that under certain conditions, small even imperceptible changes in consensual social morality can lead to the implementation of programmes such as Nazi 'euthanasia'. Alexander saw the rationali-zation of health-care provision as the starting point which could lead to 'killing centers', in a suitable ideological climate such as a dictator-ship.[25] He was suspicious of utilitarian health care which is carried out 'for the best of the people as a whole' and argued that it is dictatorial to 'look at health merely in terms of utility, efficiency and productivity'. The downward slide in Germany, in Alexander's view, 'started with the acceptance of the attitude basic in the euthanasia movement, that there is such a thing as life not worthy to be lived'.[26] Then, he said, there was a move from a 'small wedged-in lever' of attitudes towards the 'severely and chronically' sick which expanded to take in 'the socially unproductive, the ideologically unwanted; the racially unwanted and finally all non-Germans'.[27] For 1949 USA, his targets were economically motivated thinking among doctors and proponents of euthanasia.[28] His argument is summed up in these words: 'From the attitude of easing patients with chronic diseases away from the doors of the best types of treatment facilities available to the actual dispatching of such patients to killing centers is a long but nevertheless logical step.'[29]

'A long but *nevertheless logical* step' (my italics) is the crux of the claim. For the logic to follow at a later time, of course, would require circumstances which were more or less historically identical. This is why both philosophers and historians generally reject the idea as a logical impossibility. However, in pointing out the precise circumstances which did facilitate medical mass-killing disguised as euthanasia, Alexander's argument can nonetheless enjoin us to consider the precise circumstances of modern euthanasia. (It should be noted, however, that most arguments about euthanasia law reform do not take place in the context of discussions about rationalizing health care.) Two recent historical examples of euthanasia law reform, in Australia and in the Netherlands, show that in two countries – both of which are democracies with solid heath-care systems – euthanasia debates can take very different directions.

## The Northern Territory Rights of the Terminally Ill Act 1995

Australia's Northern Territory (NT) was the first jurisdiction formally to bring in legislation to permit medical termination of life and physician-assisted suicide. (A vote in Oregon in 1994 resulted in the enactment of a law in 1997.[30]) In July 1995, the territory enacted legislation to make it legal for a doctor to provide or administer a lethal dose of drugs to a terminally ill patient. The passage of the Rights of the Terminally Ill Act 1995 reflected a personal campaign of the territory's Chief Minister, Marshall Perron, leader of the traditionally conservative Country-Liberal Coalition. 'Liberal' with a capital L in Australia signifies conservative, closer to Republican in the US and Tory in the UK or Canada, but Perron also represented one face of traditional liberal individualism for which a right to euthanasia has been a touchstone for over a century. Under the new law, the treating physician had to diagnose an incurable

illness; a second medical practitioner with a qualification in 'psychological medicine' had to attest that the patient, whose active request to be
killed was essential, was not *inter alia* suffering from depression. A third
medical practitioner (who could be the same person as the second) had
to sign off on the request.[31] An activist physician named Philip
Nitschke legally ended the lives of four people under this legislation.[32]

The Northern Territory is an administrative unit which has relatively
less autonomy than that of the six federated states in the Australian
commonwealth.[33] States' laws in Australia cannot be overridden feder-
ally, but territory laws can be. Thus the introduction into law of an
amendment to the territory's own constitution was enough to limit its
jurisdictional powers in relation to euthanasia. The Act had been in
place 21 months when Federal Christian (mainly Catholic) politicians
on either side of the traditional Liberal National Party/Labor (conserva-
tive/social-democrat) divide voted in March 1997 to disallow the Rights
of the Terminally Ill Act.

The prime mover behind this reversal was Kevin Andrews, a socially
conservative Catholic barrister who in 1996 was a Federal Liberal party
backbencher, in the Liberal/National Party government of John
Howard. Andrews had since the 1980s been involved in attempts to
enforce at law the broad philosophies of the 'right to life' movement,
although he is not a member of that organization. His campaign to
overturn the territory's Act (or bring down its 'death sentence' as one
subeditor referred to it),[34] took the form of a private member's bill in
the Federal House of Representatives, which would have to rely for its
success on finding the numbers for a free or conscience vote in the
house and the Senate, to disallow the Northern Territory legislation.[35]
Behind Andrews were significant political forces: the Prime Minister,
John Howard, who strongly opposed euthanasia, and also a campaign
run by two new lobby groups. One, called Euthanasia No, was based
outside the Parliament and was formed solely for the purposes of
opposing pro-euthanasia laws, initially in the New South Wales
Parliament (in 1995) and then in the Northern Territory.[36] Some of
the group's members belonged to the opposition Australian Labor
Party (ALP), providing Andrews with an opening for links to Labor
Party religionists in the event of splits within both the major parties.
Another figure in Euthanasia No was a Catholic banker named Jim
Dominguez, who held meetings with politicians where he regularly
invoked the term 'slippery slope'. Apparently as a result, one reporter
noted, the phrase took hold in parliamentary debate, being used by 26
speakers.[37]

The second group was inside the Federal Parliament, a group of Christian Liberals known as the Lyons Forum, of which Andrews was a prominent member. The Lyons Forum (which no longer exists) was named for a quote in the 1943 maiden speech of the first female member of the House of Representatives, Enid Lyons: 'The foundation of a nation's greatness is in the homes of its people.' Members of the forum believed that 'the family is the fundamental unit of society; the family is the prime agency for the development and primary socialisation of children; [and] marriage provides the optimum environment for the nurturing of children.'[38] Andrews claimed that the group was not relevant to his bill, but in 1992 he was one its founding members and the group did discuss euthanasia, likely as part of a neo-conservative 'family values' cluster.[39]

Andrews' Euthanasia Laws Bill took the form of a very simple amendment to the Northern Territory (Self-Government) Act 1978: it stated that the power of the territory to make laws 'does not extend to the making of laws which permit or have the effect of permitting (whether subject to conditions or not) the form of intentional killing of another called euthanasia (which includes mercy killing) or the assisting of a person to terminate his or her life'.[40]

The short period of legal euthanasia under the Northern Territory Act and the passage of Andrews' bill can be read as something of a microcosm of the divisions emerging across (at least) the English-speaking world within liberalism over issues of conscience, and more widely over the role of religion in public affairs. The fact that Australia's Liberal party is conservative should not obscure the fact that many of its members endorse the traditions of liberalism, for example, in relation to abortion law, censorship and homosexuality. Thus there was never a guarantee that all party members would support the bill, nor did they. By contrast, however, the then opposition Labor Party had a strong Catholic constituency nationwide. The party does not hold uniform views on social issues: however, the then leader of the ALP, Kim Beazley, supported Andrews' bill, as did a number of other Labor members.

After a strong pro-vote in the House of Representatives, heavily dominated by a newly elected Liberal Party, the Senate voted 38–33 for, with one abstention. In the Senate, the bill could not have passed without the support of the 11 ALP members who voted for it.[41] (Dr Nitschke pleaded without success that parliamentarians were deciding on the fates of two people who he said had committed to dying under the terms of the Northern Territory Act.[42]) In this case, parliamentary religious activists placed themselves in the path of what they saw as the slide of social morality down a slippery slope. However, liberals within the parliamentary Liberal Party took exception to this development, interpreting it, one might say, as an early and vigorous push down a different kind of slippery slope, from secular democracy to theocracy; a month after the House of Representatives passed the 'Andrews bill' they formed their own group, the John Stuart Mill Society, to promote traditional liberal views, such as free choice when others are not harmed by one's actions.[43] Whether or not continuation of the Rights of the Terminally Ill Act in the territory would have led to the kind of slippery slope envisaged by Alexander is impossible to say. One media commentator argued the Act was the best insurance *against* the slippery slope, as it provided for regulation and thus medical accountability.[44]However, slippery slope rhetoric appears to have helped unite otherwise politically opposed Members of Parliament. Another example of legalized euthanasia, the Netherlands, provides a different example which can help to test the validity of the idea of a 'slippery slope'.

## The Netherlands

Leo Alexander's 1949 essay turned to the Dutch medical profession as an exemplar of resistance to Nazi 'euthanasia', stating that in the face of the exigencies of occupation 'not a single euthanasia or non-therapeutic sterilization was recommended or participated in by any Dutch physician'.[45] Perhaps it is not just a simple historical irony, therefore, that the Dutch medical profession's justifiable self-image as ethical might have helped give it, just a few decades later, the moral assuredness to become consistent proponents of regulated legal euthanasia. The Netherlands has been the bellwether jurisdiction on euthanasia for some time.

In 1971, Dr Geertruida Postma, a physician, administered to her dying mother a lethal dose of drugs. In 1973, a criminal court found her 'guilty of voluntary euthanasia and ordered a one-week suspended sentence and one year's probation'.[46] The court accepted the view that while the treatment ended in death, Dr Postma intended only to 'prevent serious and irreversible suffering', concluding 'that the average Dutch physician no longer considered it as her or his duty to prolong a patient's life under all circumstances'.[47] For the benefit of future courts judging similar cases, the court then proposed criteria which might make such actions generally permissible: 'The patient is incurably ill; The patient finds his suffering (mentally or physically) unbearable; The patient requested to terminate his life; A physician acts.' Thus a decision at case law sowed the seeds of a formulation suited to implementation via statute law.

Three further legal cases (in 1983–1984, 1993–1994 and 1997) established the parameters of euthanasia and physician-assisted suicide. In particular, the successful use in 1984 of a legal 'defence of necessity' argument cemented the direction of favourable judgements for the accused. This defence holds that a conflict of duties can arise, when honouring a patient's request to die with dignity is the only way available to end 'unbearable suffering'.[48] Suffering, too, came to be increasingly widely defined: a Dutch Supreme Court judgement in 1994 accommodated psychological suffering, after a psychiatrist had administered to a 50-year-old woman at her request a lethal dose of drugs as she was suffering from acute depression related to tragic family circumstances.[49] (This stands in contrast to the 1995 Northern Territory law in which depression was an exclusion criterion.)

Notwithstanding the *de facto* legality of euthanasia, enabling law on euthanasia did not come into existence until 2000, a result in part of the dominance of the Dutch Parliament by Christian Democrats up to 1994.[50] After many decades of lobbying and debate, under a new left-wing liberal government, the upper house of the Parliament of the Netherlands finalized passage in 2001 of the Termination of Life on Request and Assisted Suicide (Review Procedures) Act 2000, to make it permissible for a doctor to administer a lethal dose of drugs with the intention of ending the life of the patient, provided this was done within certain constraints and with due medical care. The Act stipulates, in brief, that:

1. The patient's request is voluntary and well-considered; 2. The patient's suffering is unbearable and hopeless; 3. The patient is informed about his situation and prospects; 4. There are no reasonable alternatives. Further, 5. Another independent physician should be consulted; and 6. The termination of life should be performed with due medical care and attention.[51]

The patient must be in no case younger than 12 (with minors requiring parental assent); and following the patient's death the doctor must report what s/he has done and provide details of what has occurred to a local medical examiner. The examiner in turn is to pass the information to a local committee, empowered either to suggest prosecution or to let the matter end there. Crucially, outside entities or persons cannot seek legal action through the committee system, meaning no-one can mount an accusation of murder or manslaughter and additionally that the views of lobby groups in individual cases can have no legal purchase.[52] Supporters maintain that the 2000 law does not mean that medical killing is legal. As one legal supporter of the Dutch law puts it: 'It is often stated that the Act legalises euthanasia but this is not entirely true. Euthanasia and assisted suicide remain criminal offences. What the Act does is to create an exception to the punishability of euthanasia and assisted suicide for those physicians who have complied with the requirements of due care mentioned in the Act.'[53] This is something of a legal nicety, however, in that the pooling of cases in the committee system arguably limits the likelihood of punishment.

## Appraisals of the Netherlands Act

Several overview articles have now assessed the implementation of the Act according to both publicly available statistics and follow-up surveys of physicians.[54] Evidence points to four principal areas of concern across the history of Dutch euthanasia surveys, which began in 1990. First is the continued failure of a significant proportion of physicians to report their actions as required: the authors of a 2009 review article in *Journal of Bioethical Inquiry* (*JBI*) show that non-reporting by physicians, while declining, is still at around 20 per cent.[55] Given the system relies on retrospective declaration, provisions for due care might not be being met.[56]

Second, insufficient government support for the regulatory system which tracks euthanasia deaths is a significant concern: in 2010, the Regional Euthanasia Review Committees (2010) *Annual Report* stated that they had been unable to process all the cases of which they were notified, only reaching conclusions on 2,667 of 3,136 cases. The significant step to make a new law brought an expectation of honouring the regulatory endeavour and shortfalls in funds for dealing with reported euthanasia deaths threaten the possibilities of (and therefore justification by reference to) transparency. The report observes curtly: 'This is not only undesirable, but unlawful.'[57] It is a problem particularly troubling in relation to the committees' capacity to deal with a third concern: doctors who bring about the death of patients without their 'explicit consent' ('non-voluntary euthanasia' or 'unrequested termination of life' as it has also been called[58]).

The authors of the 2009 *JBI* overview article note that the number of people who have died without explicit consent has been declining since 1990 and they add that statistics gleaned from confidential surveys of physicians in countries where euthanasia is not permitted show that the Netherlands has the lowest number of deaths in this category.[59] This line of reasoning – that things are often worse where euthanasia is illegal – is regularly reprised in the argument that regulation provides for transparency.[60] Specifically, the 2009 *JBI* overview provides plausible evidence that there is 'no evidence of a slippery slope' into increased non-voluntary euthanasia and observes that the 'frequency of ending of life without explicit patient request did not increase over the studied years'. Making specific reference to the groups seen as most vulnerable, they argue that 'there is no evidence for a higher frequency of euthanasia among the elderly, people with low educational status, the poor, the physically disabled or chronically ill, minors, people with psychiatric illnesses including depression, or racial or ethnic minorities, compared with background populations'.[61] They point to a successful Dutch national health-care system which they see as reducing any sense that life-sustaining treatments place pressure on resources.[62] One group of reflective bioethics commentators (three clinical practitioners and one lawyer) endorse the view that the data in the 2009 *JBI* review 'show that no [slippery] slope has come into existence as a result of the legalisation of euthanasia in the Netherlands, but that the process has remained controllable and appears to have filled a specific, if limited, gap in the medical management of terminally ill patients'.[63]

Nevertheless, even allowing for the fact that around three-quarters of the number of deaths 'without explicit consent' had entailed some earlier discussion with the patient or their family, the extrapolated total figure of 550 deaths for the 2005 Dutch survey can leave a sense of some unease.[64] A 2012 *Lancet* overview article, which also takes in figures from 2010, notes a decline since 1990 in the number of people whose physician-initiated deaths have been non-voluntary, but the authors underscore that the matter is significant, maintaining that '[n]otwithstanding the decrease in ending of life without explicit request, information on characteristics of these cases is important to assess this practice'.[65] Given that figures from other countries with diverse legal positions on euthanasia show there is a notable number of deaths in this category in many jurisdictions, the fundamental question is perhaps one not just pertaining to the Netherlands.

Fourth, defining 'suffering' has continued to be an issue after legalization: in 2002 a doctor followed the request of an 86-year-old man to be killed because he said he was 'tired of life'. This case pinballed up through the court system: a district attorney prosecuted the doctor; a regional court acquitted him, and the appeals court overturned the regional court's decision. Finally the Dutch Supreme Court rejected an appeal against the appeal court's decision, making the decision for prosecution to go ahead on the basis that euthanasia 'must be linked to a recognisable medical or psychiatric condition'. The physician, however, was not punished.[66] As noted above in the 1994 case, the law allows for mental suffering as a criterion, and some members of the Dutch medical profession saw the prosecution as insupportable for this reason.[67] The court made a decision that if there were a slippery slope in relation to the curative role of physicians in supporting patients' choices to die, the slide should stop at this judgement. In this case, the court seemed to both draw a line under its criteria for suffering but also made a somewhat contradictory statement by adhering to the by now well-established practice of non-punishment. Thus the meaning and future of the statute as inevitably changing through interpretation remains in the balance until tested again at case law. The limits of the law (both before and after the 2000 legislation) have been tested case by case, pressing out but also testing and reinforcing the boundaries of acceptability as the slippery slope is tested and its gradient shored up through the interplay of legislature and courts. Within that system is the essential ligament of the regulatory system, to the deficiencies of which its own employees have drawn attention. Regulation has also played an important part in another arguably even more painful area of the euthanasia debate: the question of medical killing of very disabled newborn infants.

## The euthanasia of neonates

Since 2005, the question of the medical termination of the lives of newborns has taken the Netherlands debate to a new area, following the publication of the so-called Groningen Protocol.[68] The protocol, drafted by a panel of paediatricians at the University Medical Center, Groningen, sets out criteria which in the view of the authors make permissible medical termination of life of children with severe and in their view irresolvable medical conditions. The paediatricians who drafted the protocol argued on the basis that there is evidence that a majority of cases were not being reported, and that a protocol would 'prevent uncontrolled and unjustified euthanasia'.[69] They consulted the district attorney, and the Paediatric Association of the Netherlands (NVK) endorsed the protocol as suitable guidelines for the medical termination of life of certain disabled or severely afflicted neonates.[70] As a response to this move, in 2006 the Dutch government introduced

regulatory mechanisms to consider cases which had arisen in the mean-
time and now endorses the proposal, without recourse to new or
amended legislation.[71] The text of this regulation may be found on the
government website. Under the heading 'Euthanasia and newborn
infants', it reads in part:

> Children are occasionally born with such serious disorders that
> termination of life is regarded as the best option. The law permits
> physicians to terminate the lives of newborn infants ... only on
> condition that they fulfil the following due care criteria: In the light
> of prevailing medical opinion, the child's suffering must be unbear-
> able and with no prospect of improvement. This means that the deci-
> sion to discontinue treatment is justified. There must be no doubt
> about the diagnosis and prognosis; Both the physician and the
> parents must be convinced that there is no reasonable alternative
> solution given the child's situation; The parents must have given
> their consent for the termination of life; The parents must have been
> fully informed of the diagnosis and prognosis; At least one other,
> independent physician must have examined the child and given a
> written opinion on compliance with the due care criteria listed
> above. The termination must be performed with all due care.[72]

Formalization appears to follow what was already the accepted practice:
in 2005 a group of Dutch paediatricians reported in the *Nederlands
Tijdschrift voor Geneeskunde* that 'Between January 1997 and June 2004,
22 cases of deliberate termination of life in newborns were reported.'[73]
None went to court. It is perhaps notable that while all parents
consented, only four of the cases were the result of a direct parental
request.[74] Unsettling references to 'Predicted lack of self-sufficiency',
'Predicted inability to communicate' and 'Expected hospital dependency' which were among the criteria in these 22 cases, tend to support
the view that, while the clinicians' actions might have been morally
justifiable on other grounds, it is not clear why such criteria should
have entered the calculus.[75] The original case which is cited to justify
the new protocol – the tragic story of a newborn with an excruciating
skin condition which could not be attenuated by analgesics – did not
involve any of those criteria.[76]

To critics of legalized euthanasia this new development represents a
modern low point, particularly because of the problems of defining and
predicting 'unbearable suffering', and the risk of elasticity in relation to
the nature of the conditions affected.[77] It is also not wholly clear why

the government did not initiate a new law on this form of euthanasia, possibly in the form of an amendment to the 2000 Act. In regulating the change it appears that the goal might have been to avoid public objections. Yet the new regulation is not merely an accretion on the fundamental platform of the law, which is the capacity for human beings to make rational choices about themselves: it is about decisions made on behalf of those without the capacity to decide.

The protocol has received relatively little attention in the medical and bioethics press: a PubMed search for 'Groningen protocol' and 'Netherlands' yielded only 19 results, whereas 'Netherlands' and 'euthanasia' for the same period yielded 412. This might be the result of the fact that rather than pursue a change of law, as with the 2000 Act, the government has simply regulated to fall into step with what paedi-atricians recommend.[78] This decision appears to have removed from the usual consultative equation (medical profession/government/public) the risk that Dutch citizens might react adversely to this new accretion on the more traditional euthanasia view, that the mental competence of the person is a central plank in legitimation of the practice. Perhaps a reason for such a low-key approach is also a result of the wide contro-versy in the 1980s, which ensued following the release of a book by preference utilitarian philosophers Helga Kuhse and Peter Singer, about the medical killing of severely afflicted newborns, yet another case in which the Nazi analogy has been raised.

In 1985 Kuhse and Singer published the controversial book, *Should the Baby Live? The Problem of Handicapped Infants*.[79] The book, with the provocative title – which not only implies that potentially all infants with handicaps are of themselves a problem, but which also seemed to invite the answer 'no' – was a major example of an attempt to apply to the real world the reasoning of the branch of philosophy known as 'preference utilitarianism'. The logic in this mode of argument is that the quality of life and personal preferences of all parties in a given situ-ation should be balanced. Pursued to its logical extreme in the case of the birth of a severely disabled infant, this method of reasoning reaches the conclusion that, by virtue of the child's incapacity (based on his or her actual and projected condition at birth), the parents' preferences should be weighted so as to make it possible for them to determine the child's fate.

Disputation erupted in the wake of the book's release and the Nazi analogy took on a dual function, in criticisms of the work but also as part of an argument in defence of Peter Singer himself. Singer faced accusations that his views were similar to those of Nazi doctors.[80]

Protesters heckled Singer in Germany and prevented him from speaking in Switzerland, in response to which Singer made a 'counter use' of the Nazi analogy, likening this treatment (and particularly an audience's chant of 'Singer *raus!*' – Singer out, echoing the Nazis' 'Juden *raus!*') to the experiences of Jews persecuted by the Nazis.[81] Singer also pointed out his own Jewish background and referred to the deaths of three of his grand-parents at the hands of the Nazis in Austria.[82] This shows another way the Nazi analogy can be used, to turn the tables on the assumptions of heck-lers, in support of a freedom of speech argument. In the accounts Singer provides, this reversal served to open up a measure of dialogue with his audience by neutralizing the blunt instrument of the Nazi analogy.

## Discussion

This chapter began with a discussion of the US health scheme's proposed inclusion of funding for end-of-life care through a national health insurance programme. On Christmas Day 2011, *The New York Times* reported that the US government had been able to bring in a modified plan to fund patients who wished to discuss end-of-life care with their doctors, through regulation rather than law. The article quoted emails from within the system urging that the news not be spread widely, for fear of political backlash. The same paper reported on 4 January 2012 that the attempted change had been reversed, three days after its implementation, ostensibly on the grounds that the process had not been followed.[83] This rapid turn of events tells us much about bioethics today. As in the case of the Dutch regulation permitting doctors to end the lives of severely disabled neonates, a reluctance to go through more deliberative channels such as legislature shows how strongly neo-conservative religious activism affects the political scene in the Western world. This influence seems to be out of step with majority views and views of representative bodies. The insistent rhetoric of the Nazi analogy can wrongly persuade governments that stepping around the legislative barrier assists democratic process, doing a disservice to the very democracy for which the critics claim to stand. To introduce change via regulation can be read as both a move by stealth to avoid public overreaction and a reasonable step to avoid the kind of caricature and exaggeration that accompanies debate about new laws.

National conditions vary, statute law and case law provide different avenues for change: the outcomes of legal cases can function as *de facto* law or can lead to support for enabling legislation. National health-care conditions also matter: are palliative care options sufficiently funded, for example, to prevent any imputation that support for euthanasia of any kind is based on financial motives? And the role of regulation is critical. If legalized adult euthanasia is to take place in a way that truly balances the wishes of the community and of the person who asks to die in this way and the jurisdiction's reasonable expectations of adherence to its own laws, the real ethical question is the dull and mundane matter of government commitment to appropriate regulatory effort.

Much of the reportage, whether governmental or academic, about jurisdictions where euthanasia is permitted appears aimed to offer reassurance about the value of legalization. The best form of reporting needs to have the capacity to work against its creators, to provide for more room for interpretation, and more forthrightness about gaps. Thus the report of the Dutch committees is a good example of willingness in the system to expose its own weaknesses: the next thing is to find a solution. But is it enough that a committee system, however well funded, can still judge what might have otherwise gone directly to the court system, which is arguably more accountable? An argument that regulation guarantees transparency is only part of the story. It *can* provide transparency, but its mere existence provides no guarantee. Regulation must be funded to ensure that abuses do not occur. Medicine is a public matter and notwithstanding patient confidentiality its ethics for good or ill are matters of public policy. Nowhere is this less true than in euthanasia debate. Change via regulation only is not appropriate to the democratic process. The Groningen Protocol is troubling, possibly as much for the way in which it became 'policy' as for the challenges such a practice can make to public morality.

The Nazi analogy can and should be dismissed in relation to euthanasia debates today. Nazi 'euthanasia' is a cynical misnomer which should not be honoured by posterity. Glib references to Nazism can serve to stifle reasoned debate and provoke misinformation and partial knowledge. There are considered, informed and thoughtful commentators right across the spectrum of argument, capable of sustaining meaningful analysis. More nuanced argument is essential in such an inherently emotional area. And the slippery slope is perhaps less of a fallacy than it is a truism: moral boundaries change all the time. Fallacies lie in collapsing distinctions between the murderous and the non-murderous.

If the slippery slope argument can inadvertently point to the value of diachronic studies which look for trends – even or especially trends which invalidate the claim of the slippery slope – it serves a function. The very idea of the slippery slope, one might say, creates the conditions for its own repudiation. Disproving its validity places an onus on those who would use it randomly to prove its value case by case. The details of statistics permit further consideration of the slippery slope idea even if in a climate of vexed debate, any reportage on euthanasia cannot fail to be read for its underlying politics, even when it presents accurate data.

The line between case law and statute law is a cultural space where ambiguity and ambivalence can find expression. This sphere might remain the preferable locus of negotiation in relation to severely disabled neonates, precisely because of the rarity of the conditions where it might have some ethical legitimacy. What is ethical and what is legal might not always be the same. One might wonder, if a doctor acts purely out of conscience, why he or she might not be willing, however rarely, to endure the weight of legal scrutiny and possible sanction.

## Further reading

Battin, M., R. Rhodes and A. Silvers (eds) (1998) *Physician-assisted Suicide: Expanding the Debate* (Reflective Bioethics Series) (New York: Routledge).

Burleigh, M. (1994) *Death and Deliverance: 'Euthanasia' in Germany c. 1900–1945* (Cambridge: Cambridge University Press).

Cohen-Almagor, R. (2004) *Euthanasia in the Netherlands: The Policy and Practice of Mercy Killing* (Dordrecht: Springer).

Dowbiggin, I. (2007) *A Concise History of Euthanasia: Life, Death, God, and Medicine* (Lanham, MD: Rowman and Littlefield).

Griffith, G., A. Bood and H. Weyers (1998) *Euthanasia and Law in the Netherlands* (Amsterdam: Amsterdam University Press).

Huxtable, R. (2007) *Euthanasia, Ethics and the Law: From Conflict to Compromise?* (Oxford: Routledge-Cavendish).

Lavi, S. J. (2007) *The Modern Art of Dying: A History of Euthanasia in the United States* (Princeton, NJ: Princeton University Press).

Negri, S. (2012) *Self-determination, Dignity and End of Life Care* (Leiden: Brill).

Somerville, M. (2001) *Death Talk: The Case against Euthanasia and Physician-Assisted Suicide* (Montreal: McGill-Queen's University Press).

Thomasma, D., T. Kushner, G. Kimsma and C. Ciesielski-Carlucci (eds) (1998) *Asking to Die: Inside the Dutch Debate about Euthanasia.* (Dordrecht: Kluwer Academic).

Tulloch, G. (2005) *Euthanasia, Choice and Death* (Edinburgh: Edinburgh University Press).

# 4
# Heredity, Genes and Reproductive Politics

Since the early nineteenth century, Western medicine has been involved in fulfilling the desires of individuals, families and governments to control human heredity. Medicine's role in so-called 'hereditarian' undertakings has had mixed consequences: at worst, in implementing policies of compulsory eugenic sterilization; at best (although problematically to some) in developing clinical probes to identify, prior to the conception or full gestation of a foetus, the presence of genes which would cause any child born to suffer from a deleterious medical condition. There is no longer an influential worldwide eugenics movement urging governments to select who is 'fit' or 'unfit' to reproduce and very few of the social, political, ideological or technical realities that prompted the rise of eugenics a century ago are relevant today. But contemporary critics concerned about the social implications of modern genetics (particularly reproductive genetics) often invoke the history of eugenics to signal their concerns.

How useful has the eugenic comparison been in recent debates about powerful new genetic knowledge and technologies? This chapter will show the ways in which the 'eugenic analogy' has over recent years served as a spur to discussion, but will argue that in most cases references to eugenics are more valuable as historical background than for direct comparison. Several developments have reduced the value to ethical discussions of comparisons with the history of eugenics. First is greater knowledge of the complex history of eugenics itself. Saying something is 'eugenic', even referring to the period when the movement was at its height, does not describe a simple historical phenomenon. Second is that there is relatively little overlap between the actions of researchers, governments or ideologues in the past and the kind of techniques and ideologies under discussion today. In almost all respects, the negative ethical residue of eugenics history does not map neatly onto discussions of modern reproductive genetics. However, certain features of modern medical genetics bear *some* of the problematic aspects of the historic eugenics, government wariness of health-care costs being the main one. Successful use of analogy does not require absolute accuracy of course: it is at heart a rhetorical tool. But more complex understandings, of both the history and the present day, place an onus on modern commentators to clarify their terms.

Commentators today who invoked eugenics may be concerned about attitudes to disability (rejecting genetic screening as inherently anti-disability), they may oppose abortion and destructive or selective embryo testing, they may object to government intervention in reproductive decision-making or express concerns for genetic privacy or health-care equity.[1] The chapter will conclude that in most cases more precise terms than 'eugenics' can serve the purpose of nuanced discussions about reproductive rights, health-care equity and medical consumer autonomy. In this light it will also discuss moves to reclaim the use of the word 'eugenics' in a new, liberal guise (eugenics without the state), which have added a further complication to the use of the word in a way that can strip the term of its history.

The chapter begins with an overview of the history of eugenics, from its roots in the nineteenth century, to the rise in the twentieth century of a major international movement embracing new activist groups, new laws, committees and commissions, and many social scientific and biological research initiatives (some of which established the bases of modern medical genetics). The tragic history of mandatory sterilization in many countries from the early twentieth century until the 1980s marks the nadir of eugenic medicine. In the post-Second World War era, eugenics focused less on mass population 'quality' and more on the family unit and population control. Early genetic counselling for chromosomal and hereditary conditions reflected both the privatizing of eugenic goals and a shift in the direction of medical genetics testing for conditions potentially harmful to the child, rather than to 'society'.

Increased diagnostic precision, the development of a new range of interventions at every stage of the reproductive process, and the legalization of abortion have brought the ethics of medical genetics to prominence. This chapter outlines some of the innovations of the past forty years which have led to the widespread use of genetic science in reproductive medicine (sometimes called 'reprogenetics'). This is where many of the debates about the eugenic nature of genetic medicine have taken place. Medical genetics is involved in tests across the reproductive process. They are: screening of populations for carrier status of genetic conditions; the use of donor gametes (eggs or sperm) to either avoid or promote the birth of a child of a certain type; pre-implantation genetic diagnosis of embryos (PGD) carried out as part of an *in vitro* fertilization (IVF) treatment; and several forms of testing at different stages of pregnancy, all of which can inform a decision to terminate the pregnancy. Commentators from diverse perspectives interject in relation to different points on the reproductive and population spectrum, identifying issues such as: the right of government to screen particular populations or the population as a whole; health-care equity in relation to insurance and government support; possible discrimination in relation to disability, and of course the vexed question of abortion.

Emerging from these debates are diverse and sometimes contradictory notions of rights. When the rights claimed by individuals, communities, commercial entities and jurisdictions conflict, whose rights should prevail? Is the language of rights adequate to the complexities of policy? A new politics of 'genetics and community', for example, responds to questions such as: how far should small communities affected by particular genetic conditions be entitled to subject their members to local cultural law? And in a similar vein, what of the occasional deliberate attempt to conceive disabled children, in order to blend in to a group affected by that disability? And what limits if any should be placed on population screening and prenatal screening? Is it different for small communities and nations? Where do community values, national interest and indeed the rights of the 'international community' begin and end? (Would the answer be different, for example, in relation to *beta* thalassemia screening in Cyprus and the 1995 heredity screening laws in the People's Republic of China (PRC)?) The cases considered here show in their complexity that ethical pluralism is the condition of bioethics, ensuring an unrelenting order of debate. There are also a number of notable ethical issues the chapter has had to omit. These include manipulation of embryos to change their genetic contents (or germ line therapy), somatic gene therapy (the insertion of genes to treat conditions in those already born or in early stages of development), forensic DNA gathering and its implications for race politics, the controversial, privately funded Human Genome Diversity Project, genetic 'enhancement' of children to be born and the use of genes to create 'posthumans'.

Finally, what of the term 'eugenics'? The history of this word is a significant sub-theme of the chapter. Percolating through the entire history of eugenics, right up to the present time, has been a collective fascination with this resilient neologism, alongside a diversity of opinion on both its meaning and its value.[2] Since Francis Galton coined the term in 1883 eugenics has been a major international 'brand' which has come in and out of vogue, but has never failed to provoke animated reactions. Should the positives of modern reproductive genetics help retrieve the word 'eugenics' from associations with its tarnished history?

## Heredity and social reform

'Hereditarianism' is a term used to describe influential doctrines on human reproduction which took hold of the medical imagination in Europe from the late eighteenth century. This was a revolutionary era when the inherent superiority of aristocratic bloodlines came into question and heredity itself became democratized.[3] New doctrines of nationalism required all citizens, not just the elite, to prove their value to the nation. Physicians, among others, saw their profession as having something to offer the wider social good.[4] One of the early proponents of the new science of phrenology the Austrian physician, Johann Spurzheim (1776–1832), argued in 1821:

> It is indeed a pity that the laws of propagation are not more attended to. I am convinced that, by attention to them, not only the condition of single families, but of whole nations, might be improved beyond imagination, in figure, stature, complexion, health, talents, and moral feelings. ... He who can convince the world of the importance of the laws of propagation, and induce mankind to conduct themselves accordingly, will do more good to them, and contribute more to their improvement, than all institutions, and all systems of education.[5]

Spurzheim urged governmental restriction on marriages and reproduction for reasons of heredity. He paralleled this proposal with laws in Austria that required men to be able to support a family before they were permitted to marry.[6] That Spurzheim was a founder of the now discredited science of phrenology is significant. In the nineteenth century, phrenological theory noted the importance of heredity in the shape of the human skull which in turn was understood to provide an index to the individual's disposition and morality. Spurzheim referred without differentiation to moral and physical capacities ('figure, stature, complexion, health, talents, and moral feelings'), an approach typical of hereditarian thinking that had one eye to individual physical health and the other to the moral 'health' of wider human society. The view he encapsulated subsequently came to be known as 'genetic determinism', meaning (as in the quotation above) that a person's inherited traits radically limit the capacities of any subsequent social intervention, such as education, to improve him or her.

Spurzheim's view can stand for much of the social thought of the nineteenth century. At this time ideas such as 'society', 'state' and 'nation' became theorized and ultimately taken for granted as the natural forms through which the human race was collectively to shape its future. Bear in mind that at the start of the nineteenth century, there was no polity in the world in which all adults were entitled either to education or the vote. Democratization through both social reform from 'above' and insurrection from 'below' in Europe and North America brought with it expectations of what a citizen should be. Governments expected populations to believe in communal values of 'nation' or of 'race' (the latter meaning sometimes the whole human race, and sometimes a specific racial group in the modern sense). The state for its part came to provide increased access to education and electoral power, as well as incipient social welfare and public health policies. Together with a politics of inclusion, however, there came a new politics of resentment: 'public health' had a hereditarian mirror image, in an expectation that citizens' bodies and those of their offspring should in some way reflect the ambitions of the state. Hereditarian thought was already long imprinted in the nineteenth-century reform imagination when the wealthy English geographer and mathematician Francis Galton (1822–1911) carried the notion into the twentieth century as 'eugenics'.

## Francis Galton and the rise of eugenics

Galton himself had an early interest in phrenology and he also began to reflect on the new idea of evolution after reading his cousin's, Charles Darwin's, controversial book *On the Origin of Species* (1859).[7] Galton drew inferences for human society from Darwin's idea of biological evolution, believing the human species could actively accelerate its own improvement.[8] He saw an analogy of human cultivation with that of plants and animals and believed that the aim of optimizing biological heredity was 'equally applicable to men, brutes [animals], and plants'.[9] In *Hereditary Genius* (1869) Galton argued that genius in families should be cultivated for the purpose of overall national improvement.[10] In 1883, he outlined a 'science of improving [human] stock' and coined the word 'eugenics' (using the Greek roots for 'good' and 'breeding') to encapsulate his goal of increasing reproduction of those 'good in stock, hereditarily endowed with noble qualities'.[11]

For Galton, successful eugenics would entail 'the study of the agencies under social control that may improve or impair the racial qualities of future generations either physically or mentally'.[12] Practically, this came down to a concerted effort in human pedigree research to bring about 'judicious marriages' which could help produce a 'highly gifted race of men'.[13] Galton also at one point endorsed the idea of preventing 'undesirable' citizens such as criminals from reproducing.[14] The first approach is sometimes referred to as 'positive eugenics', meaning the breeding up of the more favourably endowed; the second is an example of 'negative eugenics', restricting breeding through controlling marriage.[15] Late in life, Galton even reflected candidly: 'Could not the undesirables be got rid of and the desirables multiplied?'[16] Yet he did not harbour a genocidal intent and nor did he urge state-imposed sterilization. In that sense, those, such as the members of the Galton Institute, who still honour his name, can reasonably claim he was not responsible for the practices which eugenics later justified. But it is not mere anachronism to read his views through modern, more egalitarian eyes: not everyone shared his views at the time. At a 1904 meeting of the Sociological Society, for example, Galton addressed a diverse audience of public figures, the majority of whom challenged him. The novelist H. G. Wells, for example, mildly rebuked him, making tongue-in-cheek comments on the unique skills of criminals.[17] Galton's innovative work nonetheless crystallized much nineteenth-century thought concerning heredity, class, race and political consciousness in Europe and the wider world.

Several developments lent momentum to Galton's cause among socially reformist members of the upper-middle classes of England. At the time of the Boer War (between Britain and Dutch South Africa, 1899–1902), a large number of recruits proved medically unfit to perform military duties, giving rise to fears of national decline.[18] In the new industrial cities, rising crime rates, sexual promiscuity and alcoholism were seen as significant problems, compounded by a proportional decline in the birth rate of the social elites by comparison with that of the less privileged.[19] Two eugenics advocates observed in 1909 that even 'medical and hygienic knowledge' contributed inadvertently to race decline, by enabling the 'feeble-minded and weak' to survive.[20] At the level of science, a revival of interest since 1900 in the 1866 findings of the Austrian monk and scientist, Gregor Mendel, on the principles governing transmission of inherited traits in plants, led to greater knowledge and acceptance of the significance of heredity. Mendel's ideas fuelled interest in the possible applications of similar biological knowledge for humans, particularly influencing the zoologist and early US eugenicist Charles Davenport, who established a genetics research unit in 1904 at Long Island's Cold Spring Harbor.[21]

In the early twentieth century, Galton, already well advanced in years, pursued his vision with new vigour. He urged to the Sociological Society that the

> first and main point is to secure the general intellectual acceptance of eugenics as a hopeful and most important study. Then let its principles work into the heart of the nation, which will gradually give practical effect to them in ways that we may not wholly foresee.[22]

He saw the systematic study of family histories as key to success, founding a Eugenics Record Office (ERO, renamed in 1907 the Francis Galton Laboratory for the Study of National Eugenics) where Marxist mathematician, Karl Pearson, set up a repository of 'pedigree analysis' designed to assist 'eugenic' marriage planning.[23] In 1907, Galton's followers founded a Eugenics Education Society and in 1909, the society published the first issue of a journal, *The Eugenics Review*.[24]

In this period, clubs, networks and societies sprang up readily, reflecting a belief that democracy was something that professions and the educated were not only qualified, but required, to sustain and shape. Scientific societies had been active since the seventeenth century and political clubs were a characteristic of civic life since the French Revolution. Eugenics societies perpetuated both of these forms of sociable activism. Membership generally came from the upper-middle classes and often included both men and women. Few of the features of the eugenics movement were strictly new: already in the late nineteenth century social researchers had plotted the family trees of criminals; Malthusians (embracing the theories of Thomas Malthus (1766–1834), the theorist of population control who also voiced hereditarian sentiments) had argued for the need to control population numbers, while fears about 'degeneration' touched France, in particular. And while not all those who endorsed Darwin's evolutionary theories came to promote eugenic ideals, 'eugenics' seems to have become something of an umbrella term, loosely linking all such 'bio-social' reform interests. Thus the new movement was not identical with but coincided in time or in broad ideology with a number of other social agendas and areas of research. Several new words – especially those based on Greek roots – transited seamlessly into more than one language.

In more than thirty countries, as the *Oxford Handbook of the History of Eugenics* has shown, eugenic thinking was manifested in a diversity of rubrics including: Malthusianism and neo-Malthusianism; racial hygiene; human regeneration; experimental evolution; race betterment; racial biology; science of population; race welfare; family hygiene; human betterment; homiculture (cultivation of people); *puériculture* (cultivation of children); study of *métis* (race mixing); 'hygiene, insurance and social assistance'; 'studies in normal and pathological human heredity'; race biology and mental hygiene. There were also less menacing terms, such as blood group research; population policy; anthropology and anthropogenetics; study of human problems, and family planning. Clustered in the mid-twentieth century, eugenics was the most frequently used new name. In Romania there was an early (1927) use of the now widely used adjective 'biopolitical'. Genetics and eugenics were also paired in several institutional names, and many early medical genetics experts also supported eugenics.[25]

The movement sought to entrench social stratification by promoting the expansion – or at least proportional stability – of numbers at the imagined racial, ethnic, moral, physical and intellectual 'top' of the social scale. Research institutions and commissions investigated such matters as 'care and control of the mentally defective and feeble-minded' and race mixing. Laws, codes and commissions established mandatory marriage restrictions (including on cousin marriages but more often the marriages of those seen as otherwise 'unfit'); mandatory premarital health tests; child removal; 'baby farms' and forcible sterilization. Local politics also affected the movement's direction. For example, even though England was the home of eugenics, it never adopted mandatory sterilization, while many other jurisdictions did, the first being the US state of Indiana, in 1907.[26] However in both England and the USA eugenicists from across the political spectrum saw a threat from the numbers of Irish Catholics, Jews, and Eastern Europeans. For the English, class was also a regular theme, while in the USA, the country's recently freed slave class, the African-Americans, were a target for ongoing discrimination and mistreatment.[27]

American historian Alexandra Minna Stern sees a defining feature of twentieth-century eugenics as 'faith in the application of biology and medicine to the perceived problems of modern society'.[28] This definition encapsulates the twin focus of eugenics, an imagined link between the individual human body and the 'social body' and the intention to shape that link biologically in favour of the social body. Such is the essence of 'hereditarianism', a tradition in which imagining what human characteristics are passed on – and saying which ones matter – has served as a platform for social visions and prejudices, as much as for biological truths. The eugenics movement targeted intellectual, behavioural and psychological attributes, ensuring that the idea that some people are born 'unfit' for human society became widespread. That such people were born biologically programmed to do social harm was taken for granted, but being born thus did not exonerate them from responsibility for that potential social harm: the body into which one was born bore one's guilt. 'Pauperism', for example, was seen as a personal weakness not a socially induced condition. In the USA eugenic researchers in the new social sciences of criminology and sociology targeted families they saw as bearers of hereditary moral or physical degeneracy.[29] The so-called eugenic family studies built on late nineteenth-century research into the family trees of people convicted as criminals. Many of these studies emanated from Charles Davenport's unit, tracing the family trees of 'idiots', 'imbeciles' and the 'feebleminded', paupers, prostitutes, alcoholics and criminals in order to demonstrate that such people should not be permitted to reproduce.[30] The unit still exists as a major medical genetics research centre, studying, in considerable contrast, areas such as cancer, neuroscience, quantitative biology, plant biology and genomics.[31]

## The appeal of eugenics

Until recently, cursory readings of eugenics history were likely to focus on the very worst effects of the movement in the fascist dictatorship of the German National Socialist government (1933–1945, discussed below). What can be lost in this account is that more moderate conservatives and indeed many progressives embraced eugenics as a way to enhance the overall social good in democratic societies. Eugenics was 'invoked variously in support of capitalism and socialism, pacifism and militarism, patriarchy and women's liberation'[32] and could justify a wide range of practices. While some reforming feminists, for example, aspired merely to improve birth control education, others favoured interventionist policies of mandatory sterilization.[33]

Eugenics was not only a 'top-down' movement. The upper middle class drove the movement, and elitism was at its heart, but people of all classes participated in an aspirational process which invited them to assess their own contribution to the social good. Fairground eugenics booths, 'Race Betterment' pavilions at exhibitions, and 'Fitter Families' competitions forged a link between familial and national enhancement, making involvement in eugenics at times seem almost a form of entertainment.[34] Popularized versions of new science added cachet to eugenics' socially divisive agendas. A sign at the 1929 Kansas Free Fair read: 'Unfit human traits such as feeblemindedness, epilepsy, criminality, insanity, alcoholism, pauperism and many others run in families and are inherited in exactly the same way as color in guinea pigs'.[35] This shows a typical hereditarian blend of moral and physical social ideals, along the lines of Spurzheim a hundred years before, only this time, crucially, a pop version of the new genetic sciences undergirded the social elements.

Cost-cutting in state institutions, too, was a major eugenic cause supported by both government and taxpayers. At the Philadelphia Sesquicentennial Fair in 1926 a sign read: 'every fifteen seconds a hundred dollars of your money went for the care of persons with bad heredity'.[36] In Germany, as we saw in Chapter 3, similar messages appeared in school maths books.[37] Eugenics' proponents saw an urgent need to ensure that the social hierarchy not be reversed by sheer force of numbers. In practice, this meant that the democratization of the nineteenth century demanded more of the lower orders. Regardless of the starting point for eugenics advocates, 'what they had in common was an attitude toward people with physical or mental disabilities linked to a fetish for efficiency. One might say that they "despised dependency".'[38] It was a eugenic goal to force those who could not be 'improved' out of the reproductive population and to cultivate the capacities of those who could be 'improved' so they could fulfil their potential to reproduce. Many influential intellectuals debated the implementation of eugenic ideas and there was a wide diversity of opinion even among its proponents, as well as fears about links to the emerging reprogenetic science, notably expressed in Aldous Huxley's dystopia *Brave New World* (1932).[39] Eugenics presumed more of a biological basis for human behaviour and intelligence than has ever been proven, an emphasis which gave much of the troubling history of eugenics its shape.

## Eugenic sterilization

Governments worldwide, not just that of Nazi Germany, conducted extensive campaigns of involuntary sterilization across much of the twentieth century, before during and after the Second World War.[40] Most eugenic thinking emphasized mental, moral and intellectual traits, and held that all were heritable. The moral reform of society and the nation was thus seen as literally within the scope of medical intervention, in the form of mass sterilization. The misplaced and cruel logic was simple: end the bloodlines of the socially undesirable and their 'type' will die out. In reality, even early genetic knowledge showed that if such genes existed, the statistical chances of 'breeding out' any hereditary moral characteristics from the human race were small. Thus government policies of sterilization can be seen as in essence punitive, targeting those individuals and families who were seen to embody a threat to, or impose a financial burden on, the state.[41]

One notorious case was that of Carrie Buck, a young woman who, together with her daughter, was in 1927 sterilized against her will while in the hands of the State of Virginia.[42] Buck had given birth to an illegitimate child, as a consequence of an alleged rape in the home of her foster family. Both she and her mother were said to have the 'conditions' of 'feeblemindedness and sexual promiscuity' and the state wanted to mount a test case for sterilization to uphold its 1924 *Eugenical Sterilization Act*. The case ended up in the US Supreme Court in 1927 where it was upheld as constitutional by a vote of eight to one.

Justice Oliver Wendell Holmes expressed the majority view in an often-quoted statement, which still bears close reading:

> [W]e have seen more than once that the public welfare may call upon the best citizens for their lives. It would be strange if it could not call upon those who already sap strength of the State for these lesser sacrifices ... in order to prevent our being swamped with incompetence ... The principle that sustains compulsory vaccination is broad enough to cover cutting the Fallopian tubes ... It is better for all the world, if instead of waiting to execute degenerate offspring for crime or to let them starve for their imbecility, society can prevent those who are manifestly unfit from continuing their kind ... Three generations of imbeciles are enough.[43]

Holmes invokes analogies from both the sacrifice of soldiers conscripted in war and the public health measure of vaccination to reinforce his view of US society's legitimate expectations of its citizens. Conscription and vaccination were both apt analogies for the time, as they were public policy issues which highlighted the question of rights and obligations of citizens in democracies. Holmes held that in the case of Carrie Buck, a highly invasive surgical intervention lay somewhere between these other two state-mandated physical demands. The punitive view of Buck is based on her embodiment of what Holmes judged to be an indivisible blend of intellectual and moral deficiency, incurring a consequent cost to the state. Melodramatic references to 'our being swamped', capital punishment for crime ('waiting to execute') and starvation as a result of mental problems seem to overstate the realities for effect, unless they were intended to hint that the country had other less merciful means of dealing with the same problem at different stages of a life.

Between 1907 and 1931 in the USA, 33 states adopted legislation permitting sterilization of men and women in state institutions.[44] Over 60,000 of the so-called 'unfit' who were in institutional custody of some kind were forcibly sterilized.[45] In Germany in 1933 the Nazi dictatorship (1933–1945) passed a Law for Protection against Genetically Defective Offspring. The Nazis not only sterilized people in institutions but went further, creating 220 'Hereditary Health Courts' which assessed whether people in the community should be sterilized.[46] The Nazi regime oversaw the forcible sterilization of 300,000 people, the majority for 'feeblemindedness, schizophrenia, and alcoholism'.[47] The Nazi *Lebensborn* ('wellspring of life') programme set up baby farms where eugenically 'suitable' women were housed and obliged to give birth to the children of a sequence of males, usually officers in the Gestapo and SS (Security Police).[48] Other jurisdictions to adopt policies of eugenic sterilization included Denmark, Finland, Mexico, Sweden, Norway, Japan, and provinces in Canada.[49] Mandatory sterilization in many countries continued well into the second half of the twentieth century, long after the exposure of Nazi abuses. Sweden carried out eugenic sterilization until the 1960s; in the USA, mandatory sterilization of men and women took place until the 1980s.[50] Not every jurisdiction with a eugenics movement supported mandatory sterilization, however.[51]

## Eugenics after World War II

Knowledge of the consequences of Nazi eugenics did not bring about a wholesale repudiation of the eugenic vision. Indeed, in the immediate post-war era, little changed. A process of repudiation of eugenics – at least in its harshest forms – and increasing use of the word as a pejorative took place intermittently in the post-war era but the process varied markedly from country to country and in the views of different individual and organizations. From the 1950s, however, renaming practices worked increasingly to remove any Nazi overtones. In 1950, for example, the Canadian National Committee for Mental Hygiene was renamed Canadian National Committee for Mental Health, and the Hong Kong Eugenics League became the Family Planning Association. In 1959, the Swedish Institute for Race Biology became the Department of Medical Genetics at Uppsala University; the Racial Hygiene Association of New South Wales (Australia) joined the new Family Planning Association in 1960 and the American Eugenics Society became in 1973 the Society for the Study of Social Biology. The process did not occur universally or uniformly, however. Greece, the home of the roots of the word, founded its first eugenics society in 1954, while in England the Eugenics Society did not become the Galton Institute until 1989.[52] The movement continued but came increasingly to target 'biosocial science', conservation, and individual and family health. Reasons ranged from idealistic to pragmatic. In 1949 the English society saw work with families as 'safe ground', because, as its General Secretary Carlos Paton Blacker later wrote, 'the word eugenics ... has come under a cloud'.[53] Many eugenic advocates promoted less provocative and generally less coercive goals, notably in the forms of 'family planning, population control, and genetic and marital counseling'.[54] The expanding capacities of medical genetics increasingly facilitated interventions which could limit the likelihood that children would be born with a harmful genetic condition. The cultural memory of eugenics nonetheless arose again in the 1970s, when some members of African-American communities questioned the motives of screening programmes for sickle cell disease.[55]

Modern medical genetics has tap roots in the eugenics movement, in the work of key eugenicists who studied deleterious genetic conditions. Geneticist Lionel Penrose first saw the link between maternal age and Down syndrome (previously 'mongolism', now Trisomy 21) in 1934.[56] He was the Professor of Eugenics and Director of the Galton Laboratory from 1947 to 1967. Late in his career he succeeded in having the name of the chair changed to Professor of Human Genetics. He urged a categorical distinction between eugenics and genetics asserting: 'human genetics is a science and eugenics is an ideology'.[57] His comment needs to be read as staking a rhetorical claim, based on a desire to maintain the best of genetics while consigning the worst of eugenics to the past. As early as the 1920s, genetic scientists in the USA had made similar moves, but they, like Penrose, remained for many years in the minority. Even emerging scientists such as Robert Sinsheimer, in 1969, did not shrink from the negative historic associations of the word, in claiming an era of a 'new eugenics' characterized by voluntary and individual uses of genetic science to create a new breed of human being.[58]

Most present-day uses of genetic medicine at the reproductive level are directed towards the prevention of the birth of children with severe physical or mental conditions, based on a body of genetic knowledge and with the help of several contributory clinical technologies. Much of the remaining discussion will be concerned with the medical interventions rendered possible through the application of the knowledge of molecular genetics, a field which expanded from the late nineteenth century and continues to grow.

## Medical genetics

Detection of heritable conditions has historically relied on data from two principal sources: mapping of biological family history (or 'pedigree') and knowledge of the inner molecular workings of human heredity. Modern molecular genetics largely builds on the research of Gregor Mendel who used pedigree analysis of the physical characteristics of peas, which he bred, to establish the principles of hereditary transmission. The principles implied, but did not identify or characterize, the presence of some yet-to-be-identified constitutive element in the human body which the reproductive process transmitted. In the 1870s, the German biologist August Weismann (1834–1914) speculated that there existed throughout the human body a substance that he referred to as 'germ plasm', which was in theory 'impermeable to the environment', while the Danish botanist Wilhelm Johannsen coined the word 'gene' in 1909 to refer to such a component.[59] The German physician Walther Flemming had published in 1882 on the use of microscopy to identify what came to be called chromosomes, the components of human cells which housed genetic material. In 1944 Oswald Avery showed genes to be made out of deoxyribonucleic acid (DNA) and in 1953 Maurice Wilkins, James Watson and Francis Crick, basing their work on the crystallography of molecular biologist Rosalind Franklin, postulated the structure of DNA, the famous 'double helix'. In 1989 an international programme supported by several governments sought to map the entire human genome, that is, 'all of the DNA in an organism'.[60] James Watson advised the first Human Genome Conference at San Diego in 1989: 'We have to be aware of the really terrible past of eugenics, where incomplete knowledge was used in a very cavalier and rather awful way, both here in the United States and in Germany.'[61] The project devoted from its outset 5 per cent of all funding to a side-programme to consider the ethical, legal and social implications (ELSI) of the dramatic expansion of genetic knowledge.[62] The ELSI programme gestured towards a decades-old wariness about the potential social implications of human genetic technology.

Modern genetics has expanded knowledge of the origins of single-gene physical diseases at the same time as it has largely retreated from facile assumptions about the heritability of personality traits and mental capacities which typified historic eugenics. Genetic scientists now acknowledge that precisely the kinds of behaviours and character-istics which governments identified as the reasons to carry out manda-tory sterilization are those which are the least likely to have a single genetic basis. Most reasons for intellectual impairment, mental illness, alcoholism and propensity to violence, for example, come under the category of 'multi-factorial', meaning that the extent of genetic and environmental influences is unknown. There is still considerable research into possible mental or behavioural genes, but findings tend to support the view that most identifiable genetic contributions to psychology, intellect or behaviour are complex. Intellect is not deter-mined by a single gene; and a persistent tradition of research into genes for 'criminality' has yielded only limited scientific results. This is a contentious issue, as (in the view of Troy Duster, the sociologist who coined the evocative term 'backdoor eugenics') the practice of retaining DNA samples from people accused but not convicted of crimes cannot be scientifically justified.[63]

Eugenics advocates presumed the powers of biological heredity long before scientists identified its mechanisms and even though many geneticists were also eugenicists, there has never been a clear synchronicity between what eugenics sought for human society and what medical genetics was able to offer. A presumption of genetic bases for all human characteristics, normal and pathological, still outstrips the actual knowledge-base and remains one of the reasons that even some scientists argue that genetic research is disproportionately favoured as an explanatory tool for human health and behaviour. Throughout the history of modern medical genetics, the development of new technical devices at the laboratory and clinical levels has provided the basis for the most common interventions in the human reproductive process. The first 'consumer' use of genetics took place in the development, after the Second World War, of what US eugenicist Sydney Reed called 'genetic counselling'. At the present time, the impact of genetic knowledge at the 'consumer interface' brings in a range of laboratory and clinical technologies all of which build on the genetic counselling model.

## Genetic counselling

Eugenicist physicians and geneticists founded the first 'genetic coun-selling' programmes in the 1940s: in 1946 in the USA and 1947 in England. Initially these services amounted to little more than advice to (mostly middle-class) couples as to whether or not they should repro-duce, for reasons of possible illness or disability in the child. The number of chromosomal and Mendelian disorders which could be detected in this period was relatively few and the means to do so were limited. The family background of the parents and health status of earlier children provided most of the basis for these assessments, with only a few biochemical tests available to establish whether a particular condition would be passed on to children. Counsellors provided a risk assessment intended to lead to a decision on whether or not to conceive.[64] Genetic counselling now mediates the very wide range of genetic tests which have come into existence in more recent times.

New clinical techniques, notably IVF and amniocentesis, as well as sciences such as embryology and endocrinology, have combined with genetic knowledge to create a series of possible interventions at every stage of the reproductive process, starting with genetic testing of prospective parents; through the creation and testing of embryos *in vitro*; numerous tests during pregnancy, and postnatal testing, such as the Guthrie test for PKU (a severe genetic condition which if detected at birth can be treated and cured). How these newly aggregated sciences and technologies are to be applied and what limitations can or should be imposed on their use forms the basis of much of the ethical debate in this area.

In the late 1960s, a new process, amniocentesis, permitted direct test-ing of the foetus *in utero*. In 1969, Guy's Hospital in London was the first to offer tests.[65] Therapeutic abortion became legal in England in 1967 and in the USA in 1973. These two developments – one technical and one legal – represented a sea-change in the capacity for medicine truly to intervene in the transmission of genetic conditions, through the termination of affected pregnancies.[66] Without legal abortion, much of the more recent debate about the eugenic nature of modern genetics and artificial reproductive technologies (ARTs) would probably not have occurred. According to Diane Paul, the 'convergence of prenatal diagno-sis and legalized abortion produced explosive growth in the field of genetic counseling'.[67]

Endocrinology (the study of hormones) provided the knowledge for the development of 'fertility drugs' in the 1950s. These hormones increase the number of oocytes (eggs) a woman produces in her menstrual cycle, facilitating 'fertility treatments' which can lead to multiple births. The technique also permitted expanded opportunities for the laboratory creation of embryos. The isolation of the human embryo outside a woman's body made human embryology for reprogenetic purposes possible.

Developmental biologists Robert Edwards and colleagues first reported the creation of human embryos in the laboratory in 1969.[68] At the same time, Edwards worked with an obstetric/gynaecological specialist, Patrick Steptoe to devise a new technology of *in vitro* fertilization (IVF, literally, fertilization in glass, as distinct from *in utero*, in the woman's uterus). Initially Steptoe and Edwards did not use fertility drugs to generate in the ovaries of female clients multiple ova ready for extraction and fertilization (a process known as superovulation); indeed, Robert Edwards repeatedly expressed scepticism at the overuse of this technique, which puts female clients at risk.[69] Techniques to access the multiple eggs in a woman's ovaries initially involved the new and somewhat hazardous technique of laparoscopy, developed by Steptoe, with the use of transvaginal egg 'harvesting' coming later.

In 1978 the first child (Louise Brown) was born following fertilization in a laboratory (IVF). A capacity for a woman's eggs to be fertilized *in vitro* using either her partner's or a donor's sperm (rather than using the technique of 'traditional' sperm donation directly into the vagina) in theory increased the likelihood of pregnancy. But fertilization in the laboratory also made it possible for a woman other than the one who had produced the egg to be the recipient of the embryo. Thus the idea of IVF 'surrogacy' – in which a woman who had ovaries but no womb, for example, might nonetheless have her 'own' genetic child, with another woman carrying the child to term – came to be projected, and indeed was used within five years of the first IVF birth.[70] The new technology also provided potential for the development of genetic probes at what came to be called 'preimplantation' stage. Early IVF was a treatment for infertility, particularly as a means of bypassing a woman's blocked fallopian tubes. However, it was also apparent early on that the growing knowledge-base of genetics would likely make it possible to detect genetic profiles at the embryo stage.

## Preimplantation genetic diagnosis (PGD)

In 1990 the Hammersmith Hospital IVF clinic in London provided the first successful clinical use of an embryonic genetic test, in a new technique called preimplantation genetic diagnosis (PGD; sometimes PIGD).[71] At early embryo stage within about three days of fertilization it is possible to remove enough cells from the embryo to determine whether or not the child born will be affected by a particular genetic condition. It is also possible at this stage to detect the sex of the embryo and the detection of sex-linked diseases was one of the most common early uses for PGD. The aim of this technique is that only those embryos cleared for conditions such as Huntington's disease, cystic fibrosis (CF), thalassemia, Duchenne muscular dystrophy, Fragile-X syndrome, and BRCA1/BRCA2 (hereditary breast/ovarian cancer) are reimplanted.[72] In the case of sex-linked conditions, the majority of which affect males, sex testing of embryos at three days is the basic procedure. Until relatively recently PGD was largely limited to sex-linked genetic diseases. However, it is also possible at this early stage to establish whether the genetic profile of the embryo makes a future child a possible 'saviour sibling' who would be able to donate bone marrow to a sibling already born who has a particular medical condition.[73]

In India and China son-preference led many people to use first amniocentesis and more recently PGD in order to ensure the birth of a son.[74] Not 'eugenic' in the strict historical sense, use of these technologies when no deleterious genetic condition is at issue clearly speaks of discriminatory priorities about who shall be born, and so could be classed as a form of private 'eugenics'. When this practice started to affect population balance, governments acted to restrict its use but it continues underground. In countries which do not have severe overpopulation, sex selection for social reasons is known by the term 'family balancing'. In 2011, anti-abortion activists in the USA sought to ban abortion based on sex testing, a shrewd manoeuvre to enlist the rhetoric of feminism in the service of the anti-abortion cause.[75] The bill was defeated.

In the UK and Australia, selecting the sex of an embryo for reasons other than clinical risk is currently not permitted in the UK under the authority of the Human Fertilisation and Embryology Authority, and in Australia under NHMRC guidelines 'sex selection (by whatever means) must not be undertaken except to reduce the risk of transmission of a serious genetic condition'.[76] Neither of these regulatory authorities has the force of law, however. Sex selection using IVF is legal in the USA and India for non-clinical reasons and one Australian fertility specialist, David Molloy, claims:

> On average around a dozen or so couples I treat head overseas every year for treatment with the desire to sex select. In some countries the

quality control regulations may not be as stringent as those in Australia, and in the United States, the cost of treatment at some private clinics can be upwards of US$20,000. There is also a greater risk that couples will choose to terminate a pregnancy if the fetus is not the desired sex.[77]

Thus Molloy highlights the standard problems of medical tourism while ending with an appeal to anti-abortion sentiment.

In Italy, resistance to the introduction of the practice of PGD because of risks to the human embryo led the government in 2004 to take the extraordinary step of insisting that all embryos created during IVF must be reimplanted in the woman. This was regardless of their genetic potentialities, and regardless of the potential effect on a woman of multiple pregnancies or on children born in a multiple birth. Once the embryo or embryos were created the law obliged the woman to have them implanted, meaning, in the words of legal scholar Dr Andrea Boggio: 'they cannot stop the process, even if the woman has changed her mind and no longer wants to proceed with the treatment'.[78] On the basis of ongoing complaints about this heavy-handed law, the Constitutional Court gave an opinion (n. 151/2009) in 2009 to the effect that the law 'was in breach of the constitution to the extent to which it mandated the creation of three embryos and the physician's absolute duty to implant them all'. Now, in light of these challenges, 'although the Court expressly indicates that this is a "medical decision," in reality women have "veto power" in the sense that the implantation cannot be coerced and that a woman who expresses the intent to undergo an abortion in the event the embryo is implanted can refuse implantation.'[79] The initial law was not 'eugenic' strictly speaking: in a sense it was the reverse, because it paid no heed to the health of possible children or their mother. But it did impel reproduction of a certain kind, removing both patient and medical autonomy from the calculus.

## Donor gamete programmes

One way in which the passing on of harmful genetic traits can be avoided is through donor gamete programmes. Sperm donation has been widely practised for many decades, with occasional controversies over 'genius' sperm banks. (Some eugenicists also argued for the freezing of sperm from 'healthy and intelligent males' in order to avoid the risks of 'genetic deterioration' through exposure to radiation.[80]) Maturation *in vivo* and extraction of multiple eggs from a woman are much more complicated procedures which have only recently become part of the repertoire of reproductive interventions. Donor gamete programmes also provide an opportunity for a kind of individualized 'eugenics', in the sense that most buyers of eggs or sperm will have information about the complexion, height and other personal details of donors to facilitate their choice. Indeed choices offered to clients seem often to be dictated more by cultural disposition than by science. Some of the sought-after features of gamete donors – such as religious background, temperament, intellectual or athletic ability, even star sign and fondness for animals – are either not heritable or at best multi-factorial. Clients can even face-match donors with 'someone famous'.[81] Donors, too, might be offered choice to the extent that they can sometimes stipulate whether they are willing for their sperm to be donated to lesbians or single women.

## Genes and rights

The language of 'rights' has taken many forms over recent decades, complicating ethical issues. The right to abortion, reproductive rights, patients' rights, intellectual property rights, the right to privacy, consumer rights, right to life – unsurprisingly, the sloganizing of so many rights means they cannot always be compatible. Today, in wealthy countries the rights issues relating to genetics can be more about the 'torrent' of genetic information than about eugenic population profiles.[82] Historian of eugenics and genetics commentator Daniel Kevles has shown, for example, that two competing models of rights touch on the question of gene patenting. Myriad Genetics has a patent on two breast cancer-linked genes: BRCA1 and 2.[83] Myriad asks high fees for the use of the probe for patients (which now includes PGD) and charges scientists to use the gene in their research. The tension here lies between patenting rights – in essence, intellectual property – and the rights of patients to access the best treatment. Gene patenting, Kevles argues, is publicly funded knowledge sold back to a select market at premium prices. He gives another example of a case in which a medical insurer agreed to pay for a prenatal test for cystic fibrosis only on condition that the woman had an abortion if the foetus was found to be affected. He argues:

> the increasing acquisition of genetic information could conceivably lead to a renewal of the ethical premises of the original eugenic movement, an insistence that the reproductive rights of individuals

must give way to the medical-economic welfare of the community as a whole, whether medical services are provided through public or private instruments.[84]

Such impositions by insurers ignore the fact that many women – even those with a diagnosis indicating that a foetus may be born with a harmful condition – do not always choose to have an abortion. Arguably, being forewarned might enable families better to deal with the consequences of having a sick child, but leading historian of the eugenic analogy, Diane Paul, underscores that governments would not fund screening programmes nor defend pro-choice views unless they anticipated savings as a result.[85] She also argues that insisting on an individual's absolute right to choose weakens the argument of feminist and left-liberal promoters of regulatory barriers to the introduction of new birth technologies.[86] The US bill to restrict sex-selective abortion cited above is a perfect example of just such a political 'cleft stick'. Choices, rights and equity can exist in tension.

Moreover, sociologist Rayna Rapp argues that choice is only ever part of the ethical equation: 'Attributing safety to an individual-choice model foregrounds personal liberty while backgrounding the social matrix of a technoscientific marketplace to whose requisites individual choices are increasingly enrolled.'[87] A choice model is intentionally culturally naïve, positioning ethics as more individualistic than the diversely politicized and economically weighted realities of modern medicine. Rapp thus neatly encapsulates the limits on the discourse of choice in economies which are generously endowed with medical technology. The individual's 'right to choose' cannot be the sole determinant of all practices and decisions in complex medico-political situations, in which multiple cultural forces are at work.

## Genetic communities: individual, group, nation

In a significant development, the language of individual patients' rights and consumer autonomy has migrated to include groups of people united as a result of a common genetic condition. Influential sociologist of science, Bruno Latour, applauds the new 'consumerism' of one group of genetically affected people who have built a grassroots movement around their rights to sponsor new research to help them and their families. He describes the Association Française contre les Myopathies (AFM) as 'a patient-run organization that has managed, through public charity, to raise enough money to engage in a vast program of molecular biology, with the aim not only of finding the genes responsible for the rare so-called orphan diseases but also of finding gene therapies for them'.[88] Latour caricatures anxieties about the power of genetic science, rejecting the view that, as he puts it, 'When genes enter, liberty flees away'.[89] On the contrary, he argues that for people in AFM 'gene action is a synonym for emancipation'.[90] Thus something like 'patients' rights' might have once implied rejection of medical power; now it is about who can work together to access and channel that power.

Israeli sociologist Aviad Raz reflects more deeply on the idea of 'community genetics' celebrated by Latour. Raz points to some of the tensions which can arise for individuals in some religious communities which are genetically at risk, a situation which can be entrenched by community-sanctioned endogamy. He explores the genetic community as also a moral community which can make rules to limit an individual's reproductive options, in the interests of the group. 'Reprogenetic programmes', he suggests, 'may be endorsed by communities in spite of limits on individual choice [as] such communities often have traditional values that are incongruent with the "standard view" [the informed choice model] of genetic counseling.'[91] Thus in some cases the cornerstone of medical autonomy, an individual's consent, 'cannot simply be "informed" but depends on instruction; individuals are often not "autonomous" but dependent on others. Pre-arranged cousin marriage is a traditional norm, and abortion is often banned by religion.' What is the role of the state if a 'genetic community' breaches the rights of individuals, understood in the liberal sense, within that group? Where do the rights of community end and those of nation begin? Eugenics historically relied on the nation and the state, but such larger political realms are now ironically the only recourse of those adversely affected by the working of other 'little commonwealths'.[92] Such complexities lead Raz to ask: 'Is it valid to judge programmes of 'community genetics', and particularly reprogenetics, according to generalized Western/ secular/liberal standards? Conversely, can we look the other way when individual autonomy is compromised in the name of community norms?'[93] It is simply not possible to overlay former understandings of rights, activism, or indeed of eugenics onto present day political and reform scenarios.

Another often-cited example of the different paths down which the rights discourse has travelled since the cheery slogans of the 1970s was a controversial case which involved the community of the deaf. When a deaf lesbian couple intentionally used a male sperm donor whose deafness might raise the genetic likelihood of the child born being deaf, the story made headlines around the world.[94] Choosing to have a child who has a condition such as deafness is another logical consequence of both a patients' rights stance and the validity of the idea of 'community genetics'. In an ethically plural global culture the positives and negatives vary sharply according to perspective, but a simplistic vocabulary of rights can serve more than one party. Ethical pluralism underscores the poverty of the discourse of rights as a way of solving complex issues in reproductive politics in the world as it now is. There is some irony in the fact that eugenics advocate Alexander Graham Bell proposed that the deaf should marry non-deaf people, to increase the likelihood of having a hearing child.[95]

If a community can make the same claims to autonomy as an individual, then what of the national 'communities'? Nations generally hold the last card in such debates, controlling (with more or less success) who shall have access to the products of reprogenetics and in some cases insisting on their use through screening programmes. The right to do this is accorded by the underlying ideal of national sovereignty. The case of two national 'communities' – Cyprus and the People's Republic of China – are further examples which show how hard it is to draw the ethical line between seemingly similar legal requirements for genetic screening in two very different political systems. If a nation itself can be legitimately seen as a genetic community, can this take us back to the full gamut of historic eugenics?

## Cyprus and the PRC

On the Mediterranean island of Cyprus, which has two governments (Greek and Turkish) reflecting its ethnic composition, the gene for *beta* thalassemia (a kind of anaemia) is prevalent: one in seven persons is a carrier and one in four of all children born to two-carrier couples are affected by the condition. In order to survive past the age of five an affected child will require a lifetime of intensive medical treatment with blood transfusions and demanding intravenous pharmacotherapy. In the 1970s both the Greek and Turkish sides of the newly divided island provided free treatment to sufferers. Later, in the wake of community and physician campaigns for screening, both began mandatory programmes of premarital carrier testing and funded voluntary prenatal testing, with the potential for a government-funded termination. Until 1983 the Greek Orthodox Church insisted that terminations had to be performed in another country.[96]

These programmes have reduced and nearly eliminated the number of affected births. Because treatment of people with the disease is costly there was also a financial motive for the governments. Nonetheless, there is no prohibition on marriage of carriers and if a woman decides to proceed with the pregnancy, the government will still pay for treatment.[97] The programme in this sense is 'anti-eugenic', in allowing for the least controversial balance of rights and obligations and it has none of the racial, moral or behavioural loading of the worst forms of eugenics.[98] Historian of science Ruth Schwartz Cowan proposes a reverse translation of the word 'eugenics', coining the term 'beautiful heredity', to endorse the positives of the Cyprus programme. Cyprus is somewhat 'eugenic' in imposing health screening, and the motivation is in part to reduce health-care costs, but it does not mandate that carriers may not give birth to an affected child. Cowan is both pragmatic and humane when she recommends: 'If not calling it a eugenic program allows it to continue, let's not call it a eugenic program.'[99] Most activists – barring the abortion lobby – would concede that such screening for a grave and clearly genetic illness such as *beta* thalassemia, with seemingly genuine protection of the 'right to choose' would be acceptable, on public health grounds. Even Troy Duster concedes sardonically that Cyprus is a case of 'cooperative consenting eugenics'.[100]

Historic eugenics was intimately tied up with the idea of supra-individual collectivities – nations and states within nations – and relatively few modern governments have entertained eugenic ideals in the full historic sense (wholly compulsory; wholly population-oriented and largely focused on mental, moral and intellectual traits). The People's Republic of China, however, introduced a Law on Maternal and Infant Health Care in 1995 which had the goal of 'improving the quality of the newborn population'.[101] The law mandates premarital check-ups for couples and stipulates that in the case of either partner being diagnosed with a 'serious genetic disorder', marriage can take place 'only if both sides agree to take long-term contraceptive measures or to take a ligation operation for sterility'.[102] The law also appears to require that all pregnant women must be screened for genetic defects in the foetus. Doctors are required to advise abortions in the case of a foetus being found to have a defect or genetic disease of a serious nature, although written permission for such an operation must be given by the woman concerned. Among the mental conditions referred to are schizophrenia, 'manic-depressive psychosis', epilepsy and mental retardation – none of them wholly or necessarily genetic.[103] However, the law positions concerns about parents' mental health as being related to possible problems with effective parenting rather than strict hereditability of the condition.[104] Yet the Minister of Public Health, Chen Mingzhang, perhaps inadvertently gave a sense of some underlying goals of the laws, referring to births of 'inferior quality' among 'the old revolutionary base, ethnic minorities, the frontier, and economically poor areas'.[105] This terminology resonated either with outright eugenics or with unfounded assumptions about the genetic origins of political views.

The word 'eugenics' or, more accurately, its approximate Chinese equivalent, had been removed from an initial 1993 version of the Act in the wake of criticism by geneticists.[106] The Human Genome Organization ethics committee nonetheless condemned the law in 1996 and the American Society of Human Genetics expressed concern about it in 1999, but no international pressure, whether through continued 'constructive engagement' as recommended by Canadian geneticists or other forms of moral suasion, appears to have affected its use.[107] It is not wholly clear, however, how widely the law has been enforced and one Western health researcher has defended the programme on public health lines, referring to several other jurisdictions with similar provisions, and notwithstanding what she refers to as 'overtones of eugenics'.[108] A similar law has been in place in Taiwan since 1984. The Eugenic Protection Law[109] requires health-care providers to 'persuade' couples to undertake premarital checks for 'hereditary disease', 'contagious disease' and 'mental disease'.[110] The Taiwan law also refers specifically to 'upgrading the quality of the population', a goal ostensibly counterbalanced by reference to a woman's decision to undergo an abortion or sterilization being 'at her own will' – but in turn, physicians are specifically required to 'persuade' the woman to undergo abortion or sterilization. The debate can come down to fine print: are the terms of reference for a heritable condition too wide? (e.g., the PRC law refers only to 'mental illness', for example, yet few mental illnesses are strictly hereditary). How truly voluntary is the consent of a woman advised by a doctor to have an abortion? (In some cases, by contrast, might it be unethical in some cases not to advise abortion?)

Can the ethical case for policy in Cyprus provide a template for other places? Or do the characteristics of the condition and the country have a unique ethical significance which can only apply in that case? The case of China opens these questions out on two fronts: first, unlike Cyprus, there is more than one condition at issue and there are questions about the heritability of the conditions referred to under the law; second, unlike Cyprus, only marriage but not reproduction can be undertaken without a couple 'passing' the tests. And as the categories to be tested for include non-heritable conditions, this raises the question of whether the intervention is a public health measure or a political measure. Given that there are therefore still legitimate questions about possible incursions on reproductive freedom in several contexts, Anglophone attempts to rehabilitate the word 'eugenics', by adding the adjective 'liberal' to accentuate a choice model might seem misplaced.

## 'Liberal eugenics'

The term 'liberal eugenics' serves as a defence of the voluntary and individual use of genetic reproductive technologies. Most liberal eugenics proponents appear to target anti-abortion and anti-embryo experimentation attitudes of the religious right. The juxtaposition of the word 'eugenics' and the word 'liberal' seems to embody a paradox, urging that there is room for the word 'eugenics' within the vocabulary of rights. 'Eugenics or "reprogenetics"? Call it what you will, but let's do it' is the defiant title of a piece by a philosopher writing on a University of Oxford blog.[111] He makes a case for genetic counselling to prevent the birth of children with severe physical impairment. Similarly, Caplan et al. ask provocatively: 'What is immoral about eugenics?', arguing, 'A couple may wish to have a baby who has no risk of inheriting Tay-Sachs disease or transmitting sickle cell disease. Or they may want a child with a particular hair color or gender. If their choice is free and informed then there is no reason to think that such a choice is immoral on grounds of force or coercion.'[112] The article intentionally conflates historic eugenics with modern reproductive genetics, in response, presumably, to the way that anti-abortionists identify eugenics. Can a word like 'eugenics' be toyed with in this way? Can the memory of the history of eugenics be wished away?

Liberal eugenics emphasizes choice above all, but as a cover-all term, it can (and for proponents intentionally does) conflate genetic testing for serious medical conditions with testing or interventions intended to 'enhance' a couple's offspring. Prevention of suffering remains at the heart of most modern uses of genetic medicine.[113] By contrast, in historic eugenics, any advances in medical genetics were incidental to, and outweighed by, much more destructive attempts to manipulate the physical and intellectual characteristics of society.

In a critique of liberal eugenics Robert Sparrow observes, proponents paint themselves as rationalists fearlessly championing progress and truth against a timid and confused Establishment:

There is a tendency for advocates of human enhancement to repre-sent themselves – and perhaps also to see themselves – as the philo-sophical descendants of Voltaire, bravely defying the forces of irrationality and conservatism in order to reach the difficult conclu-sions that others dare not.[114]

To rehabilitate eugenics under any banner seems to be a summons to amnesia, to forget that for the majority of its history eugenics fomented negative, socially divisive and often violent actions. Moreover, the re-use of the word in a positive light is in the end no more valuable than its deployment in opposition to aspects of medical genetics. It does matter what you call it. There is more to mourn than to celebrate in the history of twentieth-century eugenics and it is an error of sensibility to seek to rehabilitate the word. This is also the view expressed in the newsletter of the Galton Institute itself in 2000.[115]

## 'Reprogenetics': a preferable term

Lee M. Silver, a leading molecular biologist and advocate of the use of reproductive genetics, coined the word 'reprogenetics' to refer to 'the use of genetic information and technology to ensure or prevent the inheritance of particular genes in a child'. Another definition is: 'the field of research and application that involves the creation, use, manip-ulation, or storage of gametes and embryos'.[116] For convenience, I suggest that 'reprogenetics' should also cover those interventions which are not strictly hereditary, nor strictly embryo/gamete related, but are equivalent from an ethical point of view in that they bring in questions of reproductive screening or selection pre- or post-conception. Neural tube defects (NTDs) such as anencephaly, hydrocephalus and *spina bifida* are all conditions which can be detected *in utero*, but are not exclusively genetic. Any decision to test for these conditions and poten-tially terminate the pregnancy raises some of the same ethical questions as other reproductive interventions which have been part of the eugen-ics debate.

Silver stresses the individual and familial reasons for using modern reproductive genetics over the collective enterprises associated with eugenics. He argues: 'Fundamentally, reprogenetics can be understood through its sole motivation: the desire of parents to give all possible advantages to their children.'[117] Silver is a proponent of a free market in genetic practices, but he is aware of the ethical implications of the expansion of global capitalism. With some candour, he contemplates the logical endpoints of both a deregulated marketplace and a regulated one which permits equal access to technologies for genetic enhancement. He states:

> The use of genetic enhancement could greatly increase the gap between the haves and the have-nots in the world. ... [T]he economic and social advantages that wealthy countries maintain could be expanded into a genetic advantage. And the gap between wealthy and poor countries could widen further with each generation until all common heritage disappears. A severed humanity might be the ultimate legacy of unfettered global capitalism. The only alternative seems remote today and may never be viable: a single world state in which all children are provided with the same genetic enhancements and the same opportunities for health, happiness and success.

Thus Silver acknowledges that possible deleterious *social* consequences will arise if the things which he believes to be right *for individuals* come to pass. But he sees that no form of regulation can ultimately affect this direction, in part because of the open market for genetic products. Similarly reflective, geneticist Martin Delatycki remarks that 'governments are unlikely to fund screening programs that are not cost-effective'.[118]

There exists, too, a real if small 'neo-eugenics' movement. This should suggest caution in the re-adoption or rehabilitation of the term, eugenics: for these eugenicists know what they mean, even if the liberals are still sorting it out. Such groups are in fact very keen to see eugenics return, whether through the front or back door.[119] One relatively senior former academic, Richard Lynn of the University of Ulster, reclaims eugenics in a thinly veiled diatribe against races (notably Hispanics and African-Americans) and types of person (for example, youthful mothers on welfare) whom he regards as both intellectually inferior and inclined to over-reproduce.[120]

## Discussion

Comparison between eugenics and modern medical genetics has served as a historical starting point for conversations about the possible ethical implications of modern genetics. It has provided an elementary vocabulary for considering scientific developments which are often of great significance both for public health and for wider public policy.

The late nineteenth- and twentieth-century worldwide eugenics movement sought to change the 'quality' of populations by urging governments and private individuals to control the nature of children to be born. Eugenics supported the restriction of reproduction, sometimes through the relatively modest method of encouraging careful selection of marriage partners, but also in damaging and coercive ways. Eugenic ideologies at their most destructive provided the rationale for policies of enforced sterilization in many countries, as well as eugenic 'baby-farming' and even genocide. Nazi eugenics was not the only eugenics which was harmful to individuals and an offence to human dignity. It is necessary to recall the full extent of the movement's diversity and its resilience post-war, in order to provide a nuanced reading of where present-day practices might or might not fit on a continuum with aspects of eugenics' history.

Modern molecular genetics provides the basis for discovering if individuals or their offspring might be affected by deleterious genetic predispositions. Genetic analysis is used both in personal reproductive medicine and in public health policies, such as carrier-screening programmes. Genetic counsellors discuss with prospective parents the likelihood of transmission of genetic conditions to potential children, for example, and interventionist reproductive medicine can exclude genetic conditions from early and later stages in the reproductive process through the use of technologies such as IVF and embryo testing, and in prenatal screening which can lead to termination of pregnancy.

Historians of eugenics have highlighted the limitations of comparing past and present mindsets. They have drawn attention to the fact that the history of eugenics as a movement is more complex than a simple equation with right-wing or totalitarian ideologies: one can't just say 'that is eugenic' with much meaning. It can reduce the power of the comparison and confuse more than it clarifies. Eugenicists in the twentieth century were divided among themselves about the nature of their vision and the means to attain it; even its opponents at the time were opposed for reasons quite different from the reasons of opponents today. Modern commentators on reprogenetics speak from a wide range of viewpoints. At the extremes, opponents of reproductive interventions that can manipulate or destroy a human embryo or which entail the use of abortion have invoked eugenics because they see the destruction of embryos and abortion as selective killing of 'undesirable' human beings. In contrast, proponents of so-called 'liberal eugenics' reclaim the word eugenics to argue that embryo selection should be seen as a positive, for both the families and societies. Observers from a range of other political starting points engage with different issues, such as: health equity; risk of discrimination based on lack of medical privacy; the complexities of community genetics; slight on the dignity of people with a disability; coercion of a population; data collection practices which can be deleterious along racial or other lines; discrimination on gender grounds, and control of future generations through manipulation of their genetic make-up. Thus, reading current activist agendas alongside the actual uses of modern technologies provides a richer vocabulary to understand and engage with the politics of genetics.

Modern medical genetics is rarely now related to an overarching social policy question of 'what kind of person shall be born?' Most governments do not have policies that actively stipulate who can reproduce. In the era of eugenics' greatest influence, that was the issue at stake. But funding of health care is still a factor: population screening is in essence a gamble by government that most people will elect not to pursue a pregnancy that will result in the birth of a child with a disabling condition or even pass on a condition to the child's offspring. Funding is an issue for governments, just as it was in the heyday of eugenics.

Changing applications of the language of rights have led to some paradoxical situations. Legalized abortion, for example, ultimately permits the problem of mandatory abortion to arise, in relation to insurance coverage and genetic tests. Intellectual property rights inhering in genetic knowledge (notably in the recent Myriad Genetics legal cases in the USA) arguably extend health-care inequities.[121] 'Community genetics' can be beneficial for clusters of sufferers from hereditary disorders, but it can also cut across both the jurisdictional claims of traditional governments to protect individuals from group pressure and can further privatize medical services. The tastelessly named case for 'designer disability' reinforces disability rights while it disenfranchises children of rights to a more universally accepted idea of good health.

Arguably, historical eugenics in its most egregious forms could be described as government reproductive coercion carried out in the name of the majority with a principal focus on intellectual, behavioural and social hierarchies. Even this summary would not convey to us much of the bases for the views of modern activists.

Several of the problematic aspects of eugenics history intersect with modern reprogenetics, but rarely do they overlap fully. Cyprus practises government coercion, but it is limited, as it does not prevent marriages between carriers nor does it insist on abortion or sterilization. It also has something of the consensual localized mindset characteristic of 'community genetics'. There is a valid case that a 'eugenic' value system can be perpetrated somewhat on an individual basis, through gamete donation programmes which market features of potential children, unrelated to questions of genetic risk. There is a significant risk of reproductive coercion based on expectations of compliance for insurance purposes or limitations on government-funded health care. There is also the problem of reprogenetics widening the gap of inequitable access to health care, in access to tests for genetic diseases. To the extent that eugenic sterilization affected people with physical disabilities, reprogenetics can also serve to perpetuate negative social attitudes to disability.

Two historians have also suggested: 'Perhaps it is no bad thing that some of the nastier excesses and inhumanities of a notion of a better stock should ... be brought to mind from time to time as a way of dealing imaginatively with the power to intervene that genetics can provide and how weak some of the causal connections on which policy has been based in the past have been.'[122] That has been the view underpinning this chapter. The eugenic comparison has provided an ethical scaffolding to facilitate informed debate, even as its utility is being eclipsed through the use of a more targeted vocabulary and as a result of attempts at selective reclamation of the word. The 'eugenic comparison' is not always misplaced, but is often inadequate to the complexities of issues. Thus through precise considerations of history, qualified readings of contemporary practices can be made. In this light, practices such as donor gamete programmes and reprogenetic testing can be seen as a kind of eugenics by 'outcome if not intent' (in Alexandra Minna Stern's words); or be qualified as Duster's formulation 'cooperative consenting eugenics', while attending to Cowan's endorsement of a positive local program: 'If not calling it a eugenic program allows it to continue, let's not call it a eugenic program.'[123]

The argument of this chapter has been that modern debates about reproductive genetics have regularly invoked the history of eugenics as a cautionary parallel. However, partly because the term has been overused and its history oversimplified, greater understanding of the more complex relationship between historical eugenics and modern genetic science is essential for the purposes of both understanding and debate. Attempting to rehabilitate the concept of eugenics under the sign of market-based liberalism, however, seems misguided for being insufficiently attuned to history.

## Further reading

Agar, N. (2004) *Liberal Eugenics: In Defense of Human Enhancement* (Oxford: Blackwell).

Annas, G. J. and S. Elias (eds) (1992) *Gene Mapping: Using Law and Ethics as Guides* (New York: Oxford University Press).

Arribas-Ayllon, M., S. Sarangi and A. Clarke (2011) *Genetic Testing: Accounts of Autonomy, Responsibility, and Blame* (London: Routledge).

Bashford, A. and P. Levine (eds) (2010) *The Oxford Handbook of the History of Eugenics* (Oxford and New York: Oxford University Press).

Broberg, G. and N. Roll-Hansen (eds) (1996) *Eugenics and the Welfare State: Sterilization Policy in Denmark, Sweden, Norway, and Finland* (East Lansing, MI: Michigan State University Press).

Buchanan, A., D. W. Brock, N. Daniels and D. Wikler (2000) *From Chance to Choice: Genetics and Justice* (Cambridge: Cambridge University Press).

Cowan, R. S. (2008) *Heredity and Hope: The Case for Genetic Screening* (Cambridge, MA: Harvard University Press).

Donchin, A. (2009), 'Toward a Gender-sensitive Assisted Reproduction Policy', *Bioethics*, 23.1, 28–38.

Duster, T. (2003) *Backdoor to Eugenics*, 2nd edn (New York: Routledge).

Falk, R., D. B. Paul and G. Allen (eds) (1998) *Eugenic Thought and Practice: A Reappraisal*, Special Double Issue, *Science in Context*, 11, 3–4.

Kerr, A. and T. Shakespeare (2002) *Genetic Politics: From Eugenics to Genome* (Cheltenham: New Clarion Press).

Kevles, D. J. (1998) *In the Name of Eugenics: Genetics and the Uses of Human Heredity* (Cambridge, MA: Harvard University Press).

Kevles, D. J. and L. Hood (eds) (1992) *The Code of Codes: Scientific and Social Issues in the Human Genome Project* (Cambridge, MA: Harvard University Press).

Knowles, L. P. and G. E. Kaebnick (eds) (2007) *Reprogenetics: Law, Policy, and Ethical Issues* (Baltimore, MD: Johns Hopkins University Press).

Marteau, T. and M. Richards (eds) (1999) *The Troubled Helix: Social and Psychological Implications of the New Human Genetics* (Cambridge and New York: Cambridge University Press).

Neumann-Held, E. M. and C. Rehmann-Sutter (eds) (2006) *Genes in Development: Re-reading the Molecular Paradigm* (Durham, NC: Duke University Press).

Paul, D. B. (1998) *The Politics of Heredity: Essays on Eugenics, Biomedicine, and the Nature-Nurture Debate* (Albany, NY: State University of New York Press).

Pence, G. E. (2012) *How to Build a Better Human: An Ethical Blueprint* (Lanham, MD: Rowman & Littlefield).

Rafter, N. H. (ed.) (1997) *White Trash: The Eugenic Family Studies, 1877–1919* (Boston, MA: Northeastern University Press).

Raz, A. (2009) *Community Genetics and Genetic Alliances: Eugenics, Carrier Testing, and Networks of Risk* (London: Routledge).

Stern, A. M. (2005) *Eugenic Nation: Faults and Frontiers of Better Breeding in Modern America* (Berkeley, CA: University of California Press).

# 5
# Human Experimentation

'The fundamental dilemma of modern experimental medicine' observes historian and physician Christian Bonah, 'is the potential opposition between an individual's well-being, and the production and application of scientific knowledge in medicine'.[1] Experimental medicine by definition tests the responses of mind and body to identify limits and expand the knowledge base, rather than providing direct therapeutic in the first instance. Modern medical science also often relies on a basic model of comparison between an experimental cohort and a control group of some kind, to test claims about a new product or procedure. In its essence, therefore, modern medical science requires a balance of risk and benefit, while the rapidly expanded technical capacities of modern surgery and pharmacology have extended the range of both risks and benefits. New knowledge can help others, but the process required for its development might harm the research subject. Even in the absence of institutional ethics review, therefore, the implicit question of ethical balance for modern medicine would remain, as, in the formulation of Daniel Callahan, 'hazardous possibilities ... coexist with the good that research brings'. Moreover, he notes, historical and contemporary examples have shown that 'the desire to do good can be potent enough to invite the temptation to go too far'.[2] Risk and benefit are not absolutes, however. The question of how far is too far is a social one and the designation 'unethical' can only ever reflect a broad moral consensus which by definition cannot be unanimous. Drawing the ethical line has historically occurred within the professions (peer regulation) – in public and semi-public forums such as the medical and the mainstream press, as they debate research ethics – and through institutional and government oversight of research ethics. Modern medical experimentation on human subjects and the processes of its ethical evaluation and governance are the subject of this chapter.

Scientific medicine has a long and troubling history of experimental ethics breaches, involving hundreds of thousands of individuals, in many countries, at peace and at war, in many different kinds of medical research. The history of human experimentation therefore provides the emotional core for much bioethical debate, but what can we learn from this past? Is it necessary to reintroduce each new generation to the history of research abuses, when the range of effective medical interventions is widening at the same time as the gaps which allow large-scale ethical breaches and abuses are narrowing? There exists now internationally an enormous array of institutional review boards, hospital ethics committees, laws, protocols, state-mandated ethics panels, as well as local and global pronouncements intended to protect human research subjects. Why, then, recall in any detail events that occurred when such an array of monitoring and braking mechanisms did not exist?[3] Or as Susan Reverby posed it: 'Do we need to have yet another awful story of the "bad old days" of medical research before the creation of institutional review boards, which are presumed to protect human subjects?'[4]

For educators, a major challenge is to cultivate an awareness of the history of ethical breaches in medical research, while striking a balance between anachronistic alarmism on the one hand – by implying that nothing has changed – and 'presentist' complacency ('we know better now'), on the other. What is it, exactly, that should be recalled? This chapter proposes that the history of morally or physically harmful experimentation can show the ways in which ethical boundaries have been created or crossed historically. When we examine events that have been categorized as scandals, abuses or crimes, we are without exception also speaking of the process whereby a largely (or locally) accepted practice has been exposed, and, through being perceived in a different way, reinscribed in the history of bad ethics. All unethical research has taken place in a local environment where others were either party to or witnesses of unethical practices.

The term 'culturally induced moral ignorance' is sometimes used to describe the way in which micro-cultures can become impermeable, institutionally and ideologically, to views at variance with those within the insular moral universe.[5] The greater utility of the term is that it neatly if inadvertently encapsulates a cultural view of all morality. Only by recognizing that seemingly routine or at least locally approved actions are capable of taking on new meanings when perceived anew is it possible to understand how abuses come about and how they come to be perceived (or not) as problems.

Thus to understand unethical medical experimentation, we must look at the various 'cultures of permission' which have either ignored or encouraged research which *later or elsewhere* has been referred to as unethical. To understand how sensibilities develop which permit a belief that good is being done avoids simplistic moral condemnation and can open up dialogue. Accentuating this graduated and cultural view of 'bad ethics', Reverby has argued: 'The question is less what happens when science goes "bad", but what happens when it is supposed to be "good".'[6] This is the most important question to address.

By understanding how unethical experiments come about, meaningful commemoration of the contributions, most of them involuntary, made to medical science by those who have suffered physically or morally for its sake becomes possible. The majority of these people have been in a position of marginality or vulnerability. They include: the sick and infirm, particularly those in a hospital or institution; the poor; the elderly; people belonging to racial or ethnic groups in a position of isolation or subjection (notably African-Americans, indigenous people in colonized territories; Sinti or Rom people; Jews, and slaves); the educationally disadvantaged or intellectually impaired; prisoners in wartime and peacetime; soldiers in service; the mentally ill; women, and sexual minorities, such as homosexuals and people with 'intersex' conditions. Modern research ethics review, implicitly or explicitly, invokes those memories as part of an undertaking on the part of the wider community to protect people who agree to participate in medical research.

This chapter will first outline some of the constituent features of modern scientific medicine, before moving to a discussion of early ethical debates, Nazi medicine, the Nuremberg Trials and Nuremberg Code, post-war experiments, exposures and moves towards greater regulation. It investigates the kind of conditions that have facilitated unethical experiments and the cultural shifts at the intra-professional and public levels that have led to their exposure or repudiation. It asks: Are there limits on the value of media exposures and regulatory systems? Why do questions of interpretation persist? It will conclude by noting that while modern ethics review structures have pressed to the margins the likelihood of a recurrence of the precise kind of cases described, medical research continues to produce ethical challenges.

## Modern medical science

From the eighteenth century and increasingly in the nineteenth century Western medicine became identified with experimental science. Prior to 1800 medical experiments were largely one-on-one encounters in the sick person's home, at the moment a cure for the patient concerned was needed. Treatments might include some trial-and-error and a physician might even on occasion go into print. Gradually, an association of medicine with science came to prevail as the dominant image of modern medicine. As medical treatment moved from the home to the hospital, research based on available 'research populations' became more common. The scientific need for controls (that is, different cohorts for the sake of comparison) in research populations further de-individuated the medical 'subject'. And nineteenth-century laboratory discoveries in the expanding biological sciences pointed to possible new treatments. In *Subjected to Science*, Susan E. Lederer illustrates the cycle of basic research and the transfer into the clinical sphere:

> By the 1890s bacteriologists had identified the germs of tuberculosis, gonorrhoea, leprosy, malaria, bubonic plague, typhoid and diphtheria. These identifications in turn fostered the development of diagnostic tests, vaccines, and antitoxins for the treatment of these diseases.[7]

Medicine itself professionalized. Clinicians established medical societies to distance themselves from others they saw as 'quacks'. And new medical disciplines, such as gynaecology and alienism (psychiatry), created new professional associations.[8] New teaching institutions were founded. Medical journals for physicians and for public consumption began to appear in large numbers from the early nineteenth century and increased in number steeply in later decades.[9] Publication projected the idea of medicine as a science, a means both to communicate to colleagues and to enhance careers, and contributed to the distinctively modern cast of medicine. Statistics was still in its infancy but a new 'craze for quantification' pointed the way to a now indispensable element of medical scientific knowledge.[10] France was a leader in the modernization of medicine in its investigative as well as social aspects, and one historian has noted: 'Physicians' ambition to be recognized as practitioners of science was integral to the professionalization of medicine in nineteenth century France.'[11]

Large-scale institutionalization was a crucial adjunct factor in creating the physical settings in which human experiments could take place. Hospitals, which had traditionally been akin to poor houses, became sites for the treatment of patients, as well as teaching and research. People in armies, asylums, schools, prisons, orphanages and hospitals provided a naturalized reservoir for new ideas of statistically viable research populations.[12] (Confinement, ironically, also provided a new environment for the spread of infectious diseases.) Location could reinforce difference: some researchers sought knowledge about features seen as intrinsic to a particular group (e.g., those in asylums, such as the insane, as well as homosexuals or hysterical women). But much more of the experimentation on populations was opportunistic, a result of access to large numbers of people as 'subjects of convenience'.[13] Thus the conscription of groups into research could come about merely as a consequence of location and status.

## Advancement and trepidation

By the turn of the twentieth century, most of the parameters of modern medicine were therefore in place and the crucial division between therapeutic and non-therapeutic research represents one of the central cultural fissures characteristic of modern medicine. Many recognizably modern forms of problematic experimentation had occurred before 1900: use of anaesthesia to carry out experimental cancer grafts without patient consent; the intentional causing of diseases (notably syphilis and yellow fever) with a strong chance of death and the use of subjects in institutions were all documented.[14] Lederer demonstrates that the new capacities and experimental requirements of modern medicine did not evolve in a moral vacuum. People within the medical professions, as well as members of government and social activists, including reporters, were wary of the risks of so-called 'human vivisection' and regular scandals about access to the bodies of the deceased for anatomy classes also played on the conscience of people of all classes. Thus an argument that 'they didn't know better then' – that is, that a primitive medical modernity was equivalently ethically ignorant – is both condescending and inaccurate. Prior to the late twentieth-century era of regulation, modern medicine was not a wild frontier which a later more highly evolved wisdom needed to domesticate. Both within the medical and scientific fraternities and among lay people questions arose as to the limits which might be suitable for non-therapeutic experimentation.

English physician Thomas Percival in *Medical Ethics* (1803) had made an early call for peer review of experiments and the American army surgeon William Beaumont in 1833 expressed the need for a subject's voluntary consent.[15] In 1865, the French physiologist Claude Bernard urged that no experiment should be carried out 'which might be harmful to [the subject] to any extent, even though the result might be highly advantageous to science, i.e., to the health of others'.[16] The term 'human vivisection' derived from opposition to animal experiments in England and the USA, and the term 'human guinea pigs', coined by George Bernard Shaw in 1913, underlined fears of the objectification of both human beings and non-human animals.[17] The American Medical Association in 1896–1900, confronted with challenges from anti-vivisectionists, debated whether or not to introduce a code of experimental ethics, deciding in that instance in the negative.[18] In 1900, Senator Jacob Gallinger, himself a physician, introduced a bill to the US senate which would have radically regulated medical experiments, along lines very similar to regulations in operation today. In particular, it would have banned experiments on people unable to give consent. Activism on the part of AMA prevented passage of the bill but the AMA itself in the early twentieth century went on to issue its own experimental codes for laboratory research. However, it did not introduce governance of clinical medicine.[19] With this historical background of debate and heightened ethical awareness in mind, it becomes apparent that the historical gears were substantially thrown into reverse under the Nazi regime in Germany prior to what became the watershed era for ethics regulation of the mid-twentieth century.

## Nazi medicine

Germany at the turn of the twentieth century was 'one of the most "civilized", technologically advanced, and scientifically sophisticated societies on the face of the globe', with a burgeoning pharmaceutical industry developing new vaccines and drugs.[20] Germany was also the first country to bring in a law to protect subjects of medical experimentation. From 1900, Prussian law required that only consenting adults who had enough information about the potential risks could participate in medical experiments. Experiments themselves required authorization from clinic directors. Under the Weimar Republic (1918–1933) in 1931, in the wake of a disastrous tuberculosis vaccination campaign in Lübeck as a result of which 77 infants died, a new set of rules known as the *Richtlinien* (regulatory guidelines) came into force.[21] These rules required prior animal testing; informed consent and special protection for children. Technically, they 'remained binding law in Germany even during the period of the Third Reich'.[22]

In the 1930s, however, the fascist National Socialist (Nazi) Party gained increasing influence and the German medical profession provided the movement with some of its most influential members.

Doctors saw the nation through the powerful 'organicist metaphor' which legitimated medicine as a 'curative' for the ills of Germany, to ensure a nation purified of the perceived undesirable elements, who were seen as literally sapping its physical and intellectual the strength. As discussed in Chapters 3 and 4, the possibility of killing the disabled, particularly people in institutions, had been on the medical agenda since before the rise of Nazism, and a programme of forced eugenic sterilization commenced in 1933, the first year of Nazi rule. In the same year a group of physicians formed the Nazi Physicians' League and the profession continued with anti-Jewish policies in its own ranks, which had begun in 1932. Between 1932 and 1945 the profession expelled over 4,500 Jewish physicians, dramatically altering both its demographic profile and fashioning itself as a professional *avant garde*, ready to work, through medicine, to further the aims of Nazism.[23] (Not dissimilarly, from 1870 to 1968, branches of the United States AMA excluded African-American physicians from membership and Jews were increasingly excluded, from around 1900.[24]) The German medical profession not only worked within an evolving militaristic national culture, members worked actively to create a new culture, where medicine was part of a political Utopian vision.

In 1937, Eduard Pernkopf, an Austrian anatomist and Nazi party member, published a famous anatomical atlas, which (it emerged quite recently) appears to have been based on drawings of the bodies of political prisoners executed under the Nazi regime.[25] Moreover, the 'euthanasia' programme which began in 1939 served as a source of supply to anatomy schools of the bodies of executed children.[26] Heinrich Gross, an Austrian doctor, entered the asylums where the children were held and selected those living children whose bodies he wanted to study. He offered them a sweet as he selected them and the children were later removed. Thus medical research was already linked to Nazism before doctors in concentration camps began the notorious medical experiments on prisoners, revelations of which later led to the trials of doctors and health bureaucrats in the 1946–1947 Nuremberg war crimes trials.

Violent and often lethal medical experiments were increasingly normalized during the Nazi era (1933–1945). One medical member of the British military advised the British government in 1945 that he believed a large proportion of the German medical profession was implicated in medical crimes.[27] There were many thousands of victims – the majority were prisoners of war, notably Poles and Russians, as well as political enemies; ethnic groups such as Sinti/Rom people; Jews, children, people with dwarfism and twins.[28] No-one consented to the many experiments which included studying the effects of high-altitude decompression on the body; forcing people to drink seawater to establish toleration limits; bone, muscle and joint transplantation experiments; high-dose radiation for the purpose of sterilization; gassing; poisoning (including shooting with poison bullets), gasoline injections to bring about 'euthanasia'; studying effects of stress and starvation on ovulation and menstruation; other starvation experiments; deliberate infection with diseases, and experiments on the cheapest ways to kill. Doctors at Dachau concentration camp immersed prisoners in freezing water until they were either dead or close to death and then tested methods of resuscitation.[29] Controversially, data on hypothermia obtained through such means were used extensively in the medical literature after the war.[30]

War provided a chance to sustain or build careers begun before the war. One doctor said that he accepted the invitation to go to work in Auschwitz because the war had dried up the financial support for his medical research, and he was frustrated by having to run errands for money.[31] Working behind the lines in step with a mass killing programme provided anatomists with optimal research conditions.[32] The private diaries of anatomist Hermann Voss, written in occupied Poland, where he taught medicine, speak of his use of body parts from executed prisoners and of his academic ambitions. Experiencing his location as exile, he declared: 'How nice it would be to travel to negotiate a chair!' Voss's last formal academic post was the chair in anatomy of Jena, which he held between 1952 and 1962.[33]

The 'militarization of medical science' was not limited to Germany.[34] Japan's government carried out experiments in occupied Manchuria from the early 1930s. An estimated 200,000 Chinese people died undergoing these experiments, along with white Russians, Russian Jews and Allied POWs. At the notorious Harbin centre in Manchuria (Unit 731) alone an estimated 3,000 people died. Experiments included freezing prisoners' limbs then hitting them with clubs to test for thawing. Prisoners were given diseases such as anthrax, glanders, plague or cholera and were killed when they were too weak to keep going, and were subjected to poison gas and electric shock.[35]

Testing on troops by home governments blurred the lines about the meaning of military service. Do soldiers who might die in battle enlist for possible mistreatment by their own governments? The Australian and British armies tested mustard gas on Australian troops: several of the men claimed to have experienced side effects well after the end of the war, with some families stating that their early deaths were attributable to the experiments.[36] In the United Kingdom, experiments on the effects of nerve gas on live volunteers at Porton Down in England yielded evidence of deception of soldiers, who appear not to have understood fully the risks involved. In this case, the Official Secrets Act initially made it all but impossible for a full exposure of such experiments to take place.[37]

In the Unites States from 1941, when entry to the war seemed imminent, the Office of Scientific Research and Development (OSRD) funded research on 'children in orphanages, inmates of mental asylums, soldiers, conscientious objectors, and prisoners'.[38] Malaria research on US prisoners, which involved deliberate infection, later gave the Nazis at Nuremberg an opening to defend their research, as they questioned the validity of the US's claim that such research was ethical. This was not a case of medicalized slaughter, but deliberately caused malaria risked the lives of the prisoners and the meaningfulness of their consent while incarcerated is questionable.[39] At war's end, the US sought the Japanese data and did not press the question of trials. Some of the Japanese experimenters also went on to illustrious careers.[40]

Thus war in its many facets opened up significant questions about medical ethics: should unethically obtained data or human body parts, which might train doctors or help to save lives, or images such as Pernkopf's, which might guide surgery and anatomy, continue to be used?[41] How much is too much for a government to ask of its own soldiers? Can the seniority of researchers simply reset in peacetime? These questions continue to be debated in the bioethics literature, as is the legacy of probably the most famous, if not the most influential, human research ethics code, the Nuremberg Code of 1947.

## The Nuremberg Trials and the Nuremberg Code

At the US-led war crimes trials in Nuremberg in 1946, 23 medical officials (20 doctors and 3 health bureaucrats) stood trial for complicity in crimes leading to death. Seven were hanged; eight were sentenced to long prison terms; the rest were acquitted.[42] Appended to the judgement in 1947 was a code which set down principles for the conduct of ethical experimentation, the first of which is that 'The voluntary consent of the human subject is absolutely essential.' Andrew Ivy, an American physiologist and a witness for the prosecution at the trial, saw a code as a way to limit a general backlash which might become a 'hindrance ... in the progress of science'.[43] The Nuremberg Code had no legal authority and its influence on research practice after the war remains a subject of dispute. According to one assessment, the Nuremberg Code 'set the general agenda for all future ethical and legal questions pertaining to the conduct of human experimentation';[44] while another refers to it as 'a fragile legacy' which was consistently watered down in the years following the end of the war.[45] The execution of those convicted at Nuremberg was indeed perhaps too effective in creating a historical *cordon sanitaire*, which future doctors could not imagine themselves capable of breaching. Jay Katz, an early historian of Nazi medical experimentation, argued that the extremes of the experiments led other doctors to believe that the Nuremberg code was a 'code for barbarians' and so not relevant to the everyday conduct of medical experimentation.[46]

## The post-war era

In the aftermath of the Second World War the Cold War began, between the two global blocs of capitalism and communism. Governments moved to fund research which could serve new national security ends. Medical research in the post-war era acquired a new cachet, and in the US and UK there was a surge in government investment in medicine.[47] This was also an ideologically saturated era, when many Western nations sought to root out communist influence in their own citizenry. Left-leaning or reform-minded citizens, many of them within the medical and scientific professions, retained belief in the ideals of democracy, placing high value on the role of the press and seeking the reassurance of government control of scientific excesses. Exposure of either secret or unnoticed medical research continued the traditions of the late nineteenth-century anti-human vivisectionists. In an era of significant discovery and even more powerful therapeutic optimism good news stories were, however, the norm and medical bad press generally pushed against the tide.[48] While war-readiness provided a rationale for experiments which were both secret at the time and later condemned, research into diseases also went on in a manner continuous with the pre-war era: indeed, the most infamous of the post-war cases, the Tuskegee syphilis studies, involved research which had commenced prior to the war. The following brief case studies show something of the diversity of human experimentation from the mid- to late twentieth century, describing some of the most notable moves to expose problematic studies.

## Tuskegee (1932–1972) and Guatemala (1946–1948)

Studies in the transmission, prevention and treatment of sexually transmitted infections (STIs), such as syphilis and gonorrhoea, formed a significant part of the history of medical research with human subjects between the mid-nineteenth and late twentieth centuries. Then, as now, STIs are public health matters.[49] The most notorious of many historically controversial studies of STIs was a US Public Health Service Study in Tuskegee, Macon County, Alabama (often now just referred to as 'Tuskegee') which began in 1932.[50] The purpose of the study was to observe the 'natural history' of syphilis, that is, how a naturally acquired disease affects sufferers in the absence of treatment.[51] The subjects were poor African-American men who constituted an estimated 624 participants: 427 who were 'assumed to have the disease', and 185 who did not. The two principal ethical focuses of the history of the study are the absence of consent to be part of a study and that the researching doctors actively prevented the men from obtaining treatment, even when an effective penicillin treatment became available in the 1940s. The men did not give informed consent: they were not told the purpose of the study and did not understand, for example, that spinal taps which they underwent without anaesthesia were purely to obtain spinal fluid to study the effects of the disease. As an inducement to participate in the study the men were offered a free funeral. Not all died of the disease, but for younger men in the study assumed to have syphilis, life expectancy was c. 65 compared to c. 70 for the control group.[52] It is a common error in stories of the trials that the NIH deliberately infected the men: this did not occur. Tuskegee did not take place in secret. Through the course of the study, scientific publications appeared which became and remain part of the fabric of scientific data on syphilis.[53]

In an era of race relations activism, events such as the 1968 assassination of Martin Luther King Jr had entrenched African-American civil rights in the conscience of white liberal America. In 1972 Peter Buxtun, an employee of the United States Public Health Service (USPHS), having first complained of the ethical aspects of the study within the service, took the study to the mainstream media. Public outrage over the study contributed to an acceleration of US federal moves to regulate medical research which had been in train since at least 1968. In 1974 Congress created a National Commission for the Protection of Human Subjects of Biomedical and Behavioral Research. It published 17 reports over four years and importantly created a system of Institutional Review Boards

(IRBs).[54] Some compensation went to the study's survivors following class actions and President Clinton made an apology to the men in 1997.[55] The study has become, in historian Susan M. Reverby's words, 'increasingly iconic ... a symbolic and memorialized site that is available to give meaning to the reality of scientific endeavors, ever-present racism, state power, and the experiences of those who face illness and reach for help'.[56]

Reverby's research on Tuskegee led to her materials on another, historically overlapping study, also carried out by the USPHS. In 2011 she published a meticulously researched article in the *Journal of Policy History* which set down in detail an account of PHS experiments in Guatemala. This research revealed troubling accounts of offshoring of US medical research, carried out on soldiers, female sex workers, people with mental illness, children in orphanages, and prisoners. PHS researchers sought to infect vulnerable subjects with three venereal diseases (now called STIs): syphilis, gonorrhoea and chancroid (an ulcerative condition). Thus, unlike the Tuskegee study, this series of studies did involve deliberate infection of adults with a venereal disease. Also unlike the Tuskegee study, however, penicillin treatment on the whole was provided.

The project was coordinated by a PHS specialist in venereal diseases, John C. Cutler. The experiments had the support of the Guatemalan government with whose officials the PHS enjoyed cooperative relations. The study sought to establish whether preventive solutions applied to the male sexual organs immediately after sex were preferable to retrospective treatment, to establish why false positives occurred and to obtain precise data on the effectiveness of penicillin dosages. Researchers provided prisoners with free visits from infected female sex workers, and also applied infected bacteria to the cervixes of some of the uninfected sex workers.[57] Children in orphanages were used to establish the validity of blood-testing procedures.[58] The researchers also used male and female mental hospital inmates, to attempt to cause infection directly, without the involvement of prostitutes.[59] The researchers were able to promise medical supplies to the asylum, which was the only agent of the subjects' consent. The patients were not informed of the nature of the research. An infectious liquid was introduced to the bloodstream of the women inmates through abrading of arms, face or via the mouth and the males' penises were abraded to bring about infection.[60] Several hundred people were deliberately infected. In total, around '696 exposed to syphilis ... 722 to gonorrhoea ... and 142 to chancroid'.[61] Provision of penicillin treatment in the majority of cases does not remove doubts about the extent of physical harm to the subjects. Not all subjects obtained adequate treatment. One set of statistics, which does not yield definitive information, raises the possibility that some might have died as a result of the study.[62]

One of the arresting features of the Guatemala case is that it reveals there was a clear awareness of the ethical problems of the project. Cutler's supervisor at the PHS in the US rolled into one sentence his altruistic concerns for the participants and fear of a bad press. He wrote: 'I am a bit, in fact more than a bit, leery of the experiment with the insane people. They can not give consent, do not know what is going on, and if some goody organization got wind of the work, they would raise a lot of smoke.'[63] Others in the PHS who knew of the project also saw it as ethically unacceptable, though some turned a blind eye.[64] For a variety of reasons, including ethical wariness, the PHS withdrew Cutler from the field in 1948. Almost nothing of the studies was published.

Susan Reverby presented a paper on the study at a conference in May 2010 and also provided her findings to the Centers for Disease Control and Prevention, for verification. The paper passed via the CDC to the office of US President Obama. The Secretary of State and Secretary of the DHHS made a formal apology to the Guatemalan government.[65] They said: 'We deeply regret that it happened, and we apologize to all the individuals who were affected by such abhorrent research practices.'[66] President Obama expressed his regret direct to Guatemala's President Colom. The Guatemala experiments show that conditions such as substantial government funding, remote location, the poverty of the local facilities, which made institutional consent tempting, and the abject condition of the subjects all went to create several layers of cultural 'permission' to cause harm. The studies are of particular interest, too, because of the countervailing force of US administrators' anxieties about both bad press and genuine ethical reservations. This case matters still, not least because of regular offshoring of medical experimentation in the present day.

## Radiation experiments

Atomic weapons research from the 1940s focused attention on the medical implications of exposure to high levels of radiation. In the early days of experimentation with nuclear weapons, Australian, British and American soldiers were exposed at different sites to atomic bomb blasts, with a view to ascertaining the effects of the bomb on human populations.[67] In the 1950s, fly-throughs of atomic clouds tested the effect of radiation on men and animals in planes.[68] These tests were seen as defensible in the light of the arms race, and the threat of communism. In order to improve knowledge about the physical effects of radiation, for the purposes of civil defence, the US Atomic Energy Commission, Department of Defense and National Institutes of Health authorized research between 1944 and 1974 in which (among other studies) radioactive materials were either administered directly to subjects or the effects of workplace exposure studied. Subjects included hospital patients, pregnant women and institutionalized children, as well as uranium miners.

In 1993, Eileen Welsome, a journalist on *The Albuquerque Tribune*, published an account of the US radiation experiments, a story which led to a presidential enquiry.[69] The findings of the 1994 Advisory Committee on Human Radiation Experiments (ACHRE) showed that the levels of actual physical harm ranged from few or indeterminate effects to death (from lung cancer in the case of uranium miners whose workplaces had substandard safety features).[70] The question of moral harm related to meaningfulness of any consent given, in the substantial number of cases in which it had been sought. The commission found that even by the standards of the time, government officials and investigators were 'blameworthy for not having had policies and practices in place to protect the rights and interests of human subjects who were used in research from which the subjects could not possibly derive direct medical benefit'. It also seemed to criticize the choice of subjects from vulnerable groups.[71]

## *Psychiatry: D. Ewen Cameron (1901–1967) and Harry Bailey (1922–1985)*[72]

The post-war era also was of particular significance for psychiatry. The power of Nazi propaganda in Germany had shocked the world and suggested a need to understand the workings of mind control. Fear of the use of 'brainwashing' (a term coined in 1950) behind the Iron Curtain led the United States and its allies to imagine that the ideological power of communism might be reinforced mechanically in the brain and that espionage, for example, might be undermined, by recourse to direct manipulation of the human mind. This mechanical view made sense in an era when many psychiatrists (in capitalist and in communist countries) were adopting a biological approach to mental illness, challenging and rejecting the work of Freudian purveyors of the 'talking cure'.[73] Thus the idea of a 'battle for the mind', as the influential psychiatrist William Sargant called it in 1957, was an apt metaphor for the stance of much post-war psychiatry.[74] The literature of psychiatry is replete with examples of problematic research from this period.[75] Around 6,700 subjects were used in US government funded tests with psychoactive substances.[76] New mind-altering drugs, such as LSD, the development of irreversible psychosurgery and electro-convulsive therapy, as well as aggressive aversion therapy using electric shock, for example, to treat conditions such as homosexuality, were all part of the crude armoury of psychiatrists. In this period of largely unfounded psycho-therapeutic optimism the most 'advanced' therapists were often the developers of technical interventions to alter the mechanical composition of the mind. Egas Moniz, who developed the now widely repudiated procedures of psychosurgery, received the 1949 Nobel Prize.

There have been notable moves to counter some of the 'bad press' of psychiatry in the 1960s and 1970s, through rehabilitation of the reputation of some LSD research and researchers.[77] And some of the controversial treatments of this period, such as intensive ECT are now still used in less aggressive ways to some apparent effect. Psychosurgery, however, is rarely practised and in some jurisdictions is illegal. Two psychiatrists to be considered here, the Canada-based Scot D. Ewen Cameron and the Australian Harry Bailey were professionally successful psychiatric innovators of the mid-twentieth century. They were regarded as pioneers and for most of their careers had little or no scandal attached to them. However, colleagues and former patients gradually accumulated evidence which led to exposures of very considerable harm, carried out in the name of reputation-building and innovation.

Cameron trained in his native Scotland and then in England, becoming Professor of Psychiatry at McGill University in Montreal in 1943. Early in his career, he experimented with insulin coma therapy, a kind of shock therapy.[78] In 1945 he served as a military psychiatrist at the International Military Tribunal (Nuremberg) assessing the mental state of Nazi defendants.[79] He was also closely involved with the widely supported psychiatric goal of providing a kind of 'national therapy' to Germany and individual Germans, as the view was widespread that the country had succumbed to a form of collective mental illness, notably paranoia, and that medicine had a duty to work to reduce its aggressive national tendencies.[80] Cameron became President of the American Psychiatric Association in 1952 and inaugural president in 1961 of the World Psychiatric Association. He 'refused to follow the craze for psychoanalysis which swept US medical schools after the second world war', in the words of the author of his obituary in the *British Medical Journal* (probably William Sargant).[81] Cameron also published over 80 academic articles, in major journals. It imight be imagined that psychiatrists who used mechanical interventions were also antipathetic to the more humane practices to which anti-psychiatry and psychoanalysis laid claim, but Cameron was not a social reactionary: at the Allan Memorial Institute of which he was director, he preferred not to use locked wards.[82]

Most of what he did was at the innovative end of state-of-the-art psychiatry, and the terms 'depatterning' (to promote 'the extensive break-up of existing patterns of behaviour'[83]) and 'psychic driving' were his inventions. In a 1960 article for the new journal *Comprehensive Psychiatry*, Cameron recommended treatments that involved sleep therapy (drug-induced coma) – 'usually 25 to 40' days – in combination with ECT – '20–30 treatments', supplemented by the use of drugs.[84] 'Depatterning' took place across three phases, marked by different degrees of memory loss and functionality. In the third phase, the patient 'loses all recollection of the fact that he formerly possessed a space-time image ... his conceptual span is limited to a few minutes and entirely concrete events'.[85] Many who participated in his research suffered long-term mental damage.[86] A CIA cover organization with the seductive name Society for the Investigation of Human Ecology (later Human Ecology Fund), provided funds to Cameron from 1957 to 1962, to help sustain his work into 'depatterning'.[87]

A former senior clinical colleague, Robert Cleghorn, left a judicious but ultimately condemnatory account of Cameron's experiments at McGill. He argued that Cameron's 'blind desire to make a discovery' was a form of '*hubris* ... accompanied by a failure to assess evidence dispassionately and finally to a delusional belief in spurious evidence and a set of assumptions erected to support, justify, or explain the developed hypothesis'.[88] Several former patients sought and obtained compensation for the treatment to which Cameron submitted them. Cameron died while mountaineering in 1967.[89]

In 1954 an Australian psychiatrist, Harry Bailey, travelled on a World Health Organization fellowship to study the methods of leaders in the field, including William Sargant and Ewen Cameron. Bailey took over the headship of a major public psychiatric hospital in Sydney in 1959 and earned a reputation as someone who sought medical reform, in the interests of patient freedoms. Again, it is important to bear in mind that an identikit image of the medical miscreant as a sadist – very common in the many sensational writings about psychiatry – would completely miss the point. Radical psychiatric interventions were in principle intended to shorten institutional stays, and Bailey, like Cameron, believed he could effect lasting cures.

No longer welcome in the state system, Bailey became the psychiatrist in charge of a small private suburban clinic called Chelmsford. Here, he followed the example of his mentors and experimented with deep sleep therapy. He also prescribed many psychosurgeries. Bailey published in prestigious medical journals and had all the benefits of career success. Negligent treatments in which comatose 'deep sleep' patients were left, in essence, unattended for weeks at a time led to a documented 24 deaths, many of them the result of pneumonia as a result of having been kept under long-term sedation. Nineteen of his patients also committed suicide within a year of leaving the hospital.

Many of Bailey's patients were people in the entertainment industry who did not want their situation made public and the stigma of mental illness made others afraid to tell what had happened to them. Chelmsford staff did not generally feel able to question what their employer did. One Chelmsford nurse secretly took notes on events at the hospital and eventually (oddly, through the agency of the Church of Scientology, which opposes psychiatry) cases came to light in such great numbers that authorities were convinced to carry out a Royal Commission, which took place after Bailey's death. Bailey took his own life in 1985, the day before he was to appear in a Supreme Court damages case concerning allegations of medical malpractice for having caused brain damage in a patient. Bailey had sought the support in this case from Dr William Sargant to defend the method of feeding unconscious patients through a stomach tube, so as not to wake them. Extraordinarily, Sargant stated in a letter to Bailey's legal team that this method had killed his own patients and so he could no longer defend it.[90] Bailey wrote a suicide note in which he affirmed that he sought the good and had been persecuted: 'Always remember that the forces of evil are greater than the forces of good. I always tried to be a good doctor, and I think perhaps I was.'[91] The Royal Commission recommended in 1990 a range of requirements which led to the outlawing of psychosurgery and closer scrutiny of the use of ECT.[92] The NSW Medical Board took no action. In the New South Wales Victims' Compensation Tribunal, 152 former patients were awarded damages totalling $5.5 million.[93]

The cases of Cameron and Bailey show that individual doctors who were able to position themselves as innovators in an increasingly assertive and technically oriented medical specialism could advance because of a tradition of fraternal regard within the medical profession. A respect for independent judgements on clinical action, a premium on innovation, and a personal ability to access both funds and prestigious positions set down pathways to further advancement. Each man was subject to criticism and complaint during his working life from within and outside the profession, but their careers were nonetheless long and largely successful.

## Whistle-blowers: Henry K. Beecher and Maurice Pappworth

As Dr Cleghorn's assessment of Ewen Cameron shows, colleagues within the medical profession can accede to others' right to independent innovation without necessarily approving of it. Public breaches of the professional code are rare but often notable for that reason. In 1959, prominent anaesthesiologist Henry K. Beecher first raised concerns about the ethical aspects of some experimental practices, in a medical journal article, but to relatively little effect.[94] He later addressed a gathering organized by a drug company, catching the attention of reporters.[95] Journalists propelled Beecher's concerns into the public domain: when he submitted a written-up version of the speech to the *Journal of the American Medical Association*, it was rejected.[96] A version of the paper eventually appeared in the *New England Journal of Medicine*, detailing what Beeecher referred to as 'troubling' research, conducted in his view at a rate of about 3 per cent of all medical research.[97] He also referred to unethical research as 'universal'.[98] Beecher identified 22 typical studies which included tests and procedures on uninformed patients under anaesthesia unrelated to their condition, the deliberate introduction of disease (inducing the Willowbrook study, described below).[99] One experiment involved the insertion of catheters into and the X-raying of 26 healthy newborns, which he termed 'bizarre'.[100] Several of the studies were surgical in nature, and appeared to have been motivated by curiosity to make adventitious one-off findings rather than representing systematically designed studies, as are found in population-based studies. (This category of research is harder to advance using standard randomized controlled trial (RCT)-type study designs: the idea of sham surgery, for example, raises real questions about the limits of studying controls to produce a scientific result.[101])

Beecher identified the cultural reasons for the ethical breaches in an increasingly well-funded research environment which could fuel the quest for professional advancement. He wrote: 'Every young man knows he will never be promoted to a tenure post, to a professorship in a major medical school, unless he has proved himself as an investigator. If the ready availability of money for conducting research is added to this fact, one can see how great the pressures are on ambitious young physicians.'[102] Beecher's *NEJM* article did not name names or give article titles: only by going back to the literature – a more arduous task before the Internet – was it possible for readers to see who had conducted the experiments; thus he seemed to speak to an audience of 'insiders'.[103] Aside from the risk of legal action, this decision was in keeping with Beecher's ultimate view on ethics review: he preferred that medical researchers cultivate their consciences. Rather than isolating individuals, his purpose was to preserve the reputation of the profession in the belief that the 'more reliable safeguard' was 'an intelligent, informed, conscientious, compassionate, responsible investigator'.[104] For this reason he also did not favour the use of institutional review boards, instead emphasizing the crucial role of the academic journal editor as a sentinel against unethical research.[105]

Beecher himself felt that his own research had at times trespassed into the realm of the unethical and one of his former colleagues later said: '... we were so ethically insensitive that it never occurred to us that you ought to level with people that they were in an experiment'.[106] Such a statement is instructive as it illustrates a shift from one mindset to another in the same culture and same individuals. It is less often encountered in medical research ethics than a resistance model, when two or more mindsets come into conflict. The statement also underscores that unethical actions are rarely the result of malice. Rather it expresses a 'culturally induced moral ignorance', admitted to having been unethical as it were by omission.

Maurice Pappworth, an English GP who corresponded with Beecher,[107] recorded in a book-length study similarly troubling research, particularly centred on teaching hospitals, notably Hammersmith.[108] Pappworth was aware of the risk of research like his to research overall, admitting that if all research were ethical the number of experiments would drop.[109] His work nonetheless stimulated the formation of the English lay activist group, the Patients' Association.[110] However, Adam Hedgecoe, a scholar in history and philosophy of science, has also shown that the United Kingdom's system of Research Ethics Committees (RECs), inaugurated in the 1960s, was a product of extensive consultation between government and the medical profession and only influenced indirectly by the exposés of Maurice Pappworth.[111] Both Beecher and Pappworth had studied cases from the major teaching and research centres in the USA and UK and employed a relatively simple method, reading the medical literature against the grain, to trace the ethical scenarios behind the silences in case reports. The examples of their work show the potential for wide differences of opinion to exist within the medical fraternity about the limits on medical science research.

## Willowbrook

Like the word 'Tuskegee', the word 'Willowbrook' has assumed something of a canonical status as signifier of bad ethics, in the wake of consistent criticisms of the research of Dr Saul Krugman at the Willowbrook State School for children with mental retardation, on Staten Island, New York, from the mid-1950s to the early 1970s. However, unlike Tuskegee, there was never any link between 'Willowbrook' and new forms of regulation or legal compensation, and views on its ethics were and remain more robustly divided than for most other byword cases. A team headed by Krugman conducted an extensive series of studies on hepatitis. In some of these studies the researchers fed live hepatitis to children with mental retardation between the ages of 3 and 11. Troublingly, the live virus was derived from the faeces of infected children.[112] Hepatitis was endemic at the Willowbrook institution, but not epidemic in its symptomatic form. Children and staff contracted the disease at 10 times or more than the rate for the general population, but it remained that in 1955 only 2.5 per cent of the children had contracted it and 4 per cent of the staff.[113] The studies required participation of new residents who did not have the disease.

Infectious disease, together with exotic diseases and venereal diseases, has been historically of interest to the armed forces, thus it was not untypical for the Armed Forces Epidemiological Board to have funded Krugman's research career, consecutively for 25 years.[114] Krugman was a specialist in the field of infectious diseases and one of his goals was to investigate the kind of immunity bestowed by the immunogenic blood product gamma globulin. He confirmed first through a standard controlled experiment that gamma globulin could provide a degree of immunity to hepatitis. In order to expand knowledge of immunization, he opened a special investigative ward which was roomier and cleaner than other wards at the institution and apart from spaces where natural infection was more likely to occur.

Professionals were deeply divided over Krugman's approach. Medical correspondents to *The Lancet* and other journals subjected his work to sustained criticism, but many also lent strong support. Critics challenged the ethics of bringing about an illness, even when there was a treatment available.[115] The adequacy of parental consent was also debatable. Krugman referred to extensive conversations with parents prior to signing up their children, but the letter of invitation itself was obfuscatory, reading more as if the aim was vaccination, not infection. It states: 'virus is introduced', not only using the passive voice, but indicating neither the source nor the administration by mouth.[116] The ambiguity of the letter illustrates a common problem for the regulatory era: mere compliance with ethics procedures, which Krugman appears to have demonstrated, does not always reflect what is ethical.[117] A suggestion that early provision of a place in the home might have been contingent on participation also cast a pall over the study.[118] If one can accept the proposition that even symptomatic hepatitis B in children is mild, the question is perhaps less whether there was a great physical offence or a moral offence. Is the argument sufficient that the children were statistically more likely to contract the disease anyway?

The evidence Krugman derived helped him to establish in later studies that there was more than one strain of hepatitis. Krugman himself sums up the value of his tests as having been: identification of the two strains, A and B; identification of the means of infection; demonstration of immunogenic capacities of gamma globulin and data showing potential for a vaccine based on hepatitis B serum.[119] (However, around the same time, another researcher, Baruch Blumberg, was able to reach the same conclusion in laboratory conditions.) Krugman was still publishing in prestigious journals and receiving the plaudits of his peers many years after his work raised alarm.[120]

The ethical question, in relation to Willowbrook, revolves in part around how to determine where treatment ends and an experiment begins. The principle of vaccination confounds this question, because the active introduction of a condition through an attenuated medium is intended to prevent later major infection, by marshalling the immune system to fight the low dose. Within the bioethics literature, too, there was and continues to be disagreement about the ethics of what Krugman did. Revisionists argue the work was 'an attempt to confer long lasting immunity' while others interpret the same published material as having the goal 'to *create*, not deliver, a new form of protection'.[121] The emphasis on creation underscores the ethical line between benefit for the subject and the potentially opposing goal of a wider social benefit.

## IVF

As the use of *in vitro* fertilization (IVF) expanded in the late 1970s and early 1980s, another discussion about the border between experiment and treatment emerged.[122] IVF was novel on several counts: it was highly interventionist while the condition of infertility is not life-threatening; the safety of the drug and surgical procedures provided grounds for caution, and the perinatal outcomes in humans could not be known without carrying out the procedure. However, successful 'treatment' could reasonably be claimed in the event of a live birth. In the early 1990s, a leading WHO perinatologist and a public health researcher questioned the rapid uptake of the technology, arguing that IVF should be regarded as experimental until more data proved otherwise.[123] Lay women's health activism sought to keep these risks on the policy agenda, while most ethics conversations revolved around the status of the embryo. Later, several high-profile IVF doctors themselves became increasingly concerned by the high rate of fertility drug use, possibly reflecting differences in focus between obstetrics/gynecology and the views of endocrinologists.[124]

## *The debate over Herbert Green and the Auckland Women's Hospital Cervical Cancer research*

Similar questions about categorization arose in New Zealand in the 1980s over a series of gynaecological studies which, according to interpretation, were either observations comparing two legitimate treatment regimes or outright experimentation.

From 1965 to 1974 Herbert Green, an associate professor of obstetrics and gynaecology at Auckland Women's Hospital, withheld treatment with curative intent in a clinical study of the 'natural history of CIS' (*carcinoma in situ*, now known as cervical intraepithelial neoplasia or CIN3). One colleague referred to the study as an 'unfortunate experiment', a term which became the title of a media exposé and later a book about the study, as well as the National Committee of Enquiry which ensued on the basis of the media report.[125] This extensively documented case has divided the New Zealand medical community for over three decades and has had a divisive effect on attitudes to health-care feminism, too, particularly in the wake of a 2009 history which questioned the motives of the authors of the initial media story about the research and endorsed the scientific and ethical probity of Herbert Green. Only in 2010 was a study published which appears to have drawn the line under questions about the health effects of Green's research on patients.[126]

Green postulated that the presence of pre-cancerous cells identified by cervical smear tests was not proof that invasive cervical cancer would follow. In order to pursue this line of thinking, he decided that rather than treating the cells he would allow them to follow their own 'natural history'.[127] The study was approved by the hospital ethics committee.[128] McCredie et al. appear to have established definitively that 422 women 'underwent numerous interventions that were aimed to observe rather than treat their condition, and their risk of cancer was substantially increased', and that one core group of patients ($n = 127$) had their risk of cancer increased tenfold. If it is accepted that Green was carrying out an experiment, he not only failed to tell the women they were part of an experiment, and while carrying out tests on them, failed to adequately inform them of their treatment options.[129]

A discreet article by concerned colleagues in the journal *Obstetrics and Gynecology* in 1984 challenged Green's treatment of patients, and confirmed that CIS leads to cancer.[130] Three years later women's health writers Phillida Bunkle and Sandra Coney reported on the findings in a liberal magazine, *Metro*.[131] A subsequent Committee of Inquiry found the hospital was responsible for inadequate review of experimentation (Green was not named) and required changes nationwide to experimental ethics review. Historian Lynda Bryder has argued there was nothing unscientific about Green's thinking and that he sought to prevent unnecessary surgery (notably hysterectomy) and caused none of the women to suffer. Her revisionist 2009 history has itself had a mixed reaction, prompting both action for defamation, and criticism from those involved in the inquiry.[132] Notwithstanding Bryder's defence of Green's science, McCredie et al.'s study appears to confirm the essentially negative findings of McIndoe and colleagues, which precipitated the original inquiry.

Without seeking to minimize the offence and harm that Green is documented to have caused, to see where he stood in relation to the traditions of knowledge creation in science, buttressed by ambition and a rationalized indifference to evidence, takes us closer to understanding his thought-world. In 1935 Polish bacteriologist Ludvik Fleck urged a view of experimental ethics as intimately linked to scientific modes of thought. His views are summarized in this way by Christian Bonah:

If knowledge changes and individuals at certain stages are unaware of their own habits and standards of thought, individual scientists cannot simply be divided into two camps, 'bad' scientists who miss the truth and withhold contradicting facts and 'good scientists' who establish and publish only objective truths.[133]

In the Auckland case an accepted scientific practice of comparing two courses of clinical action (or inaction) and reporting on it in the litera-ture rendered indistinct the critical line between experiment and treat-ment. And the case underscores that, again, the power of belief that one is doing good, as a key motivation, cannot be underestimated.

## Exposé and regulation

It is time now to reflect on some of the ways historically in which some medical research has been identified as unethical. There is no perfect way to ensure that harm is not caused by some medical research. Activists from both within and outside the clinical and research profes-sions bring their own agendas: these can favour *laissez faire* or some kind of external control, or lie somewhere in between. Even agreement on principles does not mean a model will be found to suit everyone. Historically, media have played a considerable part in exposing problem research and presenting their views as those of the 'social conscience'. These media include the medical press itself, in which there is often vigorous debate intended for intra-professional consumption, as well as the mainstream media, which for many decades meant the print media and came in the past 40 years to include electronic media. In the era of the Internet, print and electronic media have remained active in expos-ing what reporters have determined to be problematic studies.

Muck-raking (now called investigative journalism) has an honourable pedigree in the United States particularly, and the post-war era was probably the high point in this genre. The abrupt modernity of an ideologically polarized world created heightened suspicion of authority and widespread alienation. From the 1950s to the 1970s, figures such as Vance Packard, writing on the advertising industry, Rachel Carson on the environment, and Jessica Mitford, who wrote about both questionable funerary practices as well as prison experi-ments (in an essay called 'Cheaper than Chimpanzees'), came to public prominence.[134] The ultimate journalists' exposé, Watergate (1972–1974), brought down a president, Richard Nixon. When increas-ing evidence of the destructive and disabling impact of the drug thalidomide came to the attention of the German weekend paper, *Welt am Sonntag*, it was its article, not items in the medical press, that led to the manufacturer withdrawing the drug in Germany.[135] *The Sunday Times* later funded a book-length study of the tragedy. All these outlets were in different ways emblematic of a new style of response to problems of modern post-war industries in general, and the modern medical industry in particular.[136]

The 1960s and 1970s are associated with hot-headedness and academics now are wary of the unsystematic hot-headed tendencies of cyberspace. When Susan Reverby exposed the Guatemala experiments, one blog which interviewed her had the title: 'Why Did Susan Reverby Wait So Long?' The author wrote: 'As a blogger, I'm almost as blown away that Reverby held on to this news for so long. It's a scoop any journalist would salivate over.' Reverby's position was: 'The context matters. I just don't work like that. It never would have even occurred to me to do that, never in a million years,' she said. 'I'm not a gotcha journalist. I'm not a blogger.'[137] Even 20 years ago the political climate was idealistic enough that it would not have been necessary to establish this kind of distance. Reverby's reply illustrates the change in cultural climate for selecting the right mode for non-medical people to raise questions of medical ethics.

Commentaries in the sciences in the 1970s debated the value of public involvement in the world of science. According to one pharmacologist, writing on the thalidomide case, 'The press should not have to substitute for an efficient and vigorous legal system'.[138] And in 1971, R. A. Morton, a British biochemist, similarly contemplated the link between exposure and regulation, writing:

> In the past, some percipient person saw a danger or thought he saw a new danger. If he was a bit of a crank (and this often happened), many did less than justice to his arguments because of his vehemence. Crank or not, he had to have a missionary zeal – to collect supporters – and, in the end, to persuade the official 'machine' to take notice. This procedure by agitation is not now good enough or quick enough. There must be a network of specialised bodies entrusted with the task of trying to foresee the consequences of technological innovations.[139]

Like Henry K. Beecher, who drew the line at lay involvement in governance, Morton had in mind networks comprised only of professional scientists.

By contrast one experimental psychiatrist voiced the hostility that regulation can sometimes elicit, arguing in 1977: 'If democracy is to survive it must grow up beyond its adolescent indignation. Scientific investigation is gradually being stifled by a mistaken bureaucracy that thinks it is responding to the wishes of the people.'[140] This second view typifies the deregulationist stance.

Since the end of the Second World War, critics of ethics codes have argued that regulation itself echoes the practices of the totalitarian states such as Nazi Germany and the USSR against which the 'West' defined itself. Here the ideology of medical autonomy and anti-communist sentiment became intertwined.[141] Seeing a link between threats to democracy and ethics regulation evoked the anxieties of the Cold War era, still resonating in the 1970s, when US withdrawal from Vietnam signalled a reversal permitting, in the eyes of critics, the further spread of global communism. These powerful ideologies have arguably contributed to the somewhat piecemeal and partial creation of guidelines for the regulation of medical research ethics worldwide.

Politicians, government authorities such as the US Food and Drug Administration and the National Institutes of Health, other NGOs, as well as medical organizations such as the World Medical Association have all contributed to the development of research ethics principles and guidelines.[142] The World Medical Association in 1964 issued the Declaration of Helsinki, which has become 'the fundamental international document in the field of ethics in biomedical research and has influenced the formulation of international, regional and national legislation and codes of conduct'.[143] Subsequent recensions of the declaration have formed the basis for the many codes which now operate worldwide, and the Council of International Organizations of Medical Sciences (CIOMS), a UNESCO/WHO body, has drafted extensive guidelines to provide advice to governments on ethics review.[144]

Administrative infrastructure is a strong starting point, but in itself does not dissolve problematic ethics. Poor ethics regulation can reinforce laxity or incompetence through its own inertia. A tragic example of this was the avoidable death in 2002 of a healthy volunteer, Ellen Roche, at Johns Hopkins University.[145] Regulation brings with it its own problems and complacencies. In the effort to understand and empathize with the *bona fides* of researchers, ethics reviewers might lose perspective. For institutions, local research funding imperatives or externally funded ethics review can compromise the independence of reviewers, if inadvertently. One report notes several salient factors:

A close look at the composition and workload of IRBs shows that not all voices are represented in board deliberations, that the existing structure of IRBs inclines researchers and research institutions to put their interests before the interests of subjects of research, and there are too few staff to monitor the many protocols IRBs are required to manage.[146]

Ethics review is imperfect for many reasons and cannot be a substitute for training in ethics. At the present time, evolving challenges such as ghost- and guest-writing in scientific journals; offshoring of human subjects research; guinea-pigging (the culture of paid research subjects); privatization of ethics review, all pose serious questions for medical research ethics.[147] The fact the military experiments, too, can use techniques protected by secrecy provisions makes findings by definition unrepeatable, and therefore scientifically and ethically opaque.[148]

## Discussion

What is most difficult, when confronting either abhorrent or dubious practices, is to try to find a way to accommodate them analytically, even if one rejects them as a matter of instinct. Nothing is ameliorated solely by condemnation or distancing. Most unethical practices lie on some kind of continuum with normal aspirations. In relation to wartime experiments, Caplan urges: 'We comfort ourselves with the belief that the individuals involved in the events of the Holocaust were mad or evil and unlike other scientists and physicians. Yet the evidence is that these professionals were educated and capable members of a technologically sophisticated society who believed they were somehow behaving morally within the context of their social-political situation.'[149] Similarly, Moreno has suggested: 'It would be comforting to assume that the brutality of [Nazi] experiments could only be tolerated by a handful of pathological personalities'.[150] David Rothman argues if we see the people behind unethical experiments as rogue elements, it ignores the extensive cultural networks and priorities that gave shape to ethical abuses.[151] In a sobering reflection, Caplan has also suggested that bioethics in its 'crude utilitarian' form encounters its limits in view of the fact that some Nazi doctors defended participation in abusive research on the grounds that it would protect many more people than the numbers of people upon whom the tests were carried out.[152] For bioethics Caplan suggests, that continuum is simply 'too hard to face' – distance is more consoling. Reverby's essential formulation is echoed here: encompassing the different understandings of what it means to do 'good' is harder than condemning the bad, but therefore all the more necessary. Although Nazi medicine was extreme it was nonetheless on a continuum of sorts: Nazis thought they were doing good and argued as much in court; modern medicine by definition too relies on the validity of the 'extended good' which can be taken to extremes. So the Nazis cannot be set aside as irrelevant.

How these histories are remembered points to policy questions today and can be a sensitive subject. In August 2006 *The Australian* newspaper's Higher Education Supplement reported on the development of new national medical research ethics guidelines. The article 'Ethics Draft Provokes Anger' reported that the scientific community had responded defensively to a reference made in the draft National Health and Medical Research Council (NHMRC) guidelines on human experimentation to experiments performed by Nazi physicians. The text had proposed a very brief historical background, which stated: 'The idea that ethical conduct in research might be a distinct sub-field within ethics arose most sharply after [World War II] in the discussion of the role of Nazi physicians in unethical human experimentation.' Molecular geneticist Professor Bob Williamson, speaking on behalf of the Australian Academy of Science, used a powerful and witty simile to press a case against inclusion of the Nazi reference, saying it 'would be equivalent to discussing the benefits of electricity and talking only about the electric chair'.[153] The academy sought to defend the medical research community against any suggestion that all medical researchers harbour questionable motives, by rendering unfounded the link between modern ethics review and its early twentieth-century antecedents. In the next draft the word 'Nazi' was replaced with a reference to 'Second World War experiments in detention and concentration camps' and 'increased attention to ethical reflection about human research since the Second World War'.[154] Technically, these changes were based on more accurate history, as other governments besides the Nazis carried out unethical research during the Second World War, but the removal of the 'chill factor' of the word 'Nazi' seems to have been the purpose of the change.

Professor Williamson's case was that medical science is capable of great good but it is being presented as if all it could do was harm. The electric chair analogy is weak, however, because all of the cases which have been considered here, including Nazi medical experiments, have been defended in terms which are recognizable, in bioethics debate, as having a moral justification. The electric chair itself is widely seen as doing social good. And it is perhaps no accident that Professor Williamson's statement carried weight in Australia, where capital punishment had been abolished, so that 'the chair' is more readily understood as a metaphor for barbarism. More importantly, the comment is a distortion of the reasoning behind the incorporation of the reference to the Nazis in the ethics guidelines. The Nuremberg Code is widely seen as a pivotal moment in modern medical ethics history, as the NHRMC statement itself acknowledged. What is sometimes misunderstood is those who formulated the code (notably Andrew Ivy) formulated it for the protection of medical science, not as a means to inhibit it. Its purpose was to serve as a counterweight to the appalling evidence from the medical crimes which the same tribunal brought to light and in so doing to defend medical research. In some cases it has done this so effectively that researchers have not seen it as applicable to them.

To conclude: perception is crucial: there is nothing 'given' about the nature of a scandal. It only becomes 'scandalous' because of some kind of ethical shift or distance, such as a shift in perception in an individual; a shift in majority social mores; a challenge from cultural outsiders or from insiders prepared to risk their status; or a challenge levelled in retrospect. Research can 'become' unethical with hindsight, because of a changing social climate which permits people to reflect on things they once accepted as appropriate.[155] The very emergence of scandals is evidence that there are at least two competing interpretations about the nature of the research at issue. Most people who have been at the centre of scandals have not only defended their actions, but found others willing to do so. Few, if any, harmful experiments have gone undefended by perpetrators or their colleagues, whether in courtrooms, the media or the medical press.[156] Many of the cases considered here might well be regarded as unproblematic by some readers: indeed, there is still active disagreement about the ethics of several well known cases. The very idea of 'scandal' or exposure relies on an assumption that public accountability is necessary, yet there is no reason to assume that something even 'certified' as a scandal reflects a universal cultural perception. In the extreme, one person's scandal is another's historic breakthrough. For Hans Muench – a doctor who worked at the Auschwitz concentration camp in the Second World War, but acquitted at the Nuremberg war crimes trials – the work done at Auschwitz remained, in his view, as 'important for science'. This was in 1998.[157]

The process of translation from one context to another, from the practices of experimentation in the clinical context, to the polite questions of colleagues in the medical literature, to the headlines of a newspaper, to a public forum such as a commission of enquiry, equally entails the literal translation of language employed in any one of these cases. Language helps to form the cultural zones within which ethics is determined; as with institutions, language is part of how 'good and bad ethics' are created and mediated. In traversing cultures, the 'troubling research' or 'unfortunate experiment' of the insider becomes a breach of ethics, medical misadventure (in the law courts), scandal (for government or the news media), disaster, or indeed in some cases, a crime or war crime.[158]

This chapter has argued that the nature of risk-benefit in modern medical research is part of the condition of medicine. The examples chosen here have shown a selection of historical 'conditions of permission' for unethical or questionable research. These cultures include: physical location, such as in another country (as in the case of Guatemala); behind the lines in time of war or occupation; in non-metropolitan communities, such as Tuskegee; and in institutions, such as prisons, children's homes, hospitals, homes for the aged and asylums. Ideological and professional circumstances also create conceptual zones which can provide both inspiration and protection, including: the desire to serve a war effort (as well as official secrecy in time of war or cold war); entrenched social prejudice, commercial pressure or pressure for self-advancement, or the attraction of having done good as one perceives it.

We have also considered countervailing conditions or actions, which have facilitated awareness of problematic research cultures or limited the opportunities for unethical practices. They include in particular exposure in the medical and mainstream media and the introduction of guidelines and review processes, generated from within the medical research professions and at government level.

To envisage a continuum between extreme cases and those closer to the mainstream is thus not to impute 'Nazi' medical behaviours attitudes to others. Rather, to accept the idea of a continuum makes it possible to recognize the singularity of extremes (notably, deliberate killing to generate knowledge, and total absence of consent) as well as areas of overlap: service of national or military goals; misuse of 'subjects of convenience'; academic ambition; zeal for knowledge for a greater good. Once non-therapeutic research became part of normal medical thinking, the capacity for research to yield information of benefit to others created a canopy under which service of the nation, for example, made a kind of sense. In the most extreme form, the nation could benefit not only metaphorically but literally as a biological entity, through the sacrifice of those perceived to be human infestations of the social body.[159]

# Further reading

Annas, G. J., and M. A. Grodin (eds) (1992) *The Nazi Doctors and the Nuremberg Code: Human Rights in Human Experimentation* (New York: Oxford University Press).

Campbell, A. V. (2009) *The Body in Bioethics* (Oxford: Routledge-Cavendish).

Callahan, D. (2003) *What Price Better Health? Hazards of the Research Imperative* (Berkeley, CA: University of California Press).

Emanuel, E. J., C. Grady, R. A. Crouch, R. Lie, F. Miller and F. Wendler (eds) (2008) *The Oxford Textbook of Clinical Research Ethics* (Oxford: Oxford University Press).

Goodman, J., A. McElligott and L. Marks (eds) (2008) *Useful Bodies: Humans in the Service of Medical Science in the Twentieth Century* (Baltimore, MD: Johns Hopkins University Press).

Lederer, S. E. (1995) *Subjected to Science: Human Experimentation in America before the Second World War* (Baltimore, MD: Johns Hopkins University Press).

McNeill, P. M. (1993) *The Ethics and Politics of Human Experimentation* (Cambridge: Cambridge University Press).

Moreno, J. D. (1999) *Undue Risk: Secret State Experiments on Humans* (New York: W. H. Freeman).

Proctor, R. (1988) *Racial Hygiene: Medicine under the Nazis* (Cambridge, MA: Harvard University Press).

Reverby, S. M. (ed.) (2000) *Tuskegee's Truths: Rethinking the Tuskegee Syphilis Study* (Chapel Hill, NC: University of North Carolina Press).

Roelcke, V., and G. Maio (eds) (2004) *Twentieth Century Ethics of Human Subjects Research: Historical Perspectives on Values, Practices, and Regulations* (Stuttgart: Franz Steiner Verlag).

Rothman, D. J. (1991) *Strangers at the Bedside: A History of How Law and Bioethics Transformed Medical Decision Making* (New York: Basic Books).

# 6
# Thalidomide

Modern pharmaceutical products are numerous, highly potent and, especially in wealthy countries, an important part of everyday life. Pharmaceutical companies have become central players in global health-care provision and their employees are as likely to be research scientists as they are to be trained clinicians. 'Bioethics' in relation to the pharmaceutical industry, therefore, is less about problematic clinical encounters than it is about the politics of sales, marketing and regulation, a mix of business ethics and public policy.[1] The names of drugs which have recently offered hope but have become surrounded by doubt – *fluoxetine hydrochloride* (best known by the trade name Prozac), rofecoxib (best known by the trade name Vioxx), oestrogen and progestin (in 'hormone replacement therapy') – are familiar to most people who read or watch the news. Of all modern drugs, however, there is one whose notoriety stands in a category of its own: thalidomide.

Thalidomide is one of the most destructive pharmaceuticals ever developed. In the late 1950s and early 1960s it was used both as a sedative and to treat morning sickness but caused in the end extensive foetal and infant death, deformity and disability. Even one dose taken in early pregnancy (c. 35–50 days after the last menstruation) was enough to cause catastrophic effects.[2] Withdrawn from sale worldwide, thalidomide was reintroduced on a small scale for the treatment of Hansen's disease (leprosy) in 1967. This development in turn left in its wake a new, though less numerous, generation of disabled children. Continued distribution of the drug occurred in both regulated and unregulated fashion until the 1980s when people with HIV/AIDS created a large informal market for it in the USA, as they experimented to find anything that might treat the new and deadly syndrome. In the 1980s and 1990s scientists also began to identify many further possible uses for thalidomide, notably for the treatment of some forms of cancer. In 1998, thalidomide re-entered the regulated US drug market. Thalidomide now presents a viable commercial proposition for treatment of a range of serious medical conditions. Celgene was the first company to obtain a licence to market thalidomide in the USA and as a result of sales of thalidomide and a new analogue, lenalidomide, it is now one of the most successful pharmaceutical companies in the world.[3] One business writer refers to Celgene as: 'the premier growth story in large-cap biotech', with a market value in 2010 of US$29 billion.[4]

Thalidomide's history is emblematic of the advance then shocked reversal of the optimism of the 'pharmaceutical revolution' of the mid twentieth century, a long and painful process followed by the negotiated return of the drug.[5] Ethics in the recent part of this history takes the form of 'risk management' in which drug regulators have balanced the known risks against valid ethical and scientific grounds for the drug's reintroduction.[6] Yet the recent history of thalidomide has drawn attention to the limitations of regulatory frameworks, with free-market advocates and patient groups unified in arguing that informed consumers can make their own decisions on whether to take potentially harmful products based on their individual attitudes to risk. Survivors of the drug's devastating effects, who refer to themselves as 'thalidomiders', have, with considerable grace, become central figures in a negotiated process to reintroduce the very drug that caused their disabilities. The present chapter will trace the history of the drug in the Western world where it had its most profound effects, through its withdrawal then reintroduction for the experimental treatment of HIV/AIDS, to current uses for a variety of other conditions, and the debates among leprosy specialists about its value in treatment. It will show how a wide range of groups – the pharmaceutical industry, health-care providers, the sick, the disabled and regulatory authorities – have come to terms with a profound cultural memory, which in the case of thalidomiders is literally embodied in the survivors.

## A 'drug in search of a disease': from early history to market withdrawal[7]

The post-Second World War era was a time of medical optimism: penicillin led to effective treatment of infection, and expanding vaccination programmes were reducing the incidence of some of the worst childhood diseases such as rubella, smallpox and polio.[8] Parents in affluent countries could reasonably expect their children to enjoy better health and longer lives than children ever had. Yet going against this favourable epidemiological trend and equally unprecedented were the tragically visible effects of thalidomide. In 46 countries, parents from around 10,000 households could be seen in suburban streets with little children whose arms or legs were either dramatically foreshortened or had not developed at all.[9] Most people who saw these families – including unaffected children – came to refer to the children as 'thalidomide babies'.[10] That such a large number of children could have been born before discovery of the cause testifies both to the commercial success of the new drug and, relatedly, to the intransigence of the drug's manufacturer in the face of advice suggesting there were problems.

Thalidomide is a synthetic molecule created from a derivative of glutamic acid, $\alpha$-phthaloylisoglutamine, in the laboratories of the private firm Chemie-Grünenthal (C-G) in West Germany in 1954.[11] As in the histories of many medical discoveries, the manufacturers came to determine the drug's applications somewhat by chance. Its development was part of a search for a low-cost antibiotic.[12] It did not fulfil this aim, and was also of no value as an antihistamine, for which it was also tested. The manufacturers noticed, however, that the drug was apparently harmless in high doses in animals, but also sent the early human trial subjects to sleep.[13] In an era when sedatives were in increasingly common use, thalidomide could be marketed as a 'suicide-proof' sleeping pill. This somewhat random decision about its target patient group has led two writers on the drug to label it a 'drug in search of a disease'.[14] The company introduced thalidomide, under the trade name Contergan, for over-the-counter sale in Germany in 1956. It became available in other countries in 1957, under 51 trade names, as a sedative and also later, crucially, to treat morning sickness.[15]

The first case of a birth defect caused by thalidomide had occurred even before the drug went on sale, though at the time the connection was not made. A Grünenthal employee gave his wife a sample of the drug for morning sickness and she gave birth to a baby who had no ears. In 1960, doctors in several countries started to notice another side effect known as peripheral neuropathy and reported it to both the company and the medical press as possibly connected to thalidomide.[16] According to the website of the major current producer of the drug, Celgene Corporation, the symptoms of peripheral neuropathy include: 'numbness, tingling, or pain or a burning sensation in the feet or hands'. It is a common side effect of the drug which can lead to permanent nerve damage.[17]

In 1960, the US pharmaceutical firm Richardson–Merrell Inc, applied for permission to market thalidomide in the USA. Pharmacologist and clinician, Dr Frances Kelsey, of United States Food and Drug Administration (FDA) set aside the application – about which she had already expressed general reservations – because of her concerns about the incidence of peripheral neuropathy.[18] Her prudence in this case became the material of legend. Even though there was as yet no registered evidence of thalidomide's effects on the developing foetus, Kelsey's professional caution helped to limit significantly the drug's overall impact in the USA, where it had been sent, nonetheless, as a sample to several hundred physicians. This led to the registered births of around 17 affected children, although the figure is regarded as possibly conservative.[19]

Recently assembled documents have suggested that C-G may have become aware of the risk of birth defects before publicity about that risk emerged, but sought to ride out the criticism by defending the drug as safe.[20] In 1961, two doctors (the paediatrician Widukind Lenz in Germany and William McBride, an obstetrician, in Australia) independently identified thalidomide as the possible cause of a rise in a rare birth defect, known as 'phocomelia'.[21] 'Phocomelia' is a standard medical Graecism which poignantly euphemizes a term that means 'seal flipper'. This refers to one of the drug's terrible effects: a failure of development of bones in the arms and legs, most notably the long bones.[22] The survival of children with foreshortened limbs tells only part of the story: many foetuses did not come to term and 40 per cent of newborns died.[23] Other birth defects included more children being born without ears, serious deformities of internal organs, and brain damage.[24] Exact numbers of children affected are unknown and estimates vary widely. Generally, figures for affected children range between 8,000 and 12,000.[25] In Germany, around 4,000 children were affected.[26] The drug was withdrawn from sale in the UK in 1961.[27] It was not withdrawn in Japan until 1963, where several hundred more affected children were born after the effects of the drug became widely known.[28]

(A similar narrative of continued drug sales beyond a time when the drug was known to cause harm occurred in the case of Diethylstilboestrol (DES), a synthetic oestrogen, which was marketed between the 1930s and 1980s – depending on the jurisdiction – to prevent miscarriage. But as early as 1953, DES was shown to have no effect on the maintenance of pregnancy. This did not lead to withdrawal from sale. In 1970 a link was established between DES and the disproportionate occurrence of a rare form of vaginal cancer: clear cell adenocarcinoma (CCAC), in daughters of women who had taken it. The FDA issued a warning against further prescriptions in 1971, but DES was still being prescribed in Europe as late as 1983, when it had long been clear that CCAC and other defects were arising in DES daughters and sons – indeed, a third generation may now being affected.[29] In 1977, women's health activists set up DES Action, which has been a lobby group and an information source since that time.)

Accounts of the lives of the young people affected by thalidomide make for heartbreaking reading. Relatively few thalidomiders have been able to become public spokespeople for a generation of harmed children, but their stories have similar themes: countless well-intentioned but often fruitless and painful surgical interventions, repeated unsuccessful attempts to attach mechanical limbs, as well as the social injury of taunting, ostracism and family breakdown.[30] One thalidomider, Randy Warren, a founder of the Canadian Thalidomide Victims Association, celebrated the fact that one of the 24 operations he underwent made two of his fingers into thumbs.[31] An English thalidomider, Mat Fraser, is now an established writer, actor and musician, who in 2005 staged and acted in a dark comedy he called 'Thalidomide! A Musical'.[32] A senior pharmacologist noted in 1977 that such signs of resilience were already in evidence when the thalidomide children were still quite young (adding 'of course some will always use [the fact they are thalidomiders] as a crutch'[33]). Randy Warren is quick to caution that the capacity for some thalidomiders to survive and experience some fulfilment as people is not representative of the experience of many others. As thalidomider Fernandez Garcia said: 'We're living the second (thalidomide) tragedy; our survival ... We are alive, but what is "life" for us?'[34]

## Drug tests and the question of liability

Tests Chemie-Grünenthal (C-G) conducted were inadequate, seemingly even for the times. According to one senior pharmacologist, neither C-G nor Distillers (the company which marketed the drug in the UK and Australia) followed 'the best drug testing procedures of the time, notwithstanding all their statements to the contrary'.[35] (C-G still maintains, however, that it acted 'in accordance with the state of scientific knowledge and all industry standards for testing new drugs that were relevant and acknowledged in the 1950s and 1960s'.[36]) There was also at this time a widespread view that a 'placental barrier' in the pregnant woman's uterus protected the developing foetus from substances which might harm the child. However, by the time thalidomide was being tested, this had been disproved for substances of a certain molecular weight, including that of thalidomide.[37] Frances Kelsey concerned herself predominantly with the known side effects of peripheral neuropathy, but FDA records show that she also queried whether the drug had been proven safe for the foetus and had been dissatisfied by the response.[38] Distillers, the English licensee, claimed that 'Distaval [thalidomide] can be given with complete safety to pregnant women and nursing mothers, without adverse effect on mother or child'.[39]

Families who sought compensation from C-G (as well as from Distillers and from Richardson-Merrell, which marketed the drug in Canada) were unable to point directly to the drug's mechanism as a cause of the damage, because these mechanisms had not been identified. But correlative rather than causal data about birth defects were persuasive: phocomelia was extremely rare before thalidomide, and the times and places in which the drug was used tallied exactly with the appearance of birth defects. In Germany, C-G agreed to pay out of court compensation measured by the victims' degree of disability, but, as a leading investigative journalist noted, 'not enough to ensure the very worst affected victims everywhere receive appropriate lifetime care'.[40] Randy Warren (whose Canadian father and German mother were living in Germany when he was born) was in 1998 receiving $300.00 per month from the fund.[41] In Canada, thalidomiders sued Richardson-Merrell on an individual basis; in the UK, the legal system took 14 years to process claims against Distillers.[42] In Australia, as late as 2011, a court in the state of Victoria refused Chemie-Grünenthal's application to have the case of a 50-year-old thalidomider heard in Germany. Lynette Rowe, born in 1961 with no arms or legs, won a settlement with two drug companies (Diageo and Distillers) on the basis of her case which alleged 'that between May 1957 and December 1961' Thalidomide was marketed in Australia 'as being safe and non-toxic and being suitable for pregnant woman, children and babies as an effective treatment of nausea, sleeplessness and anxiety'.[43] These facts must be read alongside the fact that perhaps 3,000 of the children affected did not survive childhood. Chemie-Grünenthal has been reluctant to apologize to people affected by thalidomide and was in 2007 still considering how best this might be done.[44] An apology of sorts in 2012 maintained the company's initial ignorance.[45]

## Drug regulation

The principal regulatory effect of the thalidomide tragedy was increased vigilance in many countries in relation to the transition of drugs from laboratory to market. To bring a new drug to market is costly – estimates range from US$500 million upwards and the process takes in the US around eight years.[46] There is an internationally recognized standard for new drug design and testing, involving sophisticated animal tests, and multi-phase trials with randomization, double-blinds and placebos in humans.[47]

Not all commentators welcomed the ongoing effect on drug development regulation. As early as 1977 one pharmacologist referred to a possible 'backlash' against the delays in drug launches as a result of thalidomide.[48] And an Australian pharmacist writing in 1984 referred to a 'post thalidomide knee-jerk reaction' in relation to wariness about the provision of drugs to pregnant women.[49] Professor Sir Peter Lachmann, founding president of the Academy of Medical Sciences has recently argued that the care with which drug trials are carried out has been itself costly in terms of human lives. He sees as objectionable that law firms which seek compensation in class-action cases charge on a 'no-win/no-fee' basis, arguing that this structure might induce false or frivolous claims and make the industry so cautious that useful drugs are suppressed rather than released. Lachmann makes a reasoned though not wholly convincing case that drug companies' fear of litigation might lead them to endanger lives, because of the failure to provide available benefits to the people in need of drugs, for fear of action on the part of a minority. He presses the case for pharmaceutical *laissez faire*, claiming that 'to allow patients to have access to drugs much earlier if, having been given full information about effectiveness and side effects, they sign a legally binding indemnity that they will not sue if things accidentally go wrong', that is, without the input, for example, of governments.[50]

Despite increased regulations, circumventing regulatory processes has become easier, particularly through drug buyers' groups accessing offshore laboratories, and especially since the spread of the Internet. In many countries, too, legal provision exists for so-called off-label prescribing, that is, a clinician's provision of a drug for purposes other than those for which it is licensed. Both of these practices became crucial in relation to the return of thalidomide. Drug access activism in the era of HIV/AIDS created greater openings for the less regulated use of drugs. Another significant outcome of the thalidomide exposures was that the risk of giving birth to an affected child became a factor in the USA's thinking on the liberalization of abortion laws. This became a crucial but unstated element in the drug's subsequent reintroduction.[51] There is every probability that without the legality of therapeutic abortion thalidomide would not have been reintroduced to the market in the USA. Thus, a constellation of conditions – the option of off-label prescribing, drug access activism and legalized abortion – in the end led to a new place on the mainstream medical market for thalidomide. The path was not direct, however: it began in 1964 with another accidentally identified use for thalidomide, in leprosy.

## Leprosy and HIV/AIDS

In 1965 Dr Jacob Sheskin, an Israeli doctor treating people with Hansen's disease (leprosy), wrote that he had discovered by chance that thalidomide could cure a severe complication of the disease, known as erythema nodosum leprosum (ENL). Sheskin conducted extensive tests and worked with the World Health Organization (WHO) to make a case for the prescription of thalidomide. As a consequence, since 1967, leprosy doctors have used the drug, notably in Brazil. In that country as a result more children were born affected by thalidomide, with estimates ranging from 56 to approximately 1,000, the most recent birth cited as being in 1995.[52] (One dermatologist referred in 1994 to drug controls in Brazil as 'lax'.[53]) By 1992 C-G had ceased to be the sole licensee and thalidomide was also manufactured for sale in Mexico and Brazil, and even in the USA, for the treatment of leprosy under special provision.[54] These were the sources through which in the 1980s people with HIV/AIDS began to access thalidomide.

In the devastating early years of the HIV/AIDS epidemic, people began to experiment with thalidomide as a possible treatment for their symptoms. Symptoms which appeared to respond to thalidomide included ulcers and AIDS-related wasting disease.[55] Many people with HIV/AIDS were or became experienced and articulate health consumers, seeking the maximum access to all potentially useful drug treatments for the condition. A black market in the drug emerged in the USA. Throughout the late 1980s and early 1990s considerable medical literature began to appear which suggested an even wider range of illnesses could be treated with thalidomide, include several forms of cancer, negative transplant reactions, skin diseases, and ulcerative illnesses such as Crohn's disease. The FDA, mindful of this new research, was confronted with a decision over whether it should ignore the illegal trade, with the attendant risks that if the drug reached women it might lead to yet more births of affected children. It decided instead that, given the uses to which the drug was already being put and because of evidence that it might treat yet more conditions, a regulated legal market was preferable to a bootleg market.

In November 1995 the FDA 'urged manufacturers of thalidomide to seek approval' for the drug to come into the regulated market in the

USA.[56] Celgene, a New Jersey based company with a relatively low profile, applied to market the drug. The firm is a spin-off of Celanese Research Corp, 'a chemicals, fibers, and plastics company' which had the 'original goal ... to develop biologic products to clean up hazardous waste'.[57] As the patent for thalidomide had expired, Celgene 'in-licensed' it in 1992 in its generic form.[58] Celgene applied to the FDA to use thalidomide in the treatment of Hansen's disease. The regulatory significance of this is that in the USA Hansen's disease was classified under the Orphan Drug Act 1983 as a so-called 'orphan disease', that is, a condition with relatively few sufferers (under 200,000). This status assumes the condition to be under-researched in mainstream medical science and its study is therefore encouraged through more permissive regulation. All parties were aware this was a strategy of convenience given that leprosy was not widespread in the USA. Thalidomiders say they would have preferred more upfront reference to the real target illnesses and one leprosy clinician has similarly condemned what he sees as the pragmatic use of leprosy as part of a strategy 'to reintroduce thalidomide for a multitude of other indications'.[59]

## 'Preventing the past': the 1997 FDA hearings[60]

The FDA set out an extensive consultative process which began with an open session of FDA's Dermatologic and Ophthalmic Advisory Committee held in November 1996. The meeting was intended to represent all interested parties; however, the FDA neglected to invite a thalidomider to the meeting. It is possible this occurred because so few people relatively were affected in the USA and because the FDA's record is seen in this light as an unparalleled success in the history of drug regulation. The news company CNN phoned Randy Warren, President of the Thalidomide Association of Canada, to ask how he felt about not being there. As a result Warren demanded an invitation which was duly issued.[61] On 9–10 September 1997 the FDA co-convened a further and decisive 'open public scientific workshop' to 'discuss the potential benefits and risks of thalidomide, including the medical, scientific, legal, ethical, and other policy issues related to research and treatment'.[62]

A central task of the meeting was specifically to appraise the latest in a series of draft proposals provided by Celgene for the minimization of risk of birth defects, if thalidomide were introduced to the market. Those present at the meeting included a committee: 'nine dermatologists, four ophthalmologists, one biostatistician, and one consumer representative', as well as invited thalidomiders, obstetricians, neurologists, women's health spokespeople and many others.[63] The FDA's spokesperson spelt out the task of this microcosm of the regulatory and consultative world: 'every group represented here, from the patient groups, to academia, to government research, to government regulation, to consumer groups, to lawyers, to companies doing drug development, all are going to have to contribute if we're going to make it go forward correctly, I think.'[64]

Celgene proposed a programme for the prescription and sale of thalidomide in the USA entitled STEPS® (System for Thalidomide Education and Prescribing Safety). Its goal was 'to help ensure a zero tolerance policy for thalidomide exposure during pregnancy' and is the most rigorous process for drug provision in history.[65] STEPS® requires that doctors and pharmacists who are to provide the drug be trained in the programme and also registered as providers. All patients are registered. Patients must watch a DVD about the effects of the drug and sign a consent form acknowledging they know the risks.[66]

This signing is the pivotal moment in a process which shows STEPS® to be the benchmark of an essentially post-regulatory environment. The drug may be used because it is underwritten by the consumer's agreement. For good or ill (and this is the debating point) the patient's risk-benefit judgement stands for the prior presumably more expert judgement of the regulator. Physicians centrally file a copy of the form. There is a four-week dose limit and counselling of male and female patients about contraception. (Thalidomide can be transferred in semen but its capacity for harm is apparently not passed on genetically.[67] If the drug were confirmed to affect the genome, STEPS® is unlikely to have come into being.) For women, the process is onerous, requiring proof either of infertility or of a negative pregnancy test, as well as the use of two recommended forms of contraceptive.[68]

The name was a sticking point. Celgene wanted to call the drug 'Synovir', but this was rejected as early as the November 1996 Advisory Committee meeting, on the grounds that it sounded too much like an ordinary anti-viral drug.[69] The name agreed upon was Thalomid (thalidomide), because of its evocative significance, particularly for the over-45 age group.[70] Randy Warren wanted the image of a skull and crossbones on the drug's label, but Celgene rejected the idea.[71] Every pack of the pills (which themselves each have a stick-figure prohibition on pregnancy) displays a photo of a child affected by thalidomide. Warren's group succeeded in having the label read 'Do not get pregnant' rather than Celgene's proposed 'Avoid pregnancy'.[72] The FDA approved the drug on 16 July 1998.

Thalidomide's singularity is now more symbolic than actual. Between the development of thalidomide and its re-regulation, numerous drugs have been developed which are also contra-indicated in pregnancy but are still used. In that sense what was taking place at the 1997 forum was as much about the brokerage of cultural memory as it was about the pharmacological realities. As Sol Barer, the founder of Celgene has said, with some veracity, the use of thalidomide is 'less a scientific issue than an emotional and historical issue'.[73] Nonetheless even very stringent controls on other teratogenic drugs have led to affected pregnancies. Accutane (isotretinoin), for example, is a teratogenic skin medication. Even used with tight guidelines in the period 1989–1995, there were 623 pregnancies among 210,000 users and 74 live births, as a result of which five children had related birth defects.[74] Thus no-one at the FDA meeting was prepared to claim that the STEPS® programme was failsafe: even with the tightest drug controls in history, all parties believe it is likely only a matter of time before a 'thalidomide baby' is born under this system.[75]

Two academic analysts of the meeting argue therefore that the 'risk of thalidomide is defined as the risk of a woman patient taking thalidomide' and the non-voluntary risk of the child who might be born. In their view, a 'standardized distributive system made the residual risk of congenital disability acceptable' as part of a cost-benefit analysis.[76] They point to an unexplored option of greater control of off-label use prescription. They suggest that tighter controls over the prescribing behaviour of clinicians would limit the likelihood of affected pregnancies. But the off-label option was really what the process was all about, to make the drug available for conditions other than Hansen's disease.[77] As the FDA's own Director of Drug Evaluation and Research, Janet Woodcock, underlined: 'There is no prohibition on off-label use in this program'.[78] This decision reinforced medical autonomy – an article of faith for the medical community – but also made it possible to find a way for people living with HIV/AIDS to obtain the drug legally.

In the end, 'risk management' here pertains to legal protection against the risk of being sued for redress, and the risk part of the 'risk-benefit' equation falls, in the end, wholly onto any affected child or his or her family. Thus the risk which 'we' as a society take is a purely abstract social calculus which does not – cannot – fall evenly across the board. It is a risk-benefit compromise which shows starkly the limits of that, essentially political, formula.[79] On the positive side, the chance to treat several serious conditions opened up.

A crucial element of the regulated entry of thalidomide to the marketplace, which remained largely unstated at the forum, is that the existence of prenatal tests combined with the possibility of legal therapeutic abortion underpinned reintroduction in the USA and later, elsewhere.[80] There are good reasons for leaving the abortion option unspoken: the anti-abortion lobby might have seen the move as a *de jure* institutionalization of abortion. It could be argued that this silence also respected the right of women to choose whether or not to continue with an affected pregnancy.

A 1998 *Nature Biotechnology* editorial on the announcement of the new release of thalidomide pressed the traditional case for further reductions in drug regulatory processes. It observes wryly that for 1,000 people with Hansen's disease in the USA, around 2,000 physicians and 2,000 pharmacists were to be trained for the STEPS® programme.[81] The strategy of bringing the drug to market but only labelling it for ENL means that doctors who prescribe off-label become in effect the site of new small, local, uncoordinated self-designed drug trials. The downside of this (the article contends) is a loss of accountability and a more random array of evidence on the effects of the drug. The editor makes the case that a system in which drugs can be FDA-approved quickly for an expanding range of treatments would provide for greater accountability from the drug companies, as once drugs are released, companies have less responsibility for their safety in off-label use than before. The case has some logic to it. But all risk then would fall to the patient who has elected to chance the drug. The likely outcome of such a system would be that drug companies directed a relatively greater proportion of their funds into tightening the contractual arrangement with consumers, as in the thalidomide case. Contentiously, it ends: 'The dead off-label prescription users of any numbers of drugs would thank the FDA for modernizing, if only they could.' The article's stance points to a breakdown of the very idea of drug regulation, a view in which the FDA and other national authorities are positioned as representing something like a 'nanny-state'. In the extreme, without government involvement in some form, there is in effect no-one left to lobby, opening the path for direct marketing by trained pharmacologists to time-pressed doctors and partially informed patients. The case of Celgene and thalidomide suggests this is the direction in which drug development and marketing is heading. Chiding the FDA for half-measures, on behalf of the dead, however, is an emotive case that brings with it another range of unanswerable questions about how many people have benefited from the amount of regulation that has existed to now.

Accountability, which the editorial sees as desirable, has to reside some-where and would default to the civil legal system, to individual suits and class actions. The history of thalidomiders' mixed success with claims stands as a caution. Civil law does not replicate protection from harm which is established in the first instance via regulation.

Thalidomider spokespeople nonetheless say they do not feel they can prevent others from taking a drug which might assist them.[82] The dignity with which thalidomider activists have voiced their moral authority through a gracious concession to the needs of people with other illnesses is very moving. For thalidomiders, participation in a process which was intended to have only one outcome proved a torment. According to Warren the turning point in his decision to coop-erate with Celgene was that the company offered the best hope for the development of an analogue which would have the same clinical bene-fits without the reproductive risks.[83]

It is worth recapping here some of Charles Rosenberg's descriptions of the routine development of health policy (as quoted in the introduc-tion to this book) and reading the FDA's manoeuvres in light of it:

> Policies on the ground seem less a coherent package of ideas and logi-cally related practices than a layered conglomerate of stalemated battles, ad hoc alliances, and ideological gradients, more a cumula-tive sediment of negotiated cease-fires among powerful stakeholders than a self-conscious commitment to data-sanctioned goals.[84]

There could hardly be a better example of such a scenario than the case of thalidomide. The ethical chessboard is shaded in grey, in a historical moment in which both recollection of the past and the projection of future scenarios are weighed up. Health rights activism is multi-faceted in this case: two advocacy groups – the HIV/AIDS lobby and the thalido-miders – sat at a bargaining table to bring about a treatment goal for some patients, while acknowledging the likelihood of a new disabled patient class being born. The other key players brought their own tradi-tions: clinicians stood for medical autonomy; drug companies followed the routine logic of capital, if with some sophistication, and govern-ment regulators held a position at once crucial and impossible.

Legal bioethics commentators George Annas and Sherman Elias argue that the test of a high-risk decision lies in the willingness of the 'FDA, physicians and drug companies' to truly adhere to guidelines, through vigilant postmarketing monitoring.[85] In this regard, both regu-latory and legal authorities have given Celgene somewhat 'mixed reviews', as it has pressed the case for an ever wider range of indications for thalidomide. The business media has in effect become the arbiter of Celgene's ethical fortunes by tracking the company's capacity to profit within a regulated environment.

## 'In the grand scheme of things ... it is a great drug': new indications and media views[86]

As early as the 1980s, evidence of thalidomide's possible treatment value for conditions other than ENL in Hansen's disease emerged. Throughout the 1990s, scientific evidence that thalidomide might offer potential as a treatment in a wide range of conditions, including different forms of cancer, continued to mount. Thalidomide has a capacity to inhibit both the production of tumour necrosis factor-alpha (TNF-$\alpha$), which affects immune response, and to inhibit the creation of new blood vessels (angiogenesis).[87] Conditions arising from HIV/AIDS, therefore, were only some of several avenues opening up to Celgene when it put its case to the FDA. Subsequent expansion of the global markets in which thalidomide is now sold has taken place alongside continued investigation into illnesses for which it might prove a valuable treatment. Or, in the language of the business press: 'growth looks sustainable thanks to label expansion plans and a strong pipeline'.[88] *The Pharma Letter* reported in July 2000 that 'over 140 clinical trials are being conducted to determine thalidomide's potential efficacy in a variety of cancer and inflammatory conditions' and in 2004 *The Guardian* reported, 'There are currently more than 200 research applications for trials of the drug in the UK.'[89]

In 2005 Celgene released an analogue for thalidomide, which they called lenalidomide, marketed in the USA as Revlimid.[90] The first indication for which the FDA permitted the sale of lenalidomide was a form of transfusion-dependent anaemia. In 2006, the FDA approved it for treatment of multiple myeloma (cancer of the plasma cells in bone marrow), if used in combination with dexamethasone. Lenalidomide is more powerful in treatment than thalidomide – indeed a 'blockbuster drug for the treatment of multiple myeloma' as one report describes it – but according to information on the Celgene website it has nonetheless failed to avoid being teratogenic.[91] The website reports that primate studies produced birth defects similar to those caused by thalidomide.[92]

Business and public relations media have watched in admiration as Celgene has worked to overcome the legacy of thalidomide's terrible history. In 2001 *PR Week* asked three pharmaceutical PR executives to address the problem of 'The Big Pitch' asking: 'How would you conduct a PR campaign for the new Thalidomide drugs?' Notwithstanding the indelicate editorial headline, the executives praised Celgene for its sensitivity and saw it as model practice. Doug Hochstedler of Edelman PR Worldwide argued: 'Only by remembering those devastated by Thalidomide can we hope to prevent history from repeating itself while helping those in need.' Judy Katz of Highqmedia proposed: 'The approach to marketing an old drug with new use is to be candid – never avoid its past, but highlight that the amazing results documented in trials or in actual patient use are too good to ignore.' Michael Johns of Gentiva Health Services emphasize: 'continuing to assure the medical community, regulatory bodies and the public that Thalidomide's distribution mechanism and treatment protocols are safe enough to ensure that past mistakes are not repeated.'[93]

The business press nonetheless has suffered moments of amnesia when contemplating Celgene's huge success. One article uses somewhat tactless language, describing Celgene as the 'the poster child of what a big biotech growth story should be [which] delivered yet another happy ending in the second quarter'.[94] Another, entitled 'A Great Bet in Biotech', is apparently unaware of the human gamble involved in the drug's use. It is also facetious in seeming to refer to transfusion-dependent anaemia, in its advice to purchase Celgene shares to improve an 'anemic portfolio'. The article goes on to urge that: 'with $3 billion in cash, no debt and eye-popping earnings growth ahead, Celgene isn't a hard pill to swallow'.[95]

Notwithstanding commercial success, regulatory, legal and medical challenges have been a feature of the company's history since regulation. The business press has again been the main source of news on Celgene's regulatory life. Perhaps ironically, the market itself serves in some way as a *de facto* ethical monitor, in a triangulated role with the FDA and other statutory authorities, through reportage of problems which if exposed might lower the value of stock. Business needs to know where listed companies stand in terms of relations with government in order to be able to guide investors' decisions. As we have seen, off-label marketing was always going to be part of the script for the promotion of thalidomide in new indications. However, authorities have at least twice admonished Celgene for excessive direct marketing to physicians. In 2000, the FDA division of Drug Marketing, Advertising and Communications warned Celgene to stop promoting off-label use for cancer.[96] And in March 2011, the business media reported that the US Attorney for the Central District of California was investigating Celgene regarding 'off-label marketing' and possibly 'improper payments to physicians' in relation to both lenalidomide and thalidomide.[97]

Medical as well as marketing issues have arisen: in 2004, the FDA charged Celgene with late presentation of 82 reports of serious and unexpected health problems in patients treated with Thalomid, including one death.[98] It is hard to establish if this publicity was intended to present the FDA in the best light, doing its job in a straitened regulatory environment, and if the numbers might not be similar for other companies. One report argues that investigations are quite a common occurrence, suggesting that the involvement of thalidomide makes it newsworthy.[99] Another notes more generally that the FDA has an uphill battle, because, it argues,

> gaping resource and informational deficits hamper its oversight. The FDA's responsibilities are vast and cover 25 percent of all consumer spending, including food, drugs, vaccines, and medical devices. Yet it lacks adequate staffing and resources, even as its mandate and public safety concerns continue to increase, and it does not have the information it needs for effective oversight. Consequently, it is forced to rely on manufacturers to find and disclose hazards.[100]

And in early 2011 Celgene stocks fell on reports of an increase in secondary malignancies among people using Revlimid to treat their multiple myeloma, although even for these patients, the drug proved on average to prolong life.[101] In the same year, a court in Canada judged that Celgene's prices for Canadians buying thalidomide legally cross-border in the USA had to reflect prices acceptable to Canada. The Special Access Programme of Health Canada permits doctors to prescribe thalidomide to patients who then obtain it from the USA. Celgene wanted to challenge the price of thalidomide to Canadian patients. The company argued that the drug is being 'sold' in the US and is therefore not subject to Canadian law, but the Canadian law said that because Canadians are paying for it they are buying it in Canada.[102] These examples highlight the pressure of commercial motivation to expand, diversify and optimize profit, in the context of porous national borders and legal mechanisms intended to accommodate consumers' wishes, but also to protect them from having to pay premium prices.

## Leprosy and changing WHO policies

While expanded use of thalidomide and lenalidomide relies in 'Western' countries on diversification into new treatments, there has been a whole separate politics to the use of the drug for leprosy in countries where the disease is still widespread. Clinicians are divided in their views on whether thalidomide is still a suitable treatment – even a 'drug of choice' – as part of multi-drug therapy for ENL in leprosy.[103] A series of articles in the *Leprosy Review* in 2003 and several web-list postings in 2003–2005 on a leprosy discussion site provide insights into both the mutual respect of clinicians with disparate views, working with people with Hansen's disease and their personal and professional soul-searching about thalidomide.[104] These sites show clinical 'bioethics' on the front line. The issues of concern are: whether ENL is still a significant complication of leprosy, whether treatments other than thalidomide are preferable clinically (as opposed to ethically); whether the risk of an affected pregnancy can be monitored in large markets in relatively poor or under-regulated countries; the limits of medical autonomy in decisions about the drug's use; and, broadly, how far politics should intrude into the clinical sphere.

Around the turn of the twenty-first century the WHO declared it no longer recommended the use of thalidomide in ENL.[105] Debate has arisen in the Hansen's disease-treating community over this policy change. At the centre of these discussions was Dr V. Pannikar, who was until 2009 the Geneva-based Medical Officer, Communicable Diseases (Leprosy Group) and who held that there is 'no place for thalidomide' in the treatment of ENL.[106] He argued that other drugs are preferable and that what he perceived to be the rarity of ENL has made its use redundant.[107] Pannikar advanced his views initially in the *WHO Pharmaceuticals Newsletter* in 2003 and the article was reprinted with a series of commentaries later that year in the *Leprosy Review*.

*Leprosy Review* hosted a forum on the issue. G. F. M. Pereira, an officer of the Ministry of Health in Brazil, defended thalidomide as 'a promising drug in frank redemption'. He stated that the government had purchased 8 million thalidomide tablets between 1998 and 2002.[108] Pereira challenged Pannikar's assertion of 1,000 affected births in Brazil, claiming that there had been only 56 'TH accidents' (presumably meaning children born with thalidomide-related disabilities) across four decades of use.[109] Two further articles by leprosy specialists provided detailed challenges to his clinical and scientific claims. One (by Dr Ben Naafs) contests Pannikar's claim that ENL is rare, citing a 10–60% occurrence rate.[110] Naafs also cites Dr Pannikar's own endorsement of the drug as late as 1996.[111]

Dr Pannikar maintained his views on a leprosy online discussion site.[112] A clinician in Brazil addresses his stance in these terms:

I refer to Dr. Pannikar's messages regarding the use of thalidomide ... It is interesting the way he is discussing the problem. I respect him as an excellent leprologist but I must disagree with most of his points of view regarding this drug. As doctors we are ... responsible for our prescriptions. Dermatologists are prescribing every day drugs like isotretinoin and acitretin for different diseases. Like thalidomide they can cause severe problems for pregnant women. It is our responsibility to prescribe these very important drugs. Drugs can cause lots of problems but we need them. Thalidomide is a very important drug and fortunately it is available in our country. It would be interesting to give a look on the huge number of patients suffering of the side effects related to cortisone (to treat ENL). I don't like both drugs. But fortunately in Brazil we have thalidomide. We have severe rules to prescribe it. It is the best drug for ENL.[113]

There are several elements here, notably the emphasis on medical autonomy and capacity for discernment, together with the persuasive relativist argument, that other drugs cause harm similar to that caused by thalidomide.[114] Another clinician, C. R. Revankar, develops the case for medical autonomy but refers additionally to pressure from pharmaceutical marketing, when ENL does not occur in all forms of Hansen's disease. Discussing the Indian market, he writes:

Indeed, it is good news that Thalidomide is freely available in India though it is expensive at present. It is equally disturbing that some physicians influenced by pharmaceutical/sale promoters use this drug in leprosy without proper indication ... It is the moral responsibility of treating physicians and professional organizations to follow medical ethics and standard guidelines rather than follow sale promoters while using Thalidomide.[115]

Finally, he makes a case for realism about the possible limits of regulation, asking: 'Can we achieve this shared monitoring in a vast country like India?'[116] Dr Pannikar himself responded to apparent evidence that thalidomide is being marketed for off-label use, by asking a pharmaceutical business manager about risking the birth of affected children through irresponsible marketing:

We are very surprised to see your message [online posting, 14 December 2003[117]] and unconditional marketing strategy. Can you kindly let us know what precautions you and your company are taking to prevent the tragedy of 1960's caused by thalidomide. Will your company take the ethical and legal responsibility if anything goes wrong?

The pharmaceutical representative defends his company's actions, stating:

We are indeed thankful for your concern and wish to inform you that we are as well concerned being a reputed marketing organization working towards Anti Cancer treatment. Firstly, we wish to inform you that we are not into random marketing to get business since we are quite sufficient with the sales we generate in our country. Moreover, we have not informed anyone outside the country regarding our product. ... We inform you in this regard that in no way we have supplied even a single pill to anyone without the request from a proper channel, i.e., either through their government or through an NGO or through a qualified doctor with written undertaking from their side.[118]

Notably, by the end of the exchange, Dr Pannikar seems to accept that the drug is available, even though he opposed its use through the agency of the WHO. He seeks only to be reassured that regulatory efforts will be observed, closing with: 'We very much hope that you will continue to follow the strictest policy for thalidomide's distribution and use in the community.'[119] The pharmaceutical representative, S. Krishnamurthi, thus defends himself against the accusation of excessive marketing by making the plausible case that with a market the size of India's, the need to push the drug isn't there. For the same reason, however, Dr Revankar had been able to question even the possibility of successful regulation in the Indian market. The authors refer to no company by name: the fact that several companies now market the drug suggests the pressure referred to for off-label marketing could come from a range of sources.

An overview of the use of thalidomide in ENL refers to the 'conflicting statements' of the WHO, seemingly with particular respect to Dr Pannikar.[120] As we have seen, he, too, was prepared to concede on the clinical exigencies of the Indian situation. As with the USA, it is possible that an unspoken politics of abortion lies beneath the WHO's shifts. While there is no published evidence of this, it seems that clinicians' attitudes to the possible use of abortion might be a factor in how they appraise the overall clinical value of the drug, in their own risk-benefit assessment.[121] Most articles on thalidomide in ENL refer to the need to avoid providing women of childbearing age with thalidomide. The STEPS® programme and the Brazilian government's policy since 2001 by contrast, permit such use, as do the 2006 WHO Operational Guidelines.[122] Clearly, that affected children were born in Brazil shows that at least until the mid 1990s, restrictions were tragically inadequate.

For a debilitating condition like ENL (or indeed many of the other conditions in which thalidomide is used) the moral case is strong. The option of termination as part of a treatment regime is not desirable in itself, but the procedure is generally accessible. As of 2007, no new thalidomide affected births had been reported under the STEPS® programme in the USA, where 6,000 women of childbearing age have used the drug for a range of conditions, including a small number for ENL. However, there had been one spontaneous abortion.[123] The risk of reporting only in the learned journals is that unlike regulation via government, potential conflicts of interest in relation to the influence of manufacturers might be harder to identify.[124] The 2006 WHO Operational Guidelines appeared to concede on the use of thalidomide, referring to ENL as a syndrome of 'complex medical problems requiring careful management by experienced clinicians'.[125]

The reason these discussions are important is for what they tell us about the complexities of pharmaceutical ethics on the ground. These articles show that experts disagree on even the most fundamental issues. Their exchanges show that ethical debate is intricately woven into the very fabric of clinical practice as well as being framed through government and transnational policy guidelines and international marketing. Clinical ethics among a specialist group is here projected – as it inevitably must be – onto a wider screen of international 'bio-politics' and pharmaceutical marketing.

## Discussion

A shift in public policy to 'risk management' thinking is indicative of contemporary mood, identified as a key feature of modern bioethics by Claudia Wiesemann, who writes:

> As scientific hypotheses for risk management become ever more complex they are losing their credibility. The public has to decide between different plausible or probable scientific claims. ... which risks do we really want to live with? Who is defining which risks are negligible? Who is going to control the side effects of scientific

knowledge and technological applications? Risk management becomes an eminently political question. This is the place of medical ethics today.[126]

Risk in the case of thalidomide has two meanings. Risk in the legal sense is about a calculus that has nothing to do with ethics and everything to do with legal consequences. Thus for a company to market a new drug, avoiding the risk of legal action dictates the strategy for contractual use of the drug. All medical treatments and sales of products are a kind of contract: in the case of thalidomide and its analogues, the contract is on the table from the very start. In bioethics, 'risk-benefit' by contrast is about ethics: who bears the risk? Who can benefit? Timmermans and Leiter have argued that the solution to the FDA's dilemma provided an opportunity for some patients to benefit from a drug, while placing a burden on the woman as the risk-taker and on the potential child who had no say in the choice. The fact that thalidomiders themselves believed the drug should be marketed was critical in its acceptance. Pressure on drug regulation in the USA as a result of both the promotion of research into orphan drugs and the collapse of international boundaries with drug-buyers' groups, and the condition of off-label prescribing, all paved the way for the reintroduction of thalidomide to global markets.

There are other histories of thalidomide waiting to unfold and others yet to be written. There is no major history investigating the uses of the drug since 1997, the effects, side effects and debates since then, nor is there a history of thalidomiders in later life, as many of them struggle with the effects in adulthood of their congenital medical conditions. Further research in this arena – whether by college students or advanced scholars – will be able to provide deeper insight into modern medical cultures in a historical context of great ethical significance.

# Discussion and Conclusion: Bioethics in Historical Perspective

The book will conclude with a historical overview to synthesize some key themes. First, we shall take a look at some of the historical eras which have had a particular significance for contemporary Western bioethics. They are: the Enlightenment and the French Revolution; the nineteenth century; the Nazi era; the 1950s–1970s; and the 1980s and 1990s. Each of these eras is especially significant for bioethics history for the influence of ideas and institutions *from* these eras, and the influence of current views *in relation to* these periods. Next, this overview will reflect on some of the distinctive characteristics of the contemporary Western bioethical landscape. These are: the fragmentation of the medical subject; the importance of the abortion debate; the polyvalent discourse of rights; the changing meanings of activism; the problems of regulation; the present status of medical autonomy; ethical pluralism; and the dissolution of national boundaries.

## Historical periods

### *The Enlightenment and the French Revolution*

When US president Richard Nixon visited China in 1972, he reportedly asked Chinese premier Zhou Enlai what effects Zhou thought the 1789 French Revolution had had on the history of Western civilization. Zhou is said to have answered that it was 'too early to tell'. Twenty-first century bioethics tends to bear out this view. Many non-medical factors affecting the forms of bioethics in the present day can be dated to this crucial period in France, Europe and North America, notably nationalism, secularism, rationalism and the valorization of market forces. It was an era of intensive debate on the legitimacy of religion: in pre-revolutionary France religion was the target of Enlightenment *philosophes* who ridiculed as superstitious the practices of the Catholic Church. The French Revolution promoted a cult of reason.

We saw in Chapter 1 that debate amongst philosophical schools in bioethics is often drawn along lines which thinly mask a religious versus

153

secularist opposition. The most influential Enlightenment philosophers found different ways to replace religious morality with secular moral philosophy – for the Scottish economic philosopher Adam Smith, even the marketplace was possessed of an intrinsic ethics, a self-correcting constitution most beneficial to all when responding directly to individual choice. Smith's influence is rarely cited in mainline bioethics, but the powerful idea of the autonomy of the medical consumer has helped to shape ethical responses in the context of the modern medical marketplace. The force of these changes carried on through the nineteenth and twentieth centuries and still has weight now. The modern idea of having 'faith in science' arose as much because of the repudiation of religion, as from the merits of science, for the formidable capacities of modern science were still many decades from fruition when the idea of science as an antidote to religion became an ideological force. Moreover, across much of Western Europe, science became elevated as the rightful companion of the emerging nation states.

## The nineteenth century

Medical science and the development of the modern nation were seen as mutually sustaining; in many new democratizing nations, medicine was among the professions which participated in representative government. Some doctors directed their energies to the reform of the state out of a belief in 'social healing', seeing their capacities as healers as commensurate with the reforming mood of the nineteenth century. With increasingly real power to heal and the growing credibility of the profession's members, a significant number of doctors came to play roles as theorists and practitioners in social movements of the nineteenth to mid-twentieth century. Biological science was crucial to these efforts and to the ways of thinking which underpinned them. Energizing the idea of societal healing was the so-called 'organicist metaphor' – a view of the nation-state as a single organic entity in which all components held a significance at once biological (it was a living thing, that could perish) and ethical. What is now seen as metaphor and ideology was a literal scientific reality from the late nineteenth century until at least the 1930s.

Late nineteenth- and early twentieth-century eugenics represented an intensification of the socially hierarchical biologist thinking of the nineteenth century. Eugenics was preoccupied with collective biological fate of the nation-state, seeing the strands of future prosperity in the reproduction of the socially and biologically advantaged. Darwinism lent to biology a further ideologically charged element, as 'Social Darwinism' positioned human groupings in an evolutionary hierarchy. Thus, for example, criminals and people of non-white races came to be seen as atavistic, throwbacks to an earlier evolutionary period, either dragging others back down to their level or in need of the guiding hand of social elites to elevate them. In its increasingly knowledge-based capacity to heal or prevent sickness, as well as in the professional positioning of practitioners, medicine provided a significant driver of social organization and social change well into the twentieth century. In this respect, the first three decades of the twentieth century can be seen as part of a 'long nineteenth century' for medicine.

## *The Nazi era in Germany*

Several late nineteenth-century trends found their most vicious expression under the Nazi dictatorship. Large-scale eugenic sterilization and baby farming, mass 'euthanasia' and notorious medical experiments all had devastating effects on hundreds of thousands of people in Germany and the territories occupied under Hitler's regime in the 1939–1945 war. All of these painful histories inform contemporary bioethics: almost every time an historical low-tide mark is sought in bioethics debate, the Nazi era provides a referent.

Yet the very horror that the Nazi era inspires has at times had the paradoxical effect of making these events seem historically unique, and by implication unlikely to be repeated. Japanese medical crimes from the same period have been consistently eclipsed by consideration of the Nazis, while experiments carried out by Allies on their own soldiers (using mustard gas and nerve gas, as well as infectious diseases) and vulnerable people have all come to light only relatively recently. Revelations about US radiation experiments and other war/cold-war related experiments have pointed to uncomfortable approximations of the 'logic of war' rationale provided by the Nazis. In modern euthanasia discussions, those who have ignored gradations that lie between government medical execution and individual choice about death have done a disservice to a needed public debate about the end of life. The Nazi analogy should only be employed with the greatest care, and with a view to opening out debate rather than shutting it down.

In the post-war era, a strategy of isolating Nazi medicine as a historical peculiarity largely succeeded, and so, paradoxically, scrutiny of medical research ethics was at first relatively mild. In the 1950s and 1960s several exposures of 'routine' ethically dubious medical research reinforced a need for vigilance as a concomitant of all medical research. And much heedless, pragmatic or actively abusive medical research which took place in the 1940s and 1950s did not come to light at the time. Indeed, some is still being discovered.

## The 1950s to 1970s

Idealism and disenchantment in equal measure would best describe the crucial post-war era. It was a time of faith in the power of democratic government to enact laws or regulations for the protection of civil rights. It was the new era of rights activism: racial and ethnic rights; women's rights; indigenous peoples' rights; patients' rights; and animal rights. Governments invested vast sums of money in medical research. This was the era of big government, when the world was divided between two poles of communism and capitalist states, each vying to embody the best representation of national and trans-national collectivism. While some of the instruments of government embarked on unethical experimentation in the name of the national interest, at the domestic level, protection of research subjects and stricter drug trials increasingly formed part of the health policy agenda.

Enthusiasm for modernity in its medical forms led people to trust new products, often before the evidence was in. Thalidomide is the best known example, but DES caused less publicly visible but equally devastating effects. Legal liability became part of the language of modern medicine. A critique of medical authority formed part of a wider questioning of large institutions. The anti-psychiatry movement challenged categories of psychiatric diagnoses, and exposed harsh psychiatric treatments. The abortion law reform movement at once critiqued medical authority in the name of patient autonomy and saw doctors – for perhaps the first time – as potential 'service providers' for those who knew their own medical needs. For many African-Americans, controversy over the eugenics-informed psychological study of intelligence, exposure in 1972 of the Tuskegee syphilis studies and mandatory testing for sickle-cell anaemia all focused civil rights concerns onto medicine. Mainstream media projected an image as both the conscience and the servant of an imagined 'public interest' and investigative journalism was at its historic peak.

Medical practitioners themselves could become 'whistle-blowers' who breached the traditions of professional courtesy. Henry K. Beecher and Maurice Pappworth alerted the public to research ethics abuses among their own colleagues, and helped to keep medical experimentation on the agenda of social reform. The professional incentives to medical achievement noted by Beecher are still pertinent today.

The new bioethics, encompassing as it now does the systematic external scrutiny of medical ethics, emerged from this environment, but it was neither revolutionary nor liberationist and has been criticized for serving rather than critiquing medical industries. In some respects bioethics showed a wariness of science, but bioethics consultants also addressed themselves to government as a source of counsel, creating an opening for possible tensions between being a conscience and a broker of change. Bioethics proponents were shrewdly aware that governments might be glad of guidance as to how to balance the demands of rival supplicants for its support. For the reform-minded Catholicism of the Vatican II era, medical ethics activism responded to the new mantra of the need for 'relevance' for religion. A movement for abortion law reform, euthanasia advocacy and diversity of views on organ transplants following the new designation of 'brain death' opened the door to theological as well as ethical disputation. Opposition to abortion rights has been one of the most consistent stances of the religious right – in many ways its *raison d'être* – evolving to entail opposition to prenatal screening, cloning of embryos and embryo experimentation.

## The 1980s and 1990s: down with slogans!

If there were two major non-medical characteristics of the 1980s heading into the 1990s that had a significant (if largely undocumented) effect on bioethics history, the first would be the election of conservative governments in the USA and UK, under Ronald Reagan (1981–1989) and Margaret Thatcher (1979–1990) respectively. Their incumbencies were characterized by a reassertion of the idea of 'market forces' as the font of social good. The 1989 collapse of communism in the Soviet Union and the fall of the Berlin Wall seemed to drive home the rightness of the de-regulationist messages of Reagan and Thatcher. Neo-liberal capitalism emerged as an emphatically dominant force in policy-making. For bioethics, this development prioritized patient (client) autonomy as the prime mover in ethical debate and decision-making. Thus that autonomy which was, under the Nuremberg Code, intended to prevent coercion became autonomy in the medical marketplace. Patients' rights were identified with, or even as, consumer rights.

The Thatcher government, ostensibly at odds with its own free-market sympathies, responded to contention from both scientists and the religious lobby by creating the HFEA to regulate IVF technologies.

Regulation in this mode meant not so much restriction as it did a more subtly mediated form of introduction to the market of products with capacities to reshape the social world. In this era, arguing against religious opponents of embryo research, utilitarian philosophers began to voice liberal individualist arguments for access to medical technologies. They built on the consumer and patients' rights impulses of the 1960s and 1970s, but without the wider critique of the industrial aspects of medicine. Consumer autonomy has been a staple of the utilitarian case, but it is based less on a strict appeal to traditional liberalism than on the implicit and regular repudiation of the theological underpinnings of religiously inspired bioethics.

Has modern bioethics contributed to a silencing and exclusion of medical radicalism? It is hard to say. In the 1980s and 1990s activism of various kinds became bureaucratized. Activists obtained jobs in welfare departments, in meta-activist organizations such as Greenpeace, in environmentalist parties, in government departments and, as before, in academia. Social critique tended to fragment, and the discourse of rights changed from its 1970s assumptions about the power and moral authority of single-identity interest groups, to acknowledgement of the inevitable consequences of the emergence of social and intellectual pluralities. Individualism and consumer rights came to be – strangely but truly – the new allies of big science. The internal logic of 1980s and 1990s' 'quasi-regulation' points ultimately to deregulation, and thus the FDA's 1997 position on thalidomide stands as an index of changes in the role of regulation. Critics continue to push the FDA to take itself out of the social equation, to cease even to have the role of broker between interests. Within bioethics scholarship, one of these sea changes is a challenge to the hegemony of Western bioethics itself. Now that regulation has largely become routinized or sidelined, there is room for more voices. Perhaps paradoxically, now that bioethics is institutionally entrenched, belief in the value of regulation appears to be weaker, not stronger.

Each of the historical periods discussed so far generated ripples which persist in present-day thinking. The weight of these histories provides a range of starting points for many modern bioethics conversations.

## The present landscape

What follows is a 'panning shot' of some key characteristics of ethical issues in medicine now.

## *The fragmentation of the medical subject*

Medical knowledge-creation by the mid-twentieth century was already assumed to be fragmented. Most beneficiaries of modern medicine expect that someone who is not sick has trialled a treatment (for example, a drug or vaccine) they are offered. The medical subject and the experimental subject are in this sense different people. But several new clinical developments have similarly dispersed the identity of the person who undergoes a treatment, so that the subject of a medical intervention is also in a sense no longer an individual. New clinical and laboratory techniques have, in a different way, radically disaggregated what was once assumed to be the integrated 'medical identity' of the individual patient.

An organ transplant, the provision of a human gamete (sperm or ovum), or the conception through IVF and birth of a child through surrogacy affect a range of people in different and sometimes competing ways. The seeming paradox of legal authority to have someone perform one's own suicide comes under the same heading. These divisions – involving new technology in many cases but not all – have opened up many of the questions characteristic of modern bioethics. The transactional nature of many innovations in medicine has created new kinds of conceptual and social spaces in many of which bioethics is now practised.

In the case of organ transplantation, for example, two individuals are involved in the same medical transaction. Organ transplant experimentation and the 'brain death' definition placed an individual whose life could be saved at the centre of a transaction which begins with surgery on another person. In the case of 'beating-heart' donors, this can mean the decision by the donor to help another person, in part through the agency of their own death. Should jurisdictions seek donation on an opt-in or opt-out basis? Should the bodies of prisoners who have been legally executed be off-limits, because the deaths are the effect of compulsion by the state, or are they a legitimate source of organs? Trade in kidneys has raised the question of how meaningful is the 'informed' consent of a person who has, for reason of their poverty, to sell a kidney. So-called 'saviour siblings' offer a similarly complex case. An embryo can be genetically matched to a living sibling so that the child born can be brought to term in order to provide genetically matched tissue to save the life of another child. Thus the second-born child is subject to a medical intervention, involuntarily, but is not its principal beneficiary.

To create one child today can entail the active involvement of multiple individuals. Medically managed sperm and ovum donation, as well as the practice of so-called surrogacy, are commonplace. Parties to medicalized reproduction are linked at a very intimate level, and the final person to enter the scene, the child, is also in a sense the final subject of medical exchange. People, more significantly women, undergo medical interventions specifically in order to assist another person. Off-shoring of procreation in the purchase of eggs from women or the use of 'surrogates' in another country can overlap with the physical split between the several procreators and the family that is 'created' by the birth. Bioethical reflection – much of it taking place in the context of legal inquiry – has interrogated the several dimensions in which the medical beneficiary is separated from other medical subjects, even in another country. Offshoring accentuates the division between the diverse medical subjects: the 'commissioning couple's' child might, for example, be born using their gametes. The multiplicity of people involved in providing the biological means of conception is mirrored in the specialisms involved: for example, one IVF/PGD treatment cycle will likely require the direct involvement of a genetic counsellor, an embryologist, a geneticist, an anaesthetist, a gynaecologist, a radiologist or radiographers, and nursing professionals. Endocrinologists, the pharmaceutical industry and medical device makers are also essential.

For our purposes, what is distinctive in such cases is that the opening for bioethical reflection is created as a result of the changed nature of the medical subject. The question of who is the subject of a medical intervention opens up the question of whether all those involved in these transactions have equally meaningful levels of choice.

## The significance of abortion

Abortion politics has been and remains a significant factor in Western bioethics, particularly in the United States and in countries in which religion is influential. Euthanasia, genetics and the politics of thalidomide are all at barely one remove from the politics of abortion. Abortion forms the central plank in a closely linked series of arguments which make the case that to deny God the final say in life and death is to usurp his power. Relatively improved access to abortion to terminate personally unsustainable pregnancies has provided a legal platform for the routinization of a wide range of interventions, such as selective termination of foetuses, following the use of fertility drugs and a choice for termination as a consequence of prenatal testing for harmful genetic or congenital conditions. Euthanasia of babies who are born with extreme disabilities has been justified on the grounds that it is not morally different from an abortion while the foetus is *in utero*. The term 'post-natal abortion' has surfaced lately in the bioethics media as a euphemism for euthanasia of newborns, a term which appropriates the success of the abortion rights movement but which ignores the central plank of the pro-choice argument, which refers to the woman involved.

## *The polymorphous discourse of 'rights'*

New technologies and new forms of social activism have played a significant part in changes to the meaning of rights. The discourse of rights is now ubiquitous, serving novel, multiple and sometimes competing ends. Women's rights versus foetal rights is a familiar example; intellectual property rights of gene patent holders can limit patient access to knowledge which was discovered through publicly funded research. An employer's right to know the genetic predispositions of personnel runs up against the right to genetic privacy. Patients' rights, once a defensive stance against unwanted or unsuspected medical interventions, is now more likely to refer to access to elective medical technologies or new drugs.

Increasingly, the connections between women once expressed in the discourse of 'identity politics' are more literally connected by an industry and by the genetic and biological relations established through egg donation and surrogacy. This represents a significant transformation of the contexts in which questions about consumer rights were once posed in reaction against unsatisfactory or dangerous practices or products. And the disaggregation of the reproductive process itself has permitted a movement in support of 'rights' of human embryo: this would have been impossible before human embryos were isolated in the laboratory. 'Rights' has become so much the universal unit of ethical currency that its value has been arguably undermined.

## *Contemporary meanings of activism*

Just as the discourse of rights has changed, so, too, has the nature of activism around medicine. When we think of activism we tend to think of militants, whether left or right wing, carrying placards, lined up in a public place making a noise; or, more likely these days, spending their time in the blogosphere. However, even the professions themselves (for example) have activist elements. Bioethics is a complex field which bridges the several divides between street activism, established lobbies, medical research activism, and other forms of academic activism. Even as brokers of competing activisms, bioethics commentators are themselves also activists, who do not just respond to others but see their role as being to set agendas. Many enter the field out of a sense not only of public duty but out of a wish for their own perspective to be taken into account. Academics in bioethics occupy an uncertain terrain in which they adhere to scholarly rules that allow for indefinite evolution of knowledge, at the same time as they participate in public debates which by their very nature lead to relative fixity in policy formation and implementation.

Demands for public policy control of medical research have been channelled into regulatory mechanisms. Ethics review is intended to accommodate diversity through committee composition. Many institutions, research and clinical, allow for religious and lay members or philosophical ethicists on committees, as well as providing for gender balance. All such figures are more or less activists, whose presence on the committees means that they have been absorbed into a regulatory framework. Many clinicians and scientists, too, volunteer for ethics roles out of a belief in the value of review. Panels, committees and *ad hoc* consults can reflect the ongoing effects of – and changes in – medical activism.

## *Medical autonomy*

Medical autonomy is a doctrine which works on two levels: it positions the individual medical practitioner as the best arbiter of the patient's good and preserves the independence and self-regulatory claims of the profession as a whole. The physician is only one cog in a large industry and often only the starting point for the provision of information, discussion and decision-making. The meaning and significance of 'medical autonomy' can shift and, as we have seen in the case of thalidomide, can potentially place pressure on the physician to make judgements beyond his or her capacity, compromising the value of autonomy.

Activism by members of the medical professions cannot be ignored when considering the forms and functions of modern bioethics. Venerable medical associations are one of the reasons medicine as an industry has power. The roots of long-established professional bodies such as national and international medical associations are activist: they were founded to defend and promote the professional interests of the group. Moreover, there are medical activists who work outside these bodies, such as the several euthanasia activists in the medical profession, the well-known physicians who have attracted the nickname 'Dr Death', such as Jack Kevorkian and Philip Nitschke. But widespread and long-term physician activism in the Netherlands, through that country's national body, has arguably had much more sustained success than the work of any lone figure, however high-profile.

## Ethical pluralism

Ethical pluralism describes the reality of modern bioethics. It has some of the features of multiculturalism, acknowledging that diverse ethical communities can exist within larger jurisdictions. It is an admission of the essentially political understanding of bioethics. Ethical pluralism places individuals, groups or ideologies on a potential collision course which must be mediated if the overall political public good is to be sustained. It also has echoes of 'moral relativism', the bugbear of most of the major schools of moral philosophy. However, it differs in that the term 'ethical pluralism' is merely descriptive: it does not imply that what is right cannot be known, only that people differ in their beliefs as to what is right and that these views can change.

## Dissolution of national boundaries

The Internet, along with direct consumer challenges to local regulations, has contributed to the dilution of meaning of ethical regulation within national boundaries. Widened access to life-creating, life-prolonging or life-ending medical interventions are all a result of the internationalization of medicine. 'Medical tourism' takes consumers offshore, while the Internet brings the medical market direct to the home. Regulation of reproductive technologies is highly developed in some jurisdictions and barely existent or non-existent elsewhere. Yet new technologies make it possible to import donor gametes, or even, in theory, donor embryos. So-called 'reproductive tourism' sees women or couples travelling to poorer countries in search of gametes or even the gestation of a child, in commercial surrogacy arrangements. In the case of 'death tourism', some people who are unable to procure their medically implemented death in their own jurisdictions have travelled to where they could obtain the end of their lives medically. Access to life-ending drugs through international mail order via the web is hard to police and makes local laws on euthanasia less meaningful. Provision of donor organs from poor countries has also proven at times to be ungovernable. Even the plastinated bodies of people whose remains feature in touring bio-shows have their origins in questionable international trade.

Government has withered on the vine in the face of these new international connections between buyers and sellers. Global markets place pressure on local economies but also on ethical regulation. Ethics without borders is hard to implement, less likely to reflect local ethical consensus and more likely to permit under-regulated and therefore possibly risky or exploitative practices. However, it allows for greater consumer autonomy in the medical marketplace. On present indications government will be principally significant as the provider of a legal system in which two parties thrash out medical marketplace options and medical risks on a case-by-case basis. This will go on long after regulatory bioethics has dwindled. Thus, an IVF custody case is mediated at law; any adverse effects of a drug will be challenged case-by-case at law; and case law will press out the boundaries of euthanasia. Regulation in that sense will be 'outsourced' to the courts, just as the medical marketplace is outsourced internationally.

## Conclusion

This book began with a claim about the value of historical thinking as a way to reflect on contemporary ethics. It posed a model from Charles Rosenberg about the staggered, compromised and open-ended ways in which health policy comes about. Only by understanding how mindsets – be they local, national, ideological, religious, professional or commercial – legitimate behaviours, is it possible to advance the process of ethics conversations and ethical education. How a society creates and processes medical change is inextricably linked to that society's politics and ethics. In that sense, bioethics has become one of the defining political arenas of the twenty-first century. The bioethics specialist is asked by institutions, government and media to interpret innovations, and in so doing, to broker the interests of diverse stakeholders.

Now the regulatory mechanisms which were the outcomes of the battles of the 1980s and 1990s are by and large in place. They have become the media through which bioethics as policy is enacted. Bioethics has become more open to different views as it has become less important at the level of policy debate. Bioethics itself is also heavily institutionalized and at times underwritten by corporations. Bioethics conversations are usually complicated, consensus-oriented, and in some measure, specialist. Arguably, the best form of bioethics lies in the ethics education of clinicians, scientists and consumers. Awareness of some of the sobering events of the past and about offhand and naturalized cultures of permission can be part of this process. To imagine direct analogies where none exist, however, poses a risk to reasoned debate. Seeing bioethics in historical perspective entails both seeing when these analogies are used, and testing claims to ethical relevance, through the use of specific evidence of historic and contemporary examples.

This book has shown that direct comparisons with historical examples for the purpose of contemporary ethical evaluation can have real but also limited uses. Stories from the past must, however, remain among the coordinates of bioethics conversations, for we are living with and within inherited institutions, legal frameworks and mindsets. We reproduce, distort or challenge these conditions, according to present exigencies.

The book has sought to argue that at its best, ethics review embodies genuine conversation, offering a place and time for communication between cultures that would not normally interact. Ethics monitoring also implies a legitimate interest on the part of the public sphere. It implies more deeply that there *is* such a thing as the public interest, and that there are people who are sufficiently aware of a diversity of views, but sufficiently removed from interest, that they can provide a balanced view. Ethics review nonetheless can be – indeed cannot fail to be – imprinted with ideological and selective priorities and attitudes.

Bioethics in action is not necessarily about high drama and very rarely about good versus evil: it can be about diligence in the quotidian business of reading. Faced with a three-inch stack of company literature to address one drug trial, an ethics committee might be happy to pass over the task of scrutiny to the company experts who wrote the materials. But reading is worth doing. Modern bioethics is probably at its best when it is most *mundane*. It does not come with clear guidelines as to what is wrong and right. In a successful participatory democracy, no-one is truly satisfied. The greatest success of bioethics might thus be its apparent weakness: that it is political.

In relation to academic bioethics this book has sustained the view that bioethics is not what *others* do; rather, bioethics is what we *all* do. History provides evidence and examples to facilitate ethical conversations. Bioethics in its diversity provides an opportunity to participate in mediation of both the social and medical good.

# Notes

## Introduction

1. J. R. Goldim (2009) 'Revisiting the Beginning of Bioethics: The Contribution of Fritz Jahr (1927)', *Perspectives in Biology and Medicine*, 52, 3, 377–80; H.-M. Sass (2007) 'Fritz Jahr's 1927 Concept of Bioethics', *Kennedy Institute of Ethics Journal*, 17, 4, 279–95.

2. D. Callahan (2004) 'Bioethics' in S. G. Post (ed.) *Encyclopedia of Bioethics*, 3rd edn (New York: MacMillan Reference), 278–87, p. 280. Albert Jonsen (2005) in *Bioethics beyond the Headlines: Who Lives? Who Dies? Who Decides?* (Lanham, MD: Rowman and Littlefield) says that Potter's goal was 'to describe his idea of a broad field of study that would link human values with biological knowledge' (p. 9). See also P. J.Whitehouse (2002) 'Van Rensselaer Potter: An Intellectual Memoir', *Cambridge Quarterly of Healthcare Ethics*, 11, 4, 331–4; G. Maio (2001) 'Bioetica in Prospettiva Storica: per una valutazione critica della bioetica e dei suoi rapporti con la storia della medicine', *Medicina nei secoli*, 13, 1, 169–86. The coincidence between Maio's title and the subtitle of my former course at University of Queensland from 2000 to 2007, as well as the title of this book, is indicative of the increased interest in bioethics history occurring around the turn of the century.

3. W. T. Reich (1994) 'The Word "Bioethics": Its Birth and the Legacies of Those Who Shaped It', *Kennedy Institute of Ethics Journal*, 4, 4, 319–35, p. 320; A. R. Jonsen (1998) *The Birth of Bioethics* (New York: Oxford University Press), p. 27. Goldim, 'Revisiting the Beginning of Bioethics'; Sass, 'Fritz Jahr's 1927 Concept of Bioethics'; W. T. Reich (1999) 'The "Wider View": André Hellegers's Passionate, Integrating Intellect and the Creation of Bioethics', *Kennedy Institute of Ethics Journal*, 9, 1, 25–51; D. Callahan (1999) 'The Hastings Center and the Early Years of Bioethics', *Kennedy Institute of Ethics Journal*, 9, 1, 53–71.

4. Hans-Martin Sass says that there are four kinds of bioethics but that biomedical is the one that took root: 'Although Jahr (1927; 1928a, b, c; 1929; 1930; 1934a, b, c; 1938) and Potter (1970; 1971) had not much or only limited impact on the development of global bioethics as we understand it today, bioethics in the form of biomedical ethics, as Hellegers (1971) saw it, was introduced rapidly around the world.' Sass, 'Fritz Jahr's 1927 Concept of Bioethics', p. 289. Dawson specifically challenges this narrow, medical view of bioethics and makes positive suggestions about how the field could be improved by challenging some of its own assump-

tions. This book shares his view that there is a need to see bioethics in its medical aspects from a wider angle, but uses 'bioethics' in the medical sense because it is a recognized usage. A. Dawson (2010) 'The Future of Bioethics: Three Dogmas and a Cup of Hemlock', *Bioethics*, 24, 5, 218–25.

5. Renée Fox and Judith P. Swazey identify several possible beginning points for bioethics in America, drawing particular attention to the relative silences on some issues, such as fertility politics, in present-day recollections and histories. They have convincingly shown that most prior readings of bioethics history have privileged certain stories over others and that too simple and linear a narrative belies or is a misleading guide to this complex social phenomenon, both in its early years and the present. Their narration of the 'multiple birth' of bioethics is the most useful way truly to account for the field's history. R. C. Fox and J. P. Swazey (2008) *Observing Bioethics* (Oxford: Oxford University Press), pp. 29–32. See also M. L. T. Stevens (2000) *Bioethics in America: Origins and Cultural Politics* (Baltimore, MD: Johns Hopkins University Press), pp. 39–44; P. Borry, P. Schotsmans and K. Dierickx (2005) 'The Birth of the Empirical Turn in Bioethics', *Bioethics*, 19, 1, 49–71, p. 57.

6. R. Cooter (2010) 'Inside the Whale: Bioethics in History and Discourse', *Social History of Medicine*, 23, 3, 662–72.

7. G. Weisz, 'Introduction' in G. Weisz (ed.) (1990) *Social Science Perspectives on Medical Ethics* (Dordrecht: Kluwer Academic), 3–15, p. 6.

8. J. D. Moreno (1995) *Deciding Together: Bioethics and Moral Consensus* (New York: Oxford University Press), p. 145.

9. A. G. Morrice (2002) '"Honour and Interests": Medical Ethics and the British Medical Association', in A-H. Maehle and J. Geyer-Kordesch (eds) *Historical and Philosophical Perspectives on Biomedical Ethics: From Paternalism to Autonomy?* (Aldershot: Ashgate), pp. 11–35. Morrice describes the period from the eighteenth century to mid-twentieth century in relation to advertising, etiquette, fees, competition, paternalism; confidentiality and the physician-patient dyad. He notes similarities with bioethics, in that 'doctors' behaviour, moral principles, collective and individual moral choice, and the role of the profession in society were all implicated' in these aspects of medical ethics (p. 31). See also: H. T. Have and B. Gordijn (eds) (2001) *Bioethics in a European Perspective* (Dordrecht: Kluwer Academic), p. 2; J. L. Berlant (1975) *Profession and Monopoly: A Study of Medicine in the United States and Great Britain* (Berkeley, CA: University of California Press); R. Cooter (2004) 'Historical Keywords: Bioethics' *The Lancet*, 364, 9447, 1749. Cooter here notes that medical ethics is used more often in the UK, while Callahan argues that 'bioethics' makes an explicit distinction between traditional professional medical ethics and the contemporary, more socially encompassing, bioethics (Callahan 'Bioethics', p. 280). See also: D. Brunton (ed.) (2004) *Health, Disease and Society in Europe, 1800–1930: A Source Book* (Manchester: Manchester University Press); D. Brunton (ed.) (2004) *Medicine*

*Transformed: Health, Disease and Society in Europe, 1800–1930* (Manchester: Manchester University Press in association with the Open University).

10. R. Cooter (2000) 'The Ethical Body' in R. Cooter and J. Pickstone (eds) *Medicine in the Twentieth Century* (Amsterdam: Harwood Academic), 451–68, p. 451. J. V. Pickstone (2000) *Ways of Knowing: A New History of Science, Technology and Medicine* (Manchester: Manchester University Press), p. 220.

11. The terms 'unborn' and 'brain-dead' are contentious: whether or not to place them in inverted commas can be seen to reflect a strong view on their status as science and hence their ethical resonance. Leaving them without inverted commas is not intended to endorse any particular view, even if, in a sense, it cannot fail to.

12. Medical ethics has also traditionally referred to the activities of medically trained practitioners in the clinical setting, distinct, for example, from the ethics codes of nurses or of non-clinical medical scientists.

13. '[I]n the end I settled on "bioethics" as the least unsatisfactory term that was still usable.' J. Andre (2002) *Bioethics as Practice* (Chapel Hill, NC: University of North Carolina Press), p. xi. C. E. Rosenberg (1999) 'Meanings, Policies, and Medicine: On the Bioethical Enterprise and History', *Daedalus*, 128, 4, 27–46; Maehle and Geyer-Kordesch, *Historical and Philosophical Perspectives on Biomedical Ethics*; A. Wear, J. Geyer-Kordesch and R. French (eds) (1993) *Doctors and Ethics: The Earlier Historical Setting of Professional Ethics* (Amsterdam: Rodopi); Cooter, 'The Ethical Body'.

14. C. E. Rosenerg, 'Anticipated Consequences: Historians, History, and Health Policy' in R. A. Stevens, C. E. Rosenberg and L. R. Burns (eds) (2006) *History and Health Policy in the United States: Putting the Past Back In* (New Brunswick, NJ: Rutgers University Press), 13–31, p. 14; K. A. Richman (2004) *Ethics and the Metaphysics of Medicine: Reflections on Health and Beneficence* (Cambridge, MA: MIT Press), p. 157.

15. L. E. Kay (2000) *Who Wrote the Book of Life?: A History of the Genetic Code* (Stanford, CA: Stanford University Press); B. Latour and S. Woolgar (1986) *Laboratory Life: The Construction of Scientific Facts* (Princeton, NJ: Princeton University Press); N. Oudshoorn (1994) *Beyond the Natural Body: An Archaeology of Sex Hormones* (London: Routledge); M. Burleigh (1994) *Death and Deliverance: 'Euthanasia' in Germany c. 1900–1945* (Cambridge: Cambridge University Press); R. Proctor (1988) *Racial Hygiene: Medicine under the Nazis* (Cambridge, MA: Harvard University Press); P. Weindling (1989) *Health, Race and German Politics between National Unification and Nazism, 1870–1945* (Cambridge: Cambridge University Press); A. Scull (ed.) (1981) *Madhouses, Mad-Doctors, and Madmen: The Social History of Psychiatry in the Victorian Era* (Philadelphia, PA: University of Pennsylvania Press); A. T. Scull (1989) *Social Order/Mental Disorder: Anglo-American Psychiatry in Historical Perspective* (Berkeley, CA: University of California Press); T. M. Porter (1986) *The Rise of Statistical Thinking, 1820–1900* (Princeton, NJ: Princeton University Press); W. F. Bynum and R. Porter (eds) (1987) *Medical Fringe and*

*Medical Orthodoxy, 1750–1850* (London: Croom Helm); R. Baker, D. Porter and R. Porter (eds) (1993–1995) *The Codification of Medical Morality: Historical and Philosophical Studies of the Formalization of Western Medical Morality in the Eighteenth and Nineteenth Centuries*, 2 vols (Dordrecht: Kluwer Academic); D. J. Rothman and S. M. Rothman (1984) *The Willowbrook Wars*, 1st edn (New York: Harper & Row)

16. R. S. Cowan (2008) *Heredity and Hope: The Case for Genetic Screening* (Cambridge, MA: Harvard University Press), p. 8. It cannot be assumed that historians will be tied to an agenda which is inherently wary of medical innovation. In fact, most of the historians cited in this book have used the unique capacity of historical research to focus ethical issues in ways that undermine simplistic stances. See the activist: www.historyandpolicy.org

17. A. E. Raz (2009) 'Eugenic Utopias/Dystopias, Reprogenetics, and Community Genetics', *Sociology of Health and Illness*, 31, 4, 602–16, p. 608. Everett Mendelsohn was a historian of science who as early as 1968 sat on the Ad Hoc Committee of the Harvard Medical School to Examine the Definition of Brain Death; David Rothman wrote *Strangers at the Bedside: A History of How Law and Bioethics Transformed Medical Decision Making* (New York: Basic Books, 1991) and is a member of the medical faculty at Columbia University.

18. H. Brody (2009) *The Future of Bioethics* (Oxford: Oxford University Press), p. 26; A. Buchanan, D. Brock, N. Daniels and D. Wikler (2000) *From Chance to Choice: Genetics and Justice* (Cambridge: Cambridge University Press), p. xiv.

19. Transplant ethics; neuro-ethics; nano-ethics; synthetic biology immunisation and somatic gene therapy, for example, would each merit full chapters.

20. Philosophical ethics takes the singular, medical ethics usually the plural, and ethics, meaning general social ethics, similarly the plural. However, 'bioethics' used in the singular in this book is not intended to denote a branch of philosophical ethics, rather to encompass a distinct, if wide-ranging cultural development which has arisen since the word was first coined in English.

21. In identifying cultural bioethics, Callahan highlights the claims made over many years by social scientists and historians, such as Fox, Swazey, Bosk, Kleinman, Rosenberg, Cooter, Komesaroff, Hedgecoe and others, for a more explicitly socially aware bioethics. Two other commentators offer similar differentiations. Jonsen proposes that bioethics can be understood as both a form of applied philosophical ethics and as a field of cultural activity: he draws a distinction between 'bioethics as a discipline', and the ways in which its disciplinary status in academia has been essayed and tested since 1973 and 'bioethics as a discourse', which he situates in the various public non-academic spheres in which bioethics is practised. Jonsen, *The Birth of Bioethics*.

22. C. Wiesemann (2006) 'The Contribution of Medical History to Medical Ethics: The Case of Brain Death', in C. Rehmann-Sutter, M. Düwell and D.

Mieth (eds) (2006) *Bioethics in Cultural Contexts: Reflections on Methods and Finitude* (Dordrecht: Springer), pp. 187–96. Callahan's taxonomy is itself an embodiment of cultural bioethics, in that it allows for many meanings where others might see either fewer or more meanings of the word.

23. Rosenberg, 'Meanings, Policies, and Medicine', p. 40.

24. Jonsen, *The Birth of Bioethics*, p. 27.

25. All of these histories have been documented elsewhere. Among the many works that address these aspects of bioethics history, see Baker et al., *The Codification of Medical Morality*; J. Sherwood (1999) 'Syphilization: Human Experimentation in the Search for a Syphilis Vaccine in the Nineteenth Century', *Journal of the History of Medicine and Allied Sciences*, 54, 3, 364–86; J. Hazelgrove (2002) 'The Old Faith and the New Science: The Nuremberg Code and Human Experimentation Ethics in Britain, 1946–73', *Social History of Medicine*, 15, 1, 109–35; D. J. Rothman (1991) *Strangers at the Bedside: A History of How Law and Bioethics Transformed Medical Decision Making* (New York: Basic Books); Jonsen, *The Birth of Bioethics*. Cooter has developed his 'counter-history' of bioethics in 'Inside the Whale', a 2010 review essay in *Social History of Medicine*.

26. Rosenberg. 'Anticipated Consequences: Historians, History, and Health Policy', p. 29.

27. C. Rehmann-Sutter, M. Düwell and D. Mieth (2006) 'Introduction', in Rehmann-Sutter et al., *Bioethics in Cultural Contexts*, 1–10, p. 2.

28. In this way it can also be differentiated from mainstream philosophical bioethics.

29. Pickstone, *Ways of Knowing*, p. 220.

30. Rehmann-Sutter et al., 'Introduction', p. 2.

31. Wiesemann, 'The Contribution of Medical History to Medical Ethics', p. 189.

32. Rosenberg, 'Anticipated Consequences', p. 13.

33. D. Callahan (2003) 'Principlism and Communitarianism', *Journal of Medical Ethics*, 29, 5, 287–91, p. 288.

34. On early IVF see D. Wilson (2011) 'Creating the "Ethics Industry": Mary Warnock, In Vitro Fertilization and the History of Bioethics in Britain', *BioSocieties*, 6, 2, 121–41; M. H. Johnson, S. B. Franklin, M. Cottingham and N. Hopwood (2010) 'Why the Medical Research Council Refused Robert Edwards and Patrick Steptoe Support for Research on Human Conception in 1971', *Human Reproduction*, 25, 9, 2157–74.

35. Professor Frank made this point in a talk given at the Queensland University of Technology in 2005.

36. M. Burleigh (1997) *Ethics and Extermination: Reflections on Nazi Genocide* (New York: Cambridge University Press).

37. Anon. (2004) 'Medical Errors Affect One in Ten Hospital Patients', *Bulletin of Medical Ethics*, 201, September, p. 7. See also Editorial, *Bulletin of Medical Ethics* February 2005, p. 1, which reports for the USA 120,000 deaths per

annum from mis-prescription and misuse of drugs. R. Mickelburgh (2000) 'Medical Blunders "Kill Thousands"', *Sunday Mail* (Brisbane), 20 February, reports an estimated 18,000 people die (to 2000) in Australia per year as a result of medical errors (p. 3).

# Chapter 1

1. C. L. Bosk (2002) 'Now That We Have the Data, What Was the Question?', *American Journal of Bioethics*, 2, 4, 21–3, p. 23. A thoughtful overview article on the history of bioethics with specific reference to the disciplines is K. Orfali and R. G. DeVries (2009) 'A Sociological Gaze on Bioethics' in William C. Cockerham (ed.) *The New Blackwell Companion to Medical Sociology* (Hoboken, NJ: Wiley-Blackwell), 487–510.
2. Fox and Swazey refer to the religious dimension as a 'particularly complex aspect' of bioethics history. See R.C. Fox and J. P. Swazey (2008) *Observing Bioethics* (Oxford: Oxford University Press), p. 37.
3. T. Gelfand (1993) 'The History of the Medical Profession', in W. F. Bynum and R. Porter (eds), *Companion Encyclopedia of the History of Medicine*, vol. 2 (London: Routledge), 1119–50.
4. J. E. Goldstein (1987) *Console and Classify: The French Psychiatric Profession in the Nineteenth Century* (Cambridge: Cambridge University Press).
5. P. Komesaroff (1996) 'Medicine and the Ethical Conditions of Modernity', in J. Daly (ed.) *Ethical Intersections: Health Research, Methods and Researcher Responsibility* (Boulder, CO: Westview Press), 34–48. See also: S. E. Johnston, S. R. Cruess and R. L. Cruess (2001) 'Ethical Leadership in Modern Medicine', *Canadian Journal of Administrative Studies*, 18, 4, 291–7.
6. C. E. Rosenberg (2006) 'Anticipated Consequences: Historians, History, and Health Policy', in R. A. Stevens, C. E. Rosenberg and L. R. Burns (eds) *History and Health Policy in the United States: Putting the Past Back In* (New Brunswick, NJ: Rutgers University Press), 13–31; p. 17. Physician Paul Komesaroff in 'Medicine and the Ethical Conditions of Modernity', similarly observes the inherent ethical calculus entailed in any medical encounter.
7. C. E. Rosenberg (1976) *No Other Gods: On Science and American Social Thought* (Baltimore, MD: Johns Hopkins University Press), p. 238.
8. Christian ethicists Paul Ramsey and Joseph Fletcher, as key examples, often voiced opposing views in the early years of Christian ethics debates about medicine. They are discussed extensively in A. R. Jonsen (1998) *The Birth of Bioethics* (New York: Oxford University Press).
9. See: M. L. T. Stevens (2000) *Bioethics in America: Origins and Cultural Politics* (Baltimore, MD: Johns Hopkins University Press); C. Wiesemann (2006) 'The Contribution of Medical History to Medical Ethics: The Case of Brain Death', in C. Rehmann-Sutter, M. Düwell and D. Mieth (eds) *Bioethics in Cultural Contexts: Reflections on Methods and Finitude* (Dordrecht: Springer), 187–96, and C. M. Messikomer, R. C. Fox and J. P. Swazey (2001) 'The

Presence and Influence of Religion in American Bioethics', *Perspectives in Biology and Medicine*, 44, 4, 485–508. G. S. Belkin (2003) 'Brain Death and the Historical Understanding of Bioethics', *Journal of the History of Medicine and Allied Sciences*, 58, 3, 325–61 provides a revisionist view.

10. M. Goozner, A. Caplan, J. Moreno, B. S. Kramer, T. F. Babor and W. C. Husser (2008) *A Common Standard for Conflict of Interest Disclosure*, Center for Science in the Public Interest, http://www.cspinet.org/new/pdf/ 20080711 _a_common_standard_for_conflict_of_interest_disclosure__final_for_confer ence.pdf (accessed 14 July 2010).

11. *Journal of Bioethical Inquiry*, Author Disclosure Document at http://www.springer.com/ medicine/journal/11673 (accessed 14 July 2010).

12. See A. R. Jonsen (2005) *Bioethics beyond the Headlines: Who Lives? Who Dies? Who Decides?* (Lanham, MD: Rowman and Littlefield), p. 183. See also: Damien Keown (2001)*Buddhism and Bioethics* (Basingstoke: Palgrave); S. Cromwell Crawford (2003) *Hindu Bioethics for the Twenty-first Century* (New York: SUNY Press). D. Atighetchi (2007) *Islamic Bioethics: Problems and Perspectives* (Dordrecht: Springer). For Judaism, see http://www.ijs. org.au/Bioethical-issues-in-Judaism/default.aspx (accessed 7 January 2013).

13. Jonsen, *Birth of Bioethics*, pp. 90–122.

14. A. L. Caplan and P. Patrizio (2009) 'The Art of Medicine: The Beginning of the End of the Embryo Wars', *The Lancet*, 373, 9669, 1074–75.

15. R. Weiss (2010) 'Obama's Bioethics Commission: Providing Practical Policy Options' http://www.whitehouse.gov/blog/2010/04/08/president-announces-choices-new-bioethics-commission (accessed 16 July 2010); J. H. Evans (2009) 'Obama's Bioethics Commission: Providing Practical Policy Outcomes', *Bioethics Forum*, 26, http://www.thehastingscenter.org/ Bioethicsforum/ Post.aspx?id=3630 (accessed 14 July 2010).

16. Jonsen, *Bioethics beyond the Headlines*, pp. 16-17.

17. Fox and Swazey, *Observing Bioethics*, p. 68, refer to earlier study programmes at Harvard.

18. As bioethics philosopher Judith Andre observed, with disarming frankness, scholars involved in bioethics tend to earn more money that their non-bioethics colleagues: asked by a colleague if her 25 years of bioethics had made the sick better off she records dryly that she didn't know, but that bioethicists certainly were. J. Andre (2002) *Bioethics as Practice* (Chapel Hill, NC: University of North Carolina Press), pp. 72–3.

19. Jonsen, *The Birth of Bioethics*, p. vii. See also Patricia Marshall's 1992 list of some of the US centres, P. A. Marshall (1992) 'Anthropology and Bioethics', *Medical Anthropology Quarterly*, New Series, 6, 1 (March), 49–73, p. 63.

20. http://bioethics.georgetown.edu/publications/biobib/bibintro.pdf (accessed 1 March 2011).

21. T. L. Beauchamp and J. F. Childress (2008) *Principles of Biomedical Ethics*, 6th edn (New York: Oxford University Press).

22. H. K. Beecher et al. (1968) 'A Definition of Irreversible Coma, Report of the Ad Hoc Committee of the Harvard Medical School to Examine the Definition of Brain Death', *Journal of the American Medical Association*, 5 August, 205: 337–40; Stevens, *Bioethics in America*, p. 104.

23. E. H. Courtiss (1977) 'Progress in Legal Definition of Brain Death and Consent to Remove Cadaver Organs', *Plastic and Reconstructive Surgery*, 60, 4, 660.

24. Office of Human Subjects Research (USA) (1979) *The Belmont Report: Ethical Principles and Guidelines for the Protection of Human Subjects of Research*, http://ohsr.od.nih.gov/guidelines/ belmont.html (accessed 12 July 2010).

25. D. Wilson (2011) 'Creating the "Ethics Industry": Mary Warnock, In Vitro Fertilization and the History of Bioethics in Britain', *BioSocieties*, 6, 2, 121–41.

26. Some influential legal figures have been: Michael Kirby; Loane Skene; Louis Waller; Gergoe Annas and Ian Kennedy.

27. G. E. Pence (1995) *Classic Cases in Medical Ethics: Accounts of Cases that Have Shaped Medical Ethics, with Philosophical, Legal, and Historical Backgrounds*, 2nd edn (New York: McGraw-Hill).

28. Jonsen, *Bioethics beyond the Headlines*, p. 19.

29. Boston Women's Health Book Collective (1973) *Our Bodies, Ourselves; A Book by and for Women* (New York: Simon and Schuster), back cover.

30. For current status of abortion laws worldwide, the Harvard School of Public Health provides a website: http://www.hsph.harvard.edu/population/abortion/abortionlaws.htm (accessed 6 May 2013). See also J. Keown (1988) *Abortion, Doctors, and the Law: Some Aspects of the Legal Regulation of Abortion in England from 1803 to 1982* (Cambridge: Cambridge University Press); N. Pfeffer (2000) 'The Reproductive Body' in R. Cooter and J. Pickstone (eds) *Medicine in the Twentieth Century* (Amsterdam: Harwood Academic), 277–90.

31. On INFAB, see H. B. Holmes and A. Donchin (2002) *History of the International Network on Feminist Approaches to Bioethics* (Pamphlet), Letras Livres, n.p. www.msu.edu/~hlinde/fab/history. pdf; www.plato.stanford. edu.

32. Exceptions were the works of Ramsey and Fletcher. Jonsen, *The Birth of Bioethics*, passim; see also S. E. Stumpf (1966) 'Some Moral Dimensions of Medicine', *Annals of Internal Medicine*, 64, 2, 460–70.

33. It could be that the involvement of philosophers in bioethics is a result of a kind of accident of etymology, for the 'ethics' of philosophers (a technical term with a long history of established procedures) is very different from the ethics of the medical fraternity (embodied in codes).

34. Jonsen, *Bioethics beyond the Headlines*, p. 185. See also D. W. Brock (1999) 'Truth or Consequences: The Role of Philosophers in Policy-making' in H. Kuhse and P. Singer (eds), *Bioethics: An Anthology* (Malden, MA: Blackwell), 587–90, which calls attention to the different goals of academics and policy makers (without privileging either).

35. S. Toulmin (1982) 'How Medicine Saved the Life of Ethics', *Perspectives in Biology and Medicine*, 25, 4, 736–50, p. 736. Italics in original.
36. Wilson, 'Creating the "Ethics Industry"', p. 125.
37. Toulmin, 'How Medicine Saved the Life of Ethics'. See also: H. Kuhse and P. Singer, 'Introduction', in *Bioethics: An Anthology* (Malden, MA: Blackwell), 1–7, pp. 1–2.
38. Quoted in Jonsen, *Bioethics beyond the Headlines*, p. 15.
39. M. B. Mahowald (1986) 'Biomedical Ethics: A Precocious Youth', in J. P. DeMarco and R. M. Fox (eds) *New Directions in Ethics: The Challenge of Applied Ethics* (New York: Routledge and Kegan Paul), 141–57, p. 152.
40. P. Borry, P. Schotsmans and K. Dierickx (2005) 'The Birth of the Empirical Turn in Bioethics', *Bioethics*, 19, 1, 49–71, p. 60.
41. Borry et al., 'The Birth of the Empirical Turn in Bioethics', pp. 63–4.
42. Quoted in Jonsen, *Bioethics beyond the Headlines*, p. 15.
43. Cf. 'Epilogue' in R. Fox (1998) *Experiment Perilous: Physicians and Patients Facing the Unknown*, with a new epilogue by the author (New Brunswick, NJ: Transaction), p. 282.
44. This line of thinking drew on the Nuremberg Code devised in 1947 following the Nazi medical abuses. See Chapter 5. It is worth pausing on the idea of 'interested citizens'. At that time, the idea of an interested citizen could be referred to in good faith without assuming they held an *a priori* political standpoint. There are still community consultations now, but it's perhaps true to say that more citizens in the 1970s and 1980s had an overall interest in the public and political resolution of medical ethics issues.
45. The National Commission for the Protection of Human Subjects of Biomedical and Behavioral Research (1979) *The Belmont Report: Ethical Principles and Guidelines for the Protection of Human Subjects of Research* (Washington: United States Department of Health, Education, and Welfare).
46. S. Toulmin (1981) 'The Tyranny of Principles', *Hastings Center Report*, 11, 6, 31–9.
47. Jonsen, *Bioethics beyond the Headlines*, p. 21.
48. Kuhse and Singer 'Introduction'. Robert Sparrow notes: 'Utilitarianism, historically the most important form of consequentialism, originated as a radical philosophy dedicated to social reform. Many of the early utilitarians struggled for social and political change, believing that the greatest happiness of the greatest number could be achieved only by redistributing wealth and that the state was sometimes the only available mechanism to help us achieve important social goals.' R. Sparrow (2010) 'A Not-So-New Eugenics: Harris and Savulescu on Human Enhancement', *Hastings Center Report*, 41, 1, 32–42, p. 36.
49. K. D. Clouser and B. Gert (1990) 'A Critique of Principlism', *Journal of Medicine and Philosophy*, 15, 2, 219–36, p. 230; Jonsen, *The Birth of Bioethics*, p. 329.
50. Toulmin, 'The Tyranny of Principles', p. 38.

51. It is a tradition much favoured in the Jesuit order which has at times been represented as a way to retreat from moral judgement altogether.

52. Clouser and Gert, 'A Critique of Principlism'.

53. Clouser and Gert, 'A Critique of Principlism', p. 221.

54. Clouser and Gert, 'A Critique of Principlism', p. 233.

55. E. R. DuBose, R. P. Hamel and L. J. O'Connell (1994) *A Matter of Principles? Ferment in US Bioethics* (Valley Forge, PA: Trinity Press International), Introduction, p. 3. See also J. H. Evans (2000) 'A Sociological Account of the Growth of Principlism', *The Hastings Center Report*, 30, 5, 31–8.

56. Callahan, 'Principlism and Communitarianism', p. 288.

57. 'Communitarianism' in *Stanford Encyclopedia of Philosophy*, http://plato.stanford.edu/ entries/communitarianism/ (accessed 11 May 2013).

58. D. Callahan (2003) *What Price Better Health? Hazards of the Research Imperative* (Berkeley, CA: University of California Press).

59. Fox and Swazey note that critiques of the disciplinary makeup of bioethics had appeared in the *Hastings Center Report* in 1981 and 1982. R. C. Fox and J. P. Swazey (1984) 'Medical Morality Is *Not* Bioethics: Medical Ethics in China and the United States', *Perspectives in Biology and Medicine*, 27, 3, 336–60.

60. Borry et al., 'The Birth of the Empirical Turn in Bioethics', pp. 56–7.

61. Borry et al., 'The Birth of the Empirical Turn in Bioethics', p. 60.

62. Fox and Swazey, 'Medical Morality Is *Not* Bioethics', p. 337 (italics in the original).

63. Fox and Swazey, *Observing Bioethics*, p. 205.

64. G. Weisz, 'Introduction' in G. Weisz (ed.) (1990) *Social Science Perspectives on Medical Ethics* (Dordrecht: Kluwer Academic) 3–15, p. 3.

65. Orfali and DeVries, 'A Sociological Gaze on Bioethics', p. 500 (emphasis in original.)

66. Borry et al., 'The Birth of the Empirical Turn in Bioethics', p. 60, refer to the influence of David Hume's *Treatise of Human Nature* (1740) in relation to this distinction; see also Kuhse and Singer, 'Introduction', pp. 1–7.

67. Fox and Swazey, 'Medical Morality Is *Not* Bioethics', p. 337.

68. Fox and Swazey, 'Medical Morality Is *Not* Bioethics', p. 339.

69. Mahowald, 'Biomedical Ethics', p. 152.

70. B. Jennings (1986) 'Applied Ethics and the Vocation of Social Science', in DeMarco and Fox (eds), *New Directions in Ethics,* pp. 205–17, p. 207.

71. Jennings, 'Applied Ethics and the Vocation of Social Science', p. 206. See the early commentary of T. H. Murray, (1982) 'Medical Ethics, Moral Philosophy and Moral Tradition', *Social Science and Medicine*, 25, 6, 637–44.

72. Weisz, *Social Science Perspectives on Medical Ethics*, p. 4.

73. Orfali and DeVries, 'A Sociological Gaze on Bioethics', p. 499.

74. See M. J. Selgelid and M. P. Battin (2005) 'From the Guest Editors', *Bioethics*, 19, 4, iii–vii; A. Dawson (2010) 'The Future of Bioethics: Three Dogmas and a Cup of Hemlock', *Bioethics*, 24, 5, 218–25. Thanks to Elli Storey for this

reference. P. M. McNeill, R. Macklin, A. Wasunna and P. A. Komesaroff (2005) 'An Expanding Vista: Bioethics from Public Health, Indigenous and Feminist Perspectives, *Medical Journal of Australia*, 183, 1, 8–9.

75. See, for example, A. Hedgecoe (2010) 'Bioethics and the Reinforcement of Socio-technical Expectations', *Social Studies of Science*, 40, 2, 163–86; U. Schüklenk (2006) 'Editorial: Ethics In Bioethics', *Bioethics* 20, 5, iii.

76. C. E. Rosenberg (1999) 'Meanings, Policies, and Medicine: On the Bioethical Enterprise and History', *Daedalus*, 128, 4, 27–46; R. Cooter (2010) 'Inside the Whale: Bioethics in History and Discourse', *Social History of Medicine*, 23, 3, 662–72. See also Cooter's lively exchange with bioethics commentator Arthur Caplan in *The Lancet*: R. Cooter (2004) 'Historical Keywords: Bioethics', *The Lancet*, 364, 9447, 1749; A. Caplan (2005) 'Reports of Bioethics' Demise are Premature' (letter), *The Lancet*, 365, 9460, 654–5.

77. T. Koch (2012) *Thieves of Virtue: When Bioethics Stole Medicine* (Cambridge, MA: MIT Press).

78. L. A. Eckenwiler and F. G. Cohn (eds) (2007) *The Ethics of Bioethics: Mapping the Moral Landscape* (Baltimore, MD: Johns Hopkins University Press).

## Chapter 2

1. H. L. Nelson (1997) 'Introduction: How to Do Things with Stories', in H. L. Nelson (ed.) *Stories and their Limits: Narrative Approaches to Bioethics* (New York: Routledge), viii–xx, p. xv. Thanks are due to Frances Cruickshank for encouraging my focus on language bioethics.

2. Nelson, 'Introduction', p. xii.

3. Nelson (ed.), *Stories and their Limits*; R. Charon and M. Montello (2002) 'Introduction: Memory and Anticipation: The Practice of Narrative Ethics' in R. Charon and M. Montello (eds) *Stories Matter: The Role of Narrative in Medical Ethics* (New York: Routledge), x–xiv; A. W. Frank (1995) *The Wounded Storyteller: Body, Illness and Ethics* (Chicago: University of Chicago Press).

4. N. L. Sunderland (2004) 'Biotechnology as Media: A Critical Study of the Movement of Meanings Associated with Contemporary Biotechnology', Doctoral dissertation, Queensland University of Technology, Brisbane, p. 263.

5. S. M. Squier (2004) *Liminal Lives: Imagining the Human at the Frontiers of Biomedicine* (Durham, NC: Duke University Press), p. 19. See also: C. Waldby (2000) *The Visible Human Project: Informative bodies and posthuman medicine* (London; New York: Routledge).

6. Fleck paraphrased by Bonah in C. Bonah (2002) '"Experimental Rage": The Development of Medical Ethics and the Genesis of Scientific Facts. Ludwik Fleck: An Answer to the Crisis of Modern Medicine in Interwar Germany? Society for the Social History of Medicine Millennium Prize 2000', *Social History of Medicine*, 15, 2, 187–207, p. 205.

7. Bonah, '"Experimental Rage"', p. 193.
8. Cf. Segal's useful glossary of terms for approaching the rhetorical aspects of medical discourse. J. Z. Segal (1993) 'Strategies of Influence in Medical Authorship', *Social Science and Medicine*, 37, 4, 521–30, p. 530.
9. C. E. Rosenberg and J. Golden (eds) (1992) *Framing Disease: Studies in Cultural History* (New Brunswick, NJ: Rutgers University Press); B. Latour (author), A. Sheridan and J. Law (trans.) (1988) *The Pasteurization of France* (Cambridge, MA: Harvard University Press), pp. 38–40.
10. A. Preda (2005) *AIDS, Rhetoric, and Medical Knowledge* (Cambridge: Cambridge University Press), p. 5.
11. See: N. Oudshoorn (1994) *Beyond the Natural Body: An Archaeology of Sex Hormones* (London: Routledge); B. Latour and S. Woolgar (1986) *Laboratory Life: The Construction of Scientific Facts* (Princeton, NJ: Princeton University Press).
12. E. Martin (1989) *The Woman in the Body: A Cultural Analysis of Reproduction* (Milton Keynes: Open University Press); Preda, *AIDS, Rhetoric, and Medical Knowledge*; J. van Dyck (1995) *Manufacturing Babies and Public Consent: Debating the New Reproductive Technologies* (New York: New York University Press).
13. R. C. Fox and J. P. Swazey (1992) *Spare Parts: Organ Replacement in American Society* (New York: Oxford University Press).
14. C. Crowe (1990) 'Whose Mind over Whose Matter?' in M. McNeil, I. Varcoe and S. Yearley (eds) *The New Reproductive Technologies* (London: Macmillan), 27–57, p. 45.
15. http://www.progress.org.uk/ (accessed 9 January 2013).
16. M. Mulkay (1994) 'The Triumph of the Pre-Embryo: Interpretations of the Human Embryo in Parliamentary Debate over Embryo Research', *Social Studies of Science*, 24, 4, 611–39, p. 613.
17. Crowe, 'Whose Mind over Whose Matter?', p. 48.
18. Crowe 'Whose Mind over Whose Matter?', p. 49; Mulkay, 'The Triumph of the Pre-Embryo'.
19. Crowe, 'Whose Mind over Whose Matter?', p. 27.
20. K. A. Richman (2004) *Ethics and the Metaphysics of Medicine: Reflections on Health and Beneficence* (Cambridge, MA: MIT Press), p. 157.
21. R. A. Aronowitz (2006) 'Situating Health Risks: An Opportunity for Disease-prevention Policy', in Stevens et al. (eds) *History and Health Policy in the United States*, 153–75, p. 171.
22. Aronowitz, 'Situating Health Risks', p. 171. Knowledge of the effects of these therapies has become more nuanced in the wake of important recent follow-up studies. See, for example, 'Updated IMS Recommendations on Postmenopausal Hormone Therapy and Preventive Strategies for Midlife Health' at International Menopause Society, http://www.imsociety.org, and the Australian government website 'Menopause – Hormone Replacement Therapy', http://www. betterhealth.vic.gov.au (both accessed 8 January 2013).

23. G. Orwell (1976) 'Politics and the English Language' in *Inside the Whale and Other Essays* (Harmondsworth: Penguin), p. 156.

24. Segal, 'Strategies of Influence in Medical Authorship', p. 530.

25. Segal, 'Strategies of Influence in Medical Authorship', p. 530.

26. Mintz has also argued that use of the passive voice in medical language can have an alienating effect, contributing to the sense of distance between medical providers and clients. D. Mintz (1992) 'What's in a Word: The Distancing Function of Language in Medicine', *Journal of Medical Humanities*, 13, 4, 223–33, p. 224.

27. N. L. Stepan (1986) 'Race and Gender: The Role of Analogy in Science', *Isis*, 77, 2, 261–77, p. 275.

28. Quoted in Stepan, 'Race and Gender', p. 271.

29. P. Geddes and J. A. Thomson (1889) *The Evolution of Sex* (London: Walter Scott) digitized full text, http://www.archive.org/stream/ evolutionsex01 geddgoog/evolutionsex01geddgoog_djvu.txt (accessed 29 July 2010).

30. See P. Weindling (1989) *Health, Race, and German Politics between National Unification and Nazism, 1870–1945* (Cambridge: Cambridge University Press), passim.

31. M. S. Lubinsky (1993–94) 'Degenerate Heredity: The History of a Doctrine in Medicine and Biology', *Perspectives in Biology and Medicine*, 37, 1, 74–90, p. 86.

32. G. V. O'Brien (1999), 'Protecting the Social Body: Use of the Organism Metaphor in Fighting the "Menace of the Feebleminded"', *Mental Retardation*, 37, 3, 188–200, p. 189; P. Weindling (1998) 'Dissecting German Social Darwinism: Historicizing the Biology of the Organic State' in R. Falk, D. B. Paul and G. Allen (eds) *Eugenic Thought and Practice: A Reappraisal*, Special Double Issue, *Science in Context*, 11, 3–4, 619–37.

33. R. A. Nye (1989) 'Sex Difference and Male Homosexuality in French Medical Discourses, 1830–1930', *Bulletin of the History of Medicine*, 63, 1, 32–51.

34. Quoted in O'Brien, 'Protecting the Social Body', p. 191.

35. O'Brien, 'Protecting the Social Body', p. 193.

36. J. P. Warbasse (1935) *The Doctor and the Public: A Study of the Sociology, Economics, Ethics, and Philosophy of Medicine, Based on Medical History* (New York: P. B. Hoeber), p. 415.

37. Warbasse, *The Doctor and the Public*, p. 415.

38. M. D. Lemonick (1997) '"It's a Miracle"', *Time*, 1 December, 150, 23.

39. S. Woodard (2006) 'A Septuplet Celebration: The Septuplets at 9', *Ladies' Home Journal*, 123, 12, 102–14.

40. Anon. (1975) 'Fertility Drugs: A Mixed Blessing', *Time*, 19 May, 105, 21, p. 48; C. Gemzell (1965) 'The Multiple-Birth Hormone', *Time*, 86, 6, p. 66.

41. The story of so-called single 'Octomom' is instructive: instantly condemned in the blogosphere, this case led to the US Fertility Society requiring that members replace a maximum number of four embryos. L. Carroll (2009) 'Too Many Babies: What Went Wrong? Birth of Octuplets Is Not a "Medical

Triumph," Caution Fertility Experts', *msnbc.com*, 29 January, http://www.msnbc.msn.com/id/28902137/ns/health-womens_health/ (accessed 14 February 2010).

42. See also P. Jasen (2009), 'From the "Silent Killer" to the "Whispering Disease": Ovarian Cancer and the Uses of Metaphor', *Medical History*, 53, 4, 489–512.

43. L. E. Kay (2000) *Who Wrote the Book of Life? A History of the Genetic Code* (Stanford, CA: Stanford University Press), pp. 326, 327–8.

44. Kay, *Who Wrote the Book of Life?*, p. 328.

45. Kay, *Who Wrote the Book of Life?*, p. 26.

46. Squier, *Liminal Lives*, p. 17.

47. Preda, *AIDS, Rhetoric, and Medical Knowledge*, p. 5. See also D. Lupton (1994) *Medicine as Culture: Illness, Disease and the Body in Western Societies* (London: Sage Publications); S. Sontag (1991) *Illness as Metaphor; and, AIDS and its Metaphors* (London: Penguin).

48. Preda, *AIDS, Rhetoric, and Medical Knowledge*, p. 246.

49. Preda, *AIDS, Rhetoric, and Medical Knowledge*, pp. 231–2.

50. T. Chambers (2001) '*The Fiction of Bioethics*: A Précis', *American Journal of Bioethics*, 1, 1, 40–3, p. 43. See also T. Chambers (1997) 'What to Expect from an Ethics Case (and What it Expects from You)', in Nelson (ed.) *Stories and their Limits*, 171–84.

51. T. Chambers (1999) *The Fiction of Bioethics: Cases as Literary Texts* (New York: Routledge), p. 21.

52. Chambers, *The Fiction of Bioethics*, p. 175.

53. Chambers, *The Fiction of Bioethics*, p. 37.

54. Chambers, *The Fiction of Bioethics*, p. 146.

55. Chambers, *The Fiction of Bioethics*, pp. 177–8.

56. Chambers, *The Fiction of Bioethics*, p. 177.

57. Chambers, *The Fiction of Bioethics*, p. 177.

58. Chambers, *The Fiction of Bioethics*, p. 183.

## Chapter 3

1. The full text of the original bill may be found at: http://www.gpo.gov/fdsys/pkg/BILLS-111hr3200ih/pdf/BILLS-111hr3200ih.pdf (accessed 30 April 2013).

2. M. Burleigh (1994) *Death and Deliverance: 'Euthanasia' in Germany c. 1900–1945* (Cambridge: Cambridge University Press), p. 173.

3. Anon. (2008) 'Editorial: No "Final Solution," but a Way Forward', *Washington Times*, 23 November, http://www.washingtontimes.com/news/2008/nov/23/no-final-solution-but-a-way-forward/ (accessed 31 January 2010).

4. http://www.facebook.com/note.php?note_id=113851103434 (accessed 30 April 2013). Palin did not use the word 'Nazi' and did not refer to Aktion

T4, but her word choice – using both key terms in inverted commas – evoked both the panels who looked at documents only, to decide the fate of the euthanasia programme's victims and the Nazi policy's justification on economic grounds.

5. F. Beckett (2009) 'Vested Interests Hate Good Healthcare', *The Guardian*, 24 August, http://www.guardian.co.uk/commentisfree/2009/aug/24/health-care-nhs-nazi-americans-health (accessed 31 January 2010).

6. N. Hentoff, D. Callahan, G. Crum and C. Cohen (1988) 'Contested Terrain: The Nazi Analogy in Bioethics', *The Hastings Center Report*, 18, 4, 29–33.

7. R. Klitzman (2010) 'Death Panels, Dignity, and You', *Huffington Post*, 25 April, http://www.huffingtonpost.com/robert-klitzman-md/death-panels-or-dignity-a_b_551265.html (accessed 31 October 2010).

8. W. R. Lafleur (2007) 'Refusing Utopia's Bait: Research, Rationalizations, and Hans Jonas' in W. R. Lafleur, G. Böhme and S. Shimazono (eds) *Dark Medicine: Rationalizing Unethical Medical Research* (Bloomington, IN: Indiana University Press, 2007), 233–46, p. 233.

9. M. Burleigh (1997) *Ethics and Extermination: Reflections on Nazi Genocide* (New York: Cambridge University Press), p. 142.

10. Burleigh, *Death and Deliverance*; M. Burleigh (1991) 'Racism as Social Policy: The Nazi "Euthanasia" Programme, 1939–1945', *Ethnic and Racial Studies*, 14, 4, 453–73.

11. F. Lebowitz (1997) 'Fran Lebowitz on Race', *Vanity Fair*, 446, October, p. 220.

12. The Hastings Center Report devoted two special issues to forums debating the use of the analogy. A. Caplan (1989) 'The Meaning of the Holocaust for Bioethics', *The Hastings Center Report*, 19, 4, 2–3; Hentoff et al., 'Contested Terrain'.

13. M. Somerville (2001) *Death Talk: The Case against Euthanasia and Physician-Assisted Suicide* (Montreal: McGill-Queen's University Press), p. 103.

14. Associated Press (2006) 'A Timeline of Dr. Jack Kevorkian's Assisted-Suicide Campaign', *Associated Press Newswires*, 14 December; K. B. Hoffman (2006) 'Assisted Suicide Advocate Jack Kevorkian to be Paroled in June', *Associated Press Newswires*, 14 December.

15. F. Godlee (2012) 'Assisted Dying', *British Medical Journal*, International edition, 344, 7861, p. 10; B. D. Onwuteaka-Philipsen, A. Brinkman-Stoppelenburg, C. Penning, G. J. F. de Jong-Krul, J. J. M. van Delden and A. van der Heide (2012) 'Trends in End-of-life Practices Before and After the Enactment of the Euthanasia Law in the Netherlands from 1990 to 2010: A Repeated Cross-sectional Survey', *The Lancet*, 380, 9845, 908–15; J. Rietjens, P. J. van der Maas, B. D. Onwuteaka-Philipsen, J. J. M. van Delden and A. van der Heide (2009) 'Two Decades of Research on Euthanasia from the Netherlands: What Have We Learnt and What Questions Remain?', *Journal of Bioethical Inquiry*, 6, 3, 271–83, p. 278.

16. Rietjens et al., 'Two Decades of Research on Euthanasia from the Netherlands', p. 281. Bagaric and Amarasekara refer also to: Law Reform

Commission of Canada 1982; Social Development Committee of the Parliament of Victoria (Australia) 1987; House of Lords Select Committee on Medical Ethics (1994); New York Task Force on Life and the Law (1994); Special Committee on Assisted Suicide and Euthanasia of the Senate of Canada (1995); Senate Legal and Constitutional Legislation Committee (1997), M. Bagaric and K. Amarasekara (2002) 'Euthanasia: Why it Doesn't Matter (Much) What the Doctor Thinks and Why There Is No Suggestion that Doctors Should Have a Duty to Kill', *Journal of Law and Medicine*, 10, 2, 221–31, p. 225. A yougov.co.uk poll in 2013 showed that a majority of people in the UK supported in different degree, physician-assisted suicide and euthanasia. http://yougov.co.uk/news/2010/03/05/majority-would-support-more-compassionate-euthana/ (accessed 4 May 2013).

17. S. Parnell (2013) 'Customs Curbs Suicide Imports', *The Australian*, 11 March, p. 3; T. Cardy (2012) 'Doctor to Test Deadly Drugs', *The Sunday Times* (Perth, WA), 22 January, p. 41; R. Huxtable (2009) 'The Suicide Tourist Trap: Compromise across Boundaries', *Journal of Bioethical Inquiry*, 6, 3, 327–36.

18. M. Burleigh (1994) 'Psychiatry, German Society, and the Nazi Euthanasia Programme', *Social History of Medicine*, 7, 2, 213–28, p. 215; also Burleigh, 'Racism as Social Policy', p. 460.

19. L. Alexander (1949) 'Medical Science under Dictatorship', *New England Journal of Medicine*, 241, 39–47, p. 39; Burleigh, 'Racism as Social Policy', pp. 462–3.

20. Burleigh, 'Psychiatry, German Society, and the Nazi Euthanasia Programme', pp. 219–20.

21. This paragraph paraphrases Burleigh, 'Racism as Social Policy', pp. 453–4.

22. Burleigh, 'Racism as Social Policy', p. 454; see also V. Roelcke, G. Hohendorf and M. Rotzoll (1994) 'Psychiatric Research and "Euthanasia": The Case of the Psychiatric Department at the University of Heidelberg, 1941–1945', *History of Psychiatry*, 5, 20, 517–32.

23. Burleigh, 'Racism as Social Policy', p. 456.

24. Burleigh, 'Racism as Social Policy', pp. 457–8.

25. Alexander, 'Medical Science under Dictatorship', p. 46.

26. Alexander, 'Medical Science under Dictatorship', p. 44.

27. Alexander, 'Medical Science under Dictatorship', p. 44.

28. See also: I. Dowbiggin (2003) *A Merciful End: The Euthanasia Movement in Modern America* (Oxford: Oxford University Press); N. D. A. Kemp (2002) *Merciful Release: The History of the British Euthanasia Movement* (Manchester: Manchester University Press).

29. Alexander, 'Medical Science under Dictatorship', p. 45.

30. http://public.health.oregon.gov/ProviderPartnerResources/Evaluation Research/DeathwithDignityAct/Documents/history.pdf (accessed 30 April 2013).

31. Northern Territory of Australia, *Rights of the Terminally Ill Act, 1995*, http://www.nt.gov.au/lant/parliamentary-business/committees/rotti/rotti95.pdf (accessed 26 November 2012).

32. ABC (2011) 'Nitschke Detained Carrying Replica Death Machine', *ABC News Online*, 15 February, http://www.abc.net.au/news/stories/2011/02/15/3139691.htm (accessed 25 February 2011).

33. M. Grattan (1996) 'Surrealism of Death by Computer', *Australian Financial Review*, 30 September, p. 15.

34. M. Ceresa and G. Windsor (1997) 'Euthanasia Awaits Death Sentence', *Australian*, 25 March, 1.

35. This, in turn, implicitly meant overturning, or at least overlooking, his own party's traditional deference to the doctrine of states' rights, bearing in mind that the Northern Territory was not technically a state.

36. M. Gordon (1997) 'Holy Alliance: The Inside Story of Euthanasia's Demise', *Australian*, 29 March, p. 19.

37. Gordon, 'Holy Alliance', p. 19. See also M. Maddox (1999) 'For God and States' Rights: Euthanasia and the Senate', *Legislative Studies*, 14, 1, 51–61.

38. N. Savva (1997) 'The God Squad', *The Age*, 2 April, p. 11; M. Grattan (2004) 'A Quiet Man's Revolution', *The Age*, 13 November (online).

39. G. Windsor and D. Shanahan (1997) 'Stone Accuses Secret Forum', *The Australian*, 26 March, 2.

40. Schedule 1 – Amendment of the Northern Territory (Self-Government) Act 1978, *Euthanasia Laws Act 1997* (Cth), No. 17, 1997.

41. G. Dodd (1997) 'Euthanasia: Senate More Representative than House' (letter-to-editor), *Canberra Times*, 4 April; J. Brough (1997) 'The Last Rights', *Sydney Morning Herald*, 29 March (online).

42. Ceresa and Windsor, 'Euthanasia Awaits Death Sentence', p. 1.

43. J. Brough (1996) 'New Lib Group Takes on the Lyons', *Sydney Morning Herald*, 10 October, p. 2.

44. K. Davidson (1997) 'New Bill Will Bury, Not Kill, Euthanasia', *The Age*, 20 March, 17.

45. Alexander, 'Medical Science under Dictatorship', p. 45.

46. Right to Die-NL (2009–2012) 'Jurisprudence', http://www.nvve.nl/nvve-english/ pagina.asp?pagkey=72086 (accessed 19 January 2013).

47. J. Legemaate (2004) 'The Dutch Euthanasia Act and Related Issues', *Journal of Law and Medicine*, 11, 3, 312–23, p. 312. See also Rietjens et al., 'Two Decades of Research on Euthanasia from the Netherlands', p. 272.

48. Legemaate, 'The Dutch Euthanasia Act and Related Issues', p. 312. Right to Die-NL (2009-2012) 'Jurisprudence'.

49. http://www.nvve.nl/nvve-english/pagina.asp?pagkey=72086 (accessed 2 May 2013).

50. Legemaate, 'The Dutch Euthanasia Act and Related Issues', p. 313. The Dutch 'Cry for Life' group claims membership of around 100,000, http://www.internationalrighttolife.com /pages/03als4.html (accessed 4 May 2013); the Dutch Right to Die group http:// www.nvve.nl/nvve-english/pagina.asp?pagnaam=homepage claims membership of 140,000

(accessed 4 May 2013). The latter sponsors the mobile euthanasia units at which the Dutch medical profession itself draws the line. A. Holligan (2012) 'Dutch Offered "Euthanasia on Wheels"', *BBC News*, online, 3 March.

51. Rietjens et al., 'Two Decades of Research on Euthanasia from the Netherlands', pp. 273–4.
52. Legemaate, 'The Dutch Euthanasia Act and Related Issues', p. 314.
53. Legemaate, 'The Dutch Euthanasia Act and Related Issues', p. 314.
54. A. van der Heide, B. D. Onwuteaka-Philipsen, M. L. Rurup, H. M. Buiting, J. E. Hanssen-de Wolf and I. M. Deerenberg (2007) 'End-of-Life Practices in the Netherlands under the Euthanasia Act', *New England Journal of Medicine*, 356, 19, 1957–65; Rietjens et al., 'Two Decades of Research on Euthanasia from the Netherlands'; Regional Euthanasia Review Committees (2010) *Annual Report* (online), The Hague.
55  Rietjens et al., 'Two Decades of Research on Euthanasia from the Netherlands', p. 276; Onwuteaka-Philipsen et al., 'Trends in End-of-life Practices', p. 913. See also J. F. M. Kerkhof (2004) 'End-of-Life Decisions in The Netherlands, 1990–2001', *Crisis*, 25, 3, 97–8. My thanks are due to Dr Judith Rietjens for explaining to me in greater detail the sampling methods used in the 2009 *JBI* article.
56. K. Amarasekara and M. Bagaric (2001) 'The Legalisation of Euthanasia in the Netherlands: Lessons to be Learnt', *Monash University Law Review*, 27, 2, 179–96, p. 189 and p. 192.
57. Regional Euthanasia Review Committees (2010) *Annual Report* (online), The Hague, p. 3.
58. G. van der Wal (1993) 'Unrequested Termination of Life: Is it Permissible?', *Bioethics*, 7, 4, 330–9, p. 330.
59. Rietjens et al., 'Two Decades of Research on Euthanasia from the Netherlands'; Legemaate, 'The Dutch Euthanasia Act and Related Issues', p. 315.
60. K. Thynne (2002) 'Implications of Legalising Euthanasia in the Netherlands: Greater Regulatory Control?', *Journal of Law and Medicine*, 10, 2, 232–8.
61. Rietjens et al., 'Two Decades of Research on Euthanasia from the Netherlands', p. 279.
62. Rietjens et al., 'Two Decades of Research on Euthanasia from the Netherlands', p. 281.
63. I. Kerridge, P. A. Komesaroff, M. Parker and E. Peter (2009) 'New Perspectives on the End of Life', *Journal of Bioethical Inquiry*, 6, 3, 269–70, p. 270.
64. Rietjens et al., 'Two Decades of Research on Euthanasia from the Netherlands', p. 276; Onwuteaka-Philipsen et al., 'Trends in End-of-life Practices', p. 913.
65. Onwuteaka-Philipsen et al., 'Trends in End-of-life Practices', p. 913.
66. T. Sheldon (2003) 'Being "Tired of Life" Is Not Grounds for Euthanasia', *British Medical Journal*, 326, 7380, 71.
67. Sheldon, 'Being "Tired of Life" Is Not Grounds for Euthanasia', p. 71. See

discussion in Rietjens et al., 'Two Decades of Research on Euthanasia from the Netherlands', p. 280.

68. E. Verhagen and P. J. J. Sauer (2005) 'The Groningen Protocol – Euthanasia in Severely Ill Newborns', *New England Journal of Medicine*, 352, 10, 959–62.

69. Verhagen and Sauer, 'The Groningen Protocol – Euthanasia in Severely Ill Newborns', p. 961.

70. Verhagen and Sauer, 'The Groningen Protocol – Euthanasia in Severely Ill Newborns'.

71. S. Moratti (2010) 'End-of-life Decisions in Dutch Neonatology', *Medical Law Review*, 18, 4, 471–96, p. 488.

72. The Dutch government website is: http://www.government.nl/issues/ euthanasia/ euthanasia-and-newborn-infants (accessed 26 November 2012). The sentence which refers to discontinuing treatment introduces a slight ambiguity. Discontinuing treatment is only the first step in the process, as the rest of the text points directly to active ending of life. One legal commentator argues that there is no ethical difference between the two. However, Dutch euthanasia law does observe a difference. It is also some-what ironic that someone promoting the legality of deliberate ending of life should adopt the same sliding logic that alarmist opponents use: that there is no ethical difference between the intermediate actions such as removal of life support and provision of potentially lethal pain relief and deliberate ending of life. For legal commentary, see Moratti, 'End-of-life Decisions in Dutch Neonatology'.

73. A. A. Verhagen, J. J. Sol, O. F. Brouwer and P. J. Sauer (2005) 'Deliberate Termination of Life in Newborns in the Netherlands: Review of all 22 Reported Cases between 1997 and 2004', (English abstract), *Nederlands Tijdschrift voor Geneeskunde*, 22, 149, 4, 183–8, p. 183.

74. Verhagen et al., 'Deliberate Termination of Life in Newborns in the Netherlands', p. 183.

75. Verhagen and Sauer, 'The Groningen Protocol – Euthanasia in Severely Ill Newborns', p. 960.

76. Moratti, 'End-of-life Decisions in Dutch Neonatology', p. 485.

77. D. Callahan (2008) 'Letter', *The Hastings Center Report*, 38, 4, 5–6.

78. Thus, not unlike the Harvard University Brain Death Committee which gave its recommendations to the *NEJM*, an article in a medical journal has formalized for clinicians the parameters of a practice which they expect should not be subject to prosecution.

79. H. Kuhse and P. Singer (1994) *Should the Baby Live? The Problem of Handicapped Infants* (Aldershot: Gregg Revivals); Cf. I. Studdard (director/producer) and A. Taft (producer) (1997) *A Peaceful Exit* (video-recording) (Sydney: SBS), broadcast 11 March 1997.

80. Kuhse's and Singer's argument reads like a proverbial Sunday picnic by comparison with the widely condemned article of 2012, from the *Journal of Medical Ethics*: A. Giubilini and F. Minerva (2012) 'After-birth Abortion:

Why Should the Baby Live?', *Journal of Medical Ethics,* medethics-2011-100411, online publication, 23 February. The authors argue that newborns whether sick or not could, morally, be killed if their mothers did not want them. The article can also be read as a veiled threat to women's access to abortion.

81. P. Singer (1991) 'On Being Silenced in Germany', *New York Review of Books,* 38, 14, 15 August, http://www.nybooks.com/articles/3186 (accessed 3 December 2012). It is perhaps an irony that Singer was able to complain of his lack of free speech through such a high-profile paper.

82. Singer's appointment to a chair at Princeton in 1999 also met with a hostile response. T. Gill (1999) 'Euthanizing Academic Liberty: Firebrand Bioethicist Peter Singer Adds Little Diversity to Already Liberal Faculty', *Princeton Spectator,* http://www.princeton.edu/~spectatr/vol5/30sept99/p3.html (accessed 20 April 2005).

83. R. Pear (2010), 'Obama Returns to End-of-Life Plan that Caused Stir', *New York Times,* 25 December; R. Pear (2011) 'U.S. Alters Rule on Paying for End-of-Life Planning', *New York Times,* 4 January.

## Chapter 4

1. M. Rothstein (2003) 'Keeping Your Genes Private', *Scientific American,* 299, 3, 64–9. A listing of US laws state by state may be found at: National Council of State Legislatures, Genetic Privacy Laws, http://www.ncsl.org/default.aspx?tabid=14287 (accessed 28 February 2011).

2. D. J. Kevles (1995) *In the Name of Eugenics: Genetics and the Uses of Human Heredity* (Cambridge, MA: Harvard University Press), pp. 12, 57.

3. Kevles, *In the Name of Eugenics,* p. 73.

4. V. L. Hilts (1982) 'Obeying the Laws of Hereditary Descent: Phrenological Views on Inheritance and Eugenics', *Journal of the History of the Behavioural Sciences,* 18, 1, 62–77; A. Bashford and P. Levine (eds) (2010) *The Oxford Handbook of the History of Eugenics* (Oxford: Oxford University Press), passim.

5. From J. G. Spurzheim (1821) *A View of the Elementary Principles of Education: Founded on the Study of the Nature of Man* (Edinburgh), p. 74, cited in Hilts 'Obeying the Laws', pp. 65–6.

6. Hilts, 'Obeying the Laws', pp. 67–8.

7. Kevles, *In the Name of Eugenics,* p. 7. The term 'evolution' itself was not used until the 1872 edition of the book. Herbert Spencer is credited with this neologism. See H. G. Wells' contribution in the 1904 debate with Galton at 'Eugenics: Its Definition, Scope, and Aims', http://galton.org/essays/1900-1911/galton-1904-am-journ-soc-eugenics-scope-aims.htm (accessed 10 November 2012).

8. Kevles, *In the Name of Eugenics,* p. 12.

9. D. B. Paul and J. Moore (2010) 'The Darwinian Context', in A. Bashford and

P. Levine (eds) *The Oxford Handbook of the History of Eugenics* (Oxford: Oxford University Press), 27–42, p. 36.

10. F. Galton (1869) *Hereditary Genius: An Enquiry into its Laws and Consequence* (London: Macmillan), full text online at http://galton.org.

11. R. S. Cowan (2008) *Heredity and Hope: The Case for Genetic Screening* (Cambridge, MA: Harvard University Press), p. 14.

12. D. Thom and M. Jennings (1996) 'Human Pedigree and the "Best Stock": From Eugenics to Genetics?', in T. Marteau and M. Richards (eds) *The Troubled Helix: Social and Psychological Implications of the New Human Genetics* (Cambridge: Cambridge University Press), 211–34, p. 212.

13. Francis Galton (1869) *Hereditary Genius: An Enquiry into its Laws and Consequence* (London: Macmillan), http://galton.org/cgi-bin/searchImages/search/pearson/vol2/pages/vol2_0108. htm (accessed 11 November 2012).

14. Galton et al., 'Eugenics: Its Definition, Scope, and Aims'.

15. Eugenic physician C. W. Saleeby coined the terms, and noted that Galton approved of them. C. W. Saleeby (1909) *Parenthood and Race Culture* (London: Cassell), p. 172. See also Paul and Moore, 'The Darwinian Context', p. 36 on positive eugenics.

16. K. Pearson (ed.) (1930) *The Life, Letters and Labours of Francis Galton*, Vol 3A: image 0402, at http://galton.org (accessed 14 November 2012).

17. Galton et al., 'Eugenics: Its Definition, Scope, and Aims'.

18. G. R. Searle (1976) *Eugenics and Politics in Britain, 1900–1914* (Leyden: Noordhoff), p. 9.

19. Kevles, *In the Name of Eugenics*, p. 73; Paul and Moore, 'The Darwinian Context', p. 38.

20. Thom and Jennings, 'Human Pedigree', p. 215.

21. Cold Spring Harbor website, http://www.cshl.edu/About-Us/History (accessed 4 May 2013); C. E. Rosenberg (1997) 'Charles Benedict Davenport and the Irony of American Eugenics', in his *No Other Gods: On Science and American Social Thought* (Baltimore, MD: Johns Hopkins University Press).

22. 'Eugenics: Its Definition, Scope, and Aims', p. 12.

23. D. Galton (2009) 'Eugenics Then and Now', *The Galton Institute Newsletter*, 71, 2–4, 2.

24. F. Galton (1909) 'Foreword', *The Eugenics Review*, April, 1, 1, 1–2, http://www.ncbi. nlm.nih.gov/pmc/articles/PMC2990354/ (accessed 28 November 2011).

25. Bashford and Levine, *The Oxford Handbook of the History of Eugenics*, Chronology, pp. 559–67. The countries are: Argentina, Australia, Austria, Bangladesh, Belgium, Brazil, Canada, Denmark, Dutch East Indies, Finland, France, Germany, Great Britain, Greece, Hong Kong, Hungary, India, Iran, Italy, Japan, Mexico, the Netherlands, New Zealand, Pakistan, Poland, Romania, Russia (later the USSR), South Africa, Sri Lanka, Sweden, Switzerland and the USA. In countries such as the USA and Canada, there were variations between different state/provincial jurisdictions.

26. Thom and Jennings, 'Human Pedigree', p. 220; A. M. Stern (2005) *Eugenic Nation: Faults and Frontiers of Better Breeding in Modern America* (Berkeley, CA: University of California Press), pp. 98–9.

27. Kevles, *In the Name of Eugenics*, pp. 74–6.

28. Stern, *Eugenic Nation*, p. 6.

29. N. H. Rafter (ed.) (1988) *White Trash: The Eugenic Family Studies, 1877–1919* (Boston: Northeastern University Press).

30. Rafter, *White Trash*.

31. http://www.cshl.edu/ (accessed 4 May 2013).

32. D. B. Paul (1994) 'Is Human Genetics Disguised Eugenics?' in R. F. Weir, S. C. Lawrence and E. Fales (eds), *Genes and Human Self-knowledge: Historical and Philosophical Reflections on Modern Genetics* (Iowa City, IA: University of Iowa Press), 67–78, p. 69.

33. Stern, *Eugenic Nation*, p. 23, notes for example that it was a prominent feminist, the physician Bethenia Owens-Adair, who lobbied successfully in Oregon for sterilization laws in 1917; Sylvia Bell Bannah (2010), 'Birds, Bees and Birth Control: A History of Family Planning in Queensland 1971–2001', Master of Arts thesis, University of Queensland, p. 43.

34. Kevles, *In the Name of Eugenics*, pp. 60–1.

35. Kevles, *In the Name of Eugenics*, p. 62.

36. Kevles, *In the Name of Eugenics*, p. 62.

37. L. Alexander (1949) 'Medical Science under Dictatorship', *New England Journal of Medicine*, 241, 39–47, p. 39.

38. D. B. Paul (2007) 'On Drawing Lessons from the History of Eugenics' in L. P. Knowles and G. E. Kaebnick (eds), *Reprogenetics: Law, Policy, and Ethical Issues* (Baltimore, MD: Johns Hopkins University Press), 3–19, p. 14.

39. Kevles, *In the Name of Eugenics*, pp. 118–22; p. 186; D. B. Paul (1998) *The Politics of Heredity: Essays on Eugenics, Biomedicine, and the Nature-Nurture Debate* (Albany, NY: State University of New York Press), passim.

40. Stern, *Eugenic Nation*, p. 3.

41. D. B. Paul and H. G. Spencer (1998) 'Did Eugenics Rest on an Elementary Mistake?' in Paul, *The Politics of Heredity*, 117–32.

42. A. White and I. Hofland (2004) *Carrie Buck, Virginia's Test Case*, http://www.hsl.virginia.edu/historical/eugenics/3-buckvbell.cfm (accessed 27 November 2011).

43. A. White and I. Hofland (2004) *Eugenics*, http://www.hsl.virginia.edu/historical/eugenics/ (accessed 27 November 2011).

44. Paul, 'Is Human Genetics Disguised Eugenics?', pp. 72–3.

45. D. L. Spar (2006) *The Baby Business: How Money, Science and Politics Drive the Commerce of Conception* (Boston, MA: Harvard Business School Press), p. 104.

46. M. Burleigh (1994) 'Psychiatry, German Society, and the Nazi Euthanasia Programme', *Social History of Medicine*, 7, 2, 213–28, p. 219.

47. D. B. Paul (1998) 'Eugenic Origins of Medical Genetics', in Paul, *The Politics of Heredity*, 133–56, p. 144.

48. D. Crossland (2006) 'Nazi Program to Breed Master Race: Lebensborn Children Break Silence', *Spiegel*, Online, 11 July.
49. D. J. Kevles (2009) 'Eugenics, the Genome, and Human Rights', *Medicine Studies*, 1, 85–93.
50. Stern, *Eugenic Nation*.
51. Kevles, *In the Name of Eugenics*, p. 169.
52. Bashford and Levine, *The Oxford Handbook of the History of Eugenics*, Chronology, pp. 559–67.
53. Thom and Jennings, 'Human Pedigree', pp. 225–7.
54. Stern, *Eugenic Nation*, pp. 3–4.
55. Cowan, *Heredity and Hope*, pp. 150–80.
56. Kevles, *In the Name of Eugenics*, p. 162.
57. Thom and Jennings, 'Human Pedigree', p. 230.
58. Paul, 'On Drawing Lessons', p. 10.
59. Kevles, *In the Name of Eugenics*, p. 70.The idea of the gene as a blueprint has recently also come under challenge. See E. M. Neumann-Held and C. Rehmann-Sutter (eds) (2006) *Genes in Development: Re-reading the Molecular Paradigm* (Durham, NC: Duke University Press).
60. L B. Jorde, J. C. Carey, M. J. Bamshad and R. White (2003) *Medical Genetics* (St Louis, MI: Mosby), p. 3.
61. Quoted by Paul, 'Is Human Genetics Disguised Eugenics', p. 67.
62. Anon. (2010) 'ELSI Planning and Evaluation History' *National Human Genome Research Institute*, http://www.genome.gov/10001754#al-2 (accessed 19 February 2012).
63. T. Duster (2003) *Backdoor to Eugenics*, 2nd edn (New York: Routledge); K. Osagie Obasogie and T. Duster (2011) 'All that Glitters Isn't Gold', *Hastings Center Report*, 41, 5, 15–18; I. Haddow (2008) 'Debating Ethics of DNA Database', *BBC News*, 9 January, http://news.bbc.co. uk/2/hi/uk_news/ 7177152.stm (accessed 1 December 2011). DNA databases can play an important role in identifying who was present at the scene of a crime or who might have committed a crime. DNA 'fingerprinting' relies on the idea that the chances of a mismatch are very small. However, DNA databases also reflect the arresting practices of police forces, who retain the data whether the person arrested is relevant to a crime scene or not. Thus in places such as the UK where people of colour are arrested disproportionately to the number who are found guilty of crimes, the risk of perpetuation of racism as a result of arresting practices has become evident. This isn't 'eugenic' strictly speaking, as it does not concern 'who shall be born'. But the shadow of eugenic ideas, conflating social groups with hereditary criminal tendencies, is evident.
64. Kevles, *In the Name of Eugenics*, p. 253.
65. Thom and Jennings, 'Human Pedigree', p. 230.
66. Many of the conditions for which amniocentesis was used, however, were chromosomal but not heritable, e.g., Down's, Kleinfelter and Turner

syndrome, and neural tube defects. Thom and Jennings, 'Human Pedigree', p. 230.

67. Paul, 'Eugenic Origins of Medical Genetics', p. 143.

68. *40 Years of IVF*, http://www.pdn.cam.ac.uk/40yearsivf/commemorative_programme.pdf (accessed 8 November 2012).

69. These concerns have been carried forward in the work of the group he helped found, The International Society for Mild Approaches in Assisted Reproduction (ISMAAR), http://naturalcycle.org/index.html (accessed 12 May 2013).

70. M. Kirkman and L. Kirkman (1988) *My Sister's Child: A Story of Full Surrogate Motherhood between Two Sisters Using in Vitro Fertilisation* (Ringwood, Vic: Penguin Books).

71. A. H. Handyside, E. H. Kontogianni, K. Hardy and R. M. Winston (1990) 'Pregnancies from Biopsied Human Preimplantation Embryos Sexed by Y-specific DNA Amplification', *Nature*, 344, 6268, 768–70.

72. S. Franklin and C. Roberts (2006) *Born and Made: An Ethnography of Preimplantation Genetic Diagnosis* (Princeton, NJ: Princeton University Press), p. 52. The list of disorders comes from major IVF provider, IVF Australia, at http://ivf.com.au/fertility-treatment/genetic-testing-pgd (accessed 9 November 2012).

73. M. de Souza (2012) 'The Regulation of Preimplantation Genetic Diagnosis: Is There Anything the United Kingdom Can Learn from the Australian Experience?', *Journal of Law and Medicine*, 20, 1, 165–77.

74. A. Malpani, A. Malpani and D. Modi (2002) 'Preimplantation Sex Selection for Family Balancing in India', *Human Reproduction*, 17, 1, 11–12.

75. J. Steinhauer (2012) 'House Rejects Bill to Ban Sex-Selective Abortions', *New York Times*, 31 May, http://www.nytimes.com/2012/06/01/us/politics/house-rejects-bill-to-ban-sex-selective-abortions.html.

76. *Ethical Guidelines on the Use of Assisted Reproductive Technology in Clinical Practice and Research*, 2007 http://www.nhmrc.gov.au/guidelines/publications/e78 (accessed 8 November 2012).

77. http://blog.ivf.com.au/its-a-boy-but-we-want-girl (accessed 20 January 2013).

78. A. Boggio (2005) 'Italy Enacts New Law on Medically Assisted Reproduction', *Human Reproduction*, 20, 5, 1156.

79. Personal communication, Dr Andrea Boggio. My sincere thanks are due to Dr Boggio, who kindly replied to an email request for clarification of the implications of the 2009 opinion. Quote used with his permission.

80. Thom and Jennings, 'Human Pedigree', p. 227.

81. C. R. Daniels and J. Golden (2004) 'Procreative Compounds: Popular Eugenics, Artificial Insemination and the Rise of the American Sperm Banking Industry', *Journal of Social History*, 38, 1, 5–27; http://donorsearch.fairfaxcryobank.com (accessed 10 November 2012).

82. Kevles, 'Eugenics, the Genome', p. 85.

83. Kevles, 'Eugenics, the Genome', pp. 92–3.
84. Kevles, 'Eugenics, the Genome', p. 92.
85. Paul, 'Eugenic Origins', pp. 148–9.
86. Paul, 'On Drawing Lessons from the History of Eugenics', pp. 11–14.
87. Quoted in A. E. Raz (2009) 'Eugenic Utopias/Dystopias, Reprogenetics, and Community Genetics', *Sociology of Health and Illness*, 31, 4, 602–16.
88. B. Latour (2002) 'Body, Cyborgs and the Politics of Incarnation', in S. T. Sweeney and I. Hodder (eds), *The Body* (Cambridge: Cambridge University Press), 127–41, p. 132.
89. Latour, 'Body, Cyborgs', p. 128.
90. Latour, 'Body, Cyborgs', p. 133.
91. Raz, 'Eugenic Utopias/Dystopias', pp. 609–10.
92. In law, the parallel development of the 'cultural defence' in reference to accusations made against people from non-dominant social groups has raised similar paradoxical questions about the traditionally 'left' belief in multiculturalism.
93. Raz, 'Eugenic Utopias/Dystopias', p. 612. See also Geneticalliance.org.
94. J. Savulescu (2002) 'Deaf Lesbians, "Designer Disability," and the Future of Medicine', *British Medical Journal*, 325, 771–3.
95. Kevles, *In the Name of Eugenics*, p. 85.
96. L. Guterman (2003) 'Choosing Eugenics: How Far Will Nations Go to Eliminate a Genetic Disease?', *Chronicle of Higher Education*, 49, 34, A22–6.
97. Cowan, *Heredity and Hope*, p. 221.
98. Cowan, *Heredity and Hope*, p. 221.
99. Guterman 'Choosing Eugenics', p. A22. Cowan takes specific issue with groups whom she identifies as concerned about the 'eugenic' implications of genetics: left-wing intellectuals concerned about human rights and totalitarianism; the anti-abortion lobby; disability activists; and those she refers to as 'reproductive feminists', *Heredity and Hope*, p. 227.
100. Duster, *Backdoor*, p. ix.
101. P. MacLeod and F. Clarke Fraser (1998) 'Forget Cloning Sheep and Pay Attention to China', *Canadian Medical Association Journal*, 159, 2, 153–5, p. 153; see also http://www.galtoninstitute.org.uk/Newsletters/GINL0006/name.htm (accessed 5 May 2013).
102. MacLeod and Fraser, 'Forget Cloning Sheep', p. 153.
103. MacLeod and Fraser, 'Forget Cloning Sheep', p. 153.
104. T. Hesketh (2003), 'Getting Married in China: Pass the Medical First', *British Medical Journal*, 326, 277–9, p. 277.
105. MacLeod and Fraser, 'Forget Cloning Sheep', p. 153; American Society of Human Genetics. Board of Directors, (1999) 'Eugenics and the Misuse of Genetic Information to Restrict Reproductive Freedom: ASHG Statement', *American Journal of Human Genetics*, 64, 2, 335–8, p. 337.
106. Anon. (1995) 'The New Chinese Law on Maternal and Infant Health Care', *Population and Development Review*, 21, 3, 698–702, p. 698. For a full text of

the law, see http://www.china.org.cn/china/2010-03/04/content_19522945. htm (accessed 24 November 2012). The government promulgated implementation rules in 2001: http://english.gov. cn/laws/2005-08/24/content_ 25746.htm (accessed 24 November 2012). (The term used in the Taiwan law and in the early version of the PRC law, 'yousheng', has a coincidental similarity to 'eugenics' but its origins predate the Common Era. It can have a wide range of meanings from quality improvement of the population to the idea of 'healthy birth'. Thanks are due to Jason Lim for this advice.)

107. Included on the website of Justice Michael Kirby, http://www.michaelkirby. com.au/images/stories/speeches/1990s/vol38/1996/1413-Report_on_ Law_of_The_ People's_Rep_of_China_on_Maternal_&_Infant_Health_- _Care_(Hum_Gen_Org).pdf (accessed 24 November 2012); MacLeod and Fraser, 'Forget Cloning Sheep', p. 155; American Society of Human Genetics, Board of Directors, 'Eugenics', p. 337.

108. Hesketh, 'Getting Married in China', p. 277.

109. See above, n. 106, re the Chinese word for 'eugenics'.

110. http://www.hsph.harvard.edu/population/abortion/taiwan.abo.htm (accessed 5 May 2013).

111. A. Erler (2010) 'Eugenics or "Reprogenetics"? Call It What You Will, But Let's Do It', *Practical Ethics*, University of Oxford, http://blog.practicalethics. ox.ac.uk/2010/02/eugenics-or-reprogenetics-call-it-what-you-will-but-lets- do-it/ (accessed 23 November 2011).

112. A. L. Caplan, G. McGee and D. Magnus (1999) 'What Is Immoral about Eugenics?', *The Western Journal of Medicine* 171, 335–7, p. 336.

113. See J. Habermas (2003) *The Future of Human Nature* (Cambridge, MA: Polity Press), pp. 19, 44; B. G. Prusak (2005) 'Rethinking "Liberal Eugenics": Reflections and Questions on Habermas on Bioethics', *Hastings Center Report*, 35, 6, 31–42.

114. R. Sparrow (2010) 'A Not-So-New Eugenics: Harris and Savulescu on Human Enhancement', *Hastings Center Report*, 41, 1, 32–42, p. 39.

115. 'Eugenics: What's in a Name', http://www.galtoninstitute.org. uk/Newsletters/GINL0006/name.htm (accessed 5 May 2013).

116. E. Parens and L.P. Knowles (2003), 'Reprogenetics and Public Policy: Reflections and Recommendations', *Hastings Center Report*, 33, 4, S1–S24, p. S4.

117. L. M. Silver (2000) 'Reprogenetics: Third Millennium Speculation: The Consequences for Humanity When Reproductive Biology and Genetics are Combined', *EMBO Reports*, 1, 5, 375–8, p. 376.

118. M. B. Delatycki (2008) 'Population Screening for Reproductive Risk for Single Gene Disorders in Australia: Now and the Future', *Twin Research and Human Genetics*, 11, 4, 422–30, p. 427.

119. One quotation will suffice: 'At the present time, we are evolving to become less intelligent with each new generation. Why is this happening? Simple: the least-intelligent people are having the most children.' Marian Van Court, 'The Case for Eugenics in a Nutshell', *Future Generations* website,

http://eugenics.net/papers/caseforeugenics.html (accessed 27 February 2011).

120. R. Lynn (2001) *Eugenics: A Reassessment* (Westport, CT: Praeger).
121. J. Conley (2013) 'Some Thoughts on Myriad after the Supreme Court Argument', *Genomics Law Report*, online 1 May.
122. Thom and Jennings, 'Human Pedigree', pp. 231–2.
123. Stern, *Eugenic Nation*, p. 215; Duster, *Backdoor*, p. ix; Ruth Cowan, quoted in Guterman, 'Choosing Eugenics', p. A26.

## Chapter 5

1. C. Bonah (2002) '"Experimental Rage": The Development of Medical Ethics and the Genesis of Scientific Facts. Ludwik Fleck: An Answer to the Crisis of Modern Medicine in Interwar Germany? Society for the Social History of Medicine Millennium Prize 2000', *Social History of Medicine*, 15, 2, 187–207, p. 187.
2. D. Callahan (2003) *What Price Better Health? Hazards of the Research Imperative* (Berkeley, CA: University of California Press), p. 259.
3. See *BioSocieties* (2013) Special Issue: Experimental Ethics, 8, 1.
4. S. M. Reverby (2011) '"Normal Exposure" and Inoculation Syphilis: A PHS "Tuskegee" Doctor in Guatemala, 1946–1948', *Journal of Policy History*, 23, 1, 6–28, p. 20.
5. R. Macklin (2012) *Ethics in Global Health: Research, Policy and Practice* (New York: Oxford University Press), p. 194.
6. Reverby, S. M. (ed.) (2000) *Tuskegee's Truths: Rethinking the Tuskegee Syphilis Study* (Chapel Hill, NC: University of North Carolina Press), p. 3.
7. S. E. Lederer (1995) *Subjected to Science: Human Experimentation in American before the Second World War* (Baltimore, MD: Johns Hopkins University Press), p. 55.
8. J. H. Cassedy (1991) *Medicine in America: A Short History* (Baltimore, MD: Johns Hopkins University Press), p. 28; G. Weisz (2006) *Divide and Conquer: A Comparative History of Medical Specialization* (New York: Oxford University Press)
9. See J. H. Cassedy (1983) 'The Flourishing and Character of Early American Medical Journalism, 1797–1860', *Journal of the History of Medicine and Allied Sciences*, 38, 2, 135–50; John Leonard Thornton (ed.), *Medical Books, Libraries and Collectors: A Study of Bibliography and the Book Trade in Relation to the Medical Sciences* (London: André Deutsch), pp. 226–8.
10. Cassedy, *Medicine in America*, p. 41.
11. J. Sherwood (1999) 'Syphilization: Human Experimentation in the Search for a Syphilis Vaccine in the Nineteenth Century', *Journal of the History of Medicine and Allied Sciences*, 54, 3, 364–86, p. 366.
12. In at least one case, an innovator in the new specialism of gynaecology purchased a slave for the sole purpose of surgical experimentation, conducted without anaesthetic. D. K. McGregor (1998) *From Midwives to*

*Medicine: The Birth of American Gynecology* (New Brunswick, NJ: Rutgers University Press), p. 60.

13. G. Baader, S. E. Lederer, M. Low, F. Schmaltz and A. V. Schwerin (2005) 'Pathways to Human Experimentation, 1933–1945: Germany, Japan, and the United States', *Osiris*, 2nd Series, 20, Politics and Science in Wartime: Comparative International Perspectives on the Kaiser Wilhelm Institute, 205–31.

14. Lederer, *Subjected to Science*, pp. 61–2.

15. P. M. McNeill (1993) *The Ethics and Politics of Human Experimentation* (Cambridge: Cambridge University Press), p. 37.

16. McNeill, *The Ethics and Politics of Human Experimentation*, pp. 38–9. See the excellent 'Timeline of Informed Consent', in E. Blacksher and J. D. Moreno (2008) 'A History of Informed Consent in Clinical Research', in E. J. Emanuel, C. Grady, R. A. Crouch, R. Lie, F. Miller and F. Wendler (eds), *The Oxford Textbook of Clinical Research Ethics* (Oxford: Oxford University Press), 591–605, pp. 592–4.

17. Lederer, *Subjected to Science*, p. xiv.

18. Lederer, *Subjected to Science*, p. 51; p. xiv.

19. Lederer, *Subjected to Science*, pp. 71–4.

20. A. L. Caplan (2005) 'Too Hard to Face', *Journal of the American Academy of Psychiatry and the Law*, 33, 3, 394–400, p. 400.

21. P. Weindling (2001) 'The Origins of Informed Consent: The International Scientific Commission on Medical War Crimes, and the Nuremberg Code', *Bulletin of the History of Medicine*, 75, 1, 37–71, p. 41. Bonah, '"Experimental Rage".

22. McNeill, *The Ethics and Politics of Human Experimentation*, p. 41, citing H.-M. Sass, 'Reichsrundschreiben 1931: Pre-Nuremberg German Regulations Concerning New Therapy and Human Experimentation', *The Journal of Medicine and Philosophy*, 8, 2, 99–111.

23. M. H. Kater (1994) 'Foreword' in G. Aly, P. Chroust and C. Pross (ed.) B. Cooper (trans.) *Cleansing the Fatherland: Nazi Medicine and Racial Hygiene* (Baltimore, MD: Johns Hopkins University Press), xii–xiii.

24. K. B. O'Reilly (2008) 'AMA apologizes for past inequality against black doctors', *Amednews*, 28 July, http://www.ama-assn.org/amednews/2008/07/28/prsb0728.htm (accessed 17 January 2013); Cassedy, *Medicine in America*, p. 96.

25. S. Hildebrandt (2006) 'How the Pernkopf Controversy Facilitated a Historical and Ethical Analysis of the Anatomical Sciences in Austria and Germany: A Recommendation for the Continued Use of the Pernkopf Atlas', *Clinical Anatomy*, 19, 2, 91–100.

26. F. P. Thomas, A. Beres and M. I. Shevell (2006) '"A Cold Wind Coming": Heinrich Gross and Child Euthanasia in Vienna', *Journal of Child Neurology*, 21, 4, 342–8; P. J. Weindling (2012) '"Cleansing" Anatomical Collections: The Politics of Removing Specimens from German Anatomical and Medical Collections 1988–92', *Annals of Anatomy*, 194, 3, 237–42; P. J. Weindling

(2011) 'From Scientific Object to Commemorated Victim: The Children of the Spiegelgrund', in I. Löwy (ed.), *Microscope Slides: Reassessing a Neglected Historical Resource* (Max Planck Institute for the History of Science), 77–88.

27. J. Hazelgrove (2002) 'The Old Faith and the New Science: The Nuremberg Code and Human Experimentation Ethics in Britain, 1946–73', *Social History of Medicine*, 15, 1, 109–35, p. 111.

28. These experiments defied the 1929 Geneva Convention on the treatment of prisoners of war to which Germany was a signatory. There were around 26 different types of experiments in all. Caplan, 'Too Hard to Face', p. 396.

29. G. J. Annas and M. A. Grodin (eds) (1992) *The Nazi Doctors and the Nuremberg Code: Human Rights in Human Experimentation* (New York: Oxford University Press), pp. 26; 70; 83; W. E. Seidelman (1988) 'Mengele Medicus: Medicine's Nazi Heritage', *The Milbank Quarterly*, 66, 2, 221–39, pp. 226–7.

30. Caplan, 'Too Hard to Face', p. 396.

31. N. Aviram (director) (1999; orig. 1996) *Healing by Killing* (videorecording), Fine Cut (series) (Sydney: SBS), broadcast 3 April.

32. G. Aly, P. Chroust and C. Pross (authors) B. Cooper (trans) (1994) *Cleansing the Fatherland: Nazi Medicine and Racial Hygiene* (Baltimore, MD: Johns Hopkins University Press), pp. 146–53.

33. Aly et al., *Cleansing the Fatherland*, p. 99.

34. Baader et al., 'Pathways to Human Experimentation', p. 206.

35. J. D. Moreno, *Undue Risk: Secret State Experiments on Humans* (New York: W.H. Freeman), pp. 104–7. See also J.-B. Nie, N. Guo, M. Selden and A. Kleinman (eds) (2010), *Japan's Wartime Medical Atrocities: Comparative Inquiries in Science, History, and Ethics* (London: Routledge).

36. B. Goodwin (1998) *Keen as Mustard: Britain's Horrific Chemical Warfare Experiments in Australia* (St Lucia, Queensland: University of Queensland Press); B. Goodwin, (director); S. Connolly and T. Graham (producers) (1989) *Keen as Mustard* (videorecording) (Lindfield, New South Wales: Yarra Bank Films/Film Australia).

37. B. Lyons (director); K. Zabihyan (producer) (1995) *The Secrets of Porton Down* (videorecording) (Sydney: SBS); I. Mason (1987) 'Porton Defends Nerve-Gas Tests on Humans', *New Scientist*, 115, 1569, 30; P. M. Hammond, and G. Carter (2002) *From Biological Warfare to Healthcare: Porton Down 1940–2000* (Basingstoke: Palgrave); Anon. (2001) 'Porton Down Scientists "Could Be Charged"', *BBC News Online*, 9 July, http://news.bbc.co.uk/ 2/hi/uk_news/ 1430382.stm (accessed 21 December 2012).

38. Baader et al., 'Pathways to Human Experimentation', p. 224.

39. Baader et al., 'Pathways to Human Experimentation', p. 228.

40. Moreno, *Undue Risk*, pp. 104–8; Baader et al., 'Pathways to Human Experimentation' pp. 221–4. The year before in 1945 Dr Leo Alexander compiled a report on the findings of the experiments to be published by the US Department of Commerce, in order that they 'be of direct benefit to US science and industry'. Seidelman, 'Mengele Medicus: Medicine's Nazi Heritage', p. 227.

41. W. E. Seidelman (2012) 'Dissecting the History of Anatomy in the Third Reich, 1989–2010: A Personal Account', *Annals of Anatomy – Anatomischer Anzeiger*, 194, 3, 228–36.
42. Moreno, *Undue Risk*, p. 53.
43. Hazelgrove, 'The Old Faith and the New Science', p. 112.
44. Annas and Grodin, *The Nazi Doctors and the Nuremberg Code*, p. 6. There is anecdotal evidence that early post-war medical scientists in Australia knew of the Code, for example, and made some attempt to inform patients and obtain at least verbal consent. N. V. Korszniak (1994) *The Use of Radioisotopes in Medicine and Medical Research, Australia 1947–73* (Yallambie, Vic.: Australian Radiation Laboratory), p. 6.
45. P. J. Weindling (2004) *Nazi Medicine and the Nuremberg Trials: From Medical War Crimes to Informed Consent* (Basingstoke: Palgrave Macmillan), pp. 319–43.
46. J. Katz (1994) 'Reflections on Unethical Experiments and the Beginnings of Bioethics in the United States', *Kennedy Institute of Ethics Journal*, 4, 2, 85–92.
47. Hazelgrove, 'The Old Faith and the New Science'; D. J. Rothman (2003) *Strangers at the Bedside: A History of How Law and Bioethics Transformed Medical Decision Making* (New Brunswick, NJ: Aldine).
48. 'Epilogue' in R. Fox (1998) *Experiment Perilous: Physicians and Patients Facing the Unknown*, with a new epilogue by the author (New Brunswick, NJ: Transaction).
49. J. Sherwood, 'Syphilization'; Lederer, *Subjected to Science,* passim; A. M. Hornblum (1999) *Acres of Skin: Human Experiments at Holmesburg Prison: A Story of Abuse and Exploitation in the Name of Medical Science* (London: Routledge), p. 91.
50. See V. N. Gamble (1997) 'Under the Shadow of Tuskegee: African Americans and Healthcare', *American Journal of Public Health*, 87, 11, 1773–8; T. A. LaViest and L. A. Isaac (eds) (2012) *Race, Ethnicity, and Health: A Public Health Reader,* 2nd edn (San Francisco: John Wiley and Sons); J. H. Jones (1993) *Bad Blood: The Tuskegee Syphilis Experiment*, new and expanded edn (New York: Free Press); S. M. Reverby (ed.) (2000) *Tuskegee's Truths: Rethinking the Tuskegee Syphilis Study* (Chapel Hill, NC: University of North Carolina Press); R. M. White (2006) 'The Tuskegee Study of Untreated Syphilis Revisited' (reflection and reaction), *Lancet Infectious Diseases*, 6, 2, 62–3; R. M. White (2000) 'Unraveling the Tuskegee Study of Untreated Syphilis', *Archives of Internal Medicine*, 160, 5, 585–98.
51. D. J. Rothman (1982) 'Were Tuskegee and Willowbrook "Studies in Nature"?' *Hastings Center Report*, 12, 2, 5–7.
52. Another 12 were 'shifted from control to subject'. S. M. Reverby (2011) 'The Tuskegee Study as a "Site of Memory"' in R. V. Katz and R. C. Warren (eds.) *The Search for the Legacy of the USPHS Syphilis Study at Tuskegee: Reflective Essays Based upon Findings from the Tuskegee Legacy Project* (Plymouth: Lexington Books), 29–40, p. 31.

53  Caplan, 'Twenty Years After', foreword, p. 29; A. L. Caplan (1992) 'When Evil Intrudes', *The Hastings Center Report*, 22, 6, 29–32, p. 30.

54. McNeill, *Ethics and Politics of Human Experimentation*, p. 63.

55. Caplan, 'Twenty Years After', p. 29; P. Wilson (1997) 'Devil's Medicine', *Weekend Australian*, 17–18 May.

56. Reverby, 'The Tuskegee Study as a "Site of Memory"', pp. 29–30.

57. Reverby, '"Normal Exposure" and Inoculation Syphilis', pp. 11–12.

58. Reverby underscores the children were not deliberately infected, '"Normal Exposure" and Inoculation Syphilis', p. 13.

59. Reverby, '"Normal Exposure" and Inoculation Syphilis', pp. 13–14.

60. Reverby, '"Normal Exposure" and Inoculation Syphilis', p. 16.

61. Reverby, '"Normal Exposure" and Inoculation Syphilis', p. 16.

62. The recent Centers for Disease Control study of records of the tests states: 'Over the course of observation, 71 subjects [of 532] were noted to have died … although the records do not allow determination of the relationship of the deaths to study procedures. There was no systematic description of other adverse events arising during the study or follow-up observation period.' US Department of Health and Human Services (2010) 'Findings from a CDC Report on the 1946–1948 U.S. Public Health Service Sexually Transmitted Disease (STD) Inoculation Study', (accessed 9 December 2012).

63. Reverby, '"Normal Exposure" and Inoculation Syphilis', p. 18.

64. Reverby, '"Normal Exposure" and Inoculation Syphilis', pp. 18–19.

65. Reverby, '"Normal Exposure" and Inoculation Syphilis', p. 22.

66. D. G. McNeil (2010) 'U.S. Apologizes for Syphilis Tests in Guatemala', *The New York Times*, 1 October, http://www.nytimes.com/2010/10/02/health/research/02infect.html?_r=0 (accessed 9 December 2012).

67. Department of Veterans' Affairs (2011) Definition of an Australian Participant in the British Nuclear Tests for the Purposes of the Non-liability Health Care Treatment for All Malignant Cancers. http://www.dva.gov.au/health_and_wellbeing/health_programs/ nuctest/Pages/definition.aspx (accessed 18 January 2013); G. Mitchell (2003) 'See an Atomic Blast and Spread the Word: Indoctrination at Ground Zero', in J. Goodman, A. McElligott and L. Marks (eds) *Useful Bodies: Humans in the Service of Medical Science in the Twentieth Century* (Baltimore, MD: Johns Hopkins University Press), 133–61.

68. Moreno, *Undue Risk*, pp. 208–9.

69. E. Welsome (2010) *The Plutonium Files: America's Secret Medical Experiments in the Cold War* (New York: Random House Publishing Group). See also T. L. Beauchamp (1996) 'Looking Back and Judging Our Predecessors', *Kennedy Institute of Ethics Journal*, 6, 3, 251–70; A. Buchanan (1996) 'The Controversy over Retrospective Moral Judgment', *Kennedy Institute of Ethics Journal*, 6, 3, 245–50, and J. Healey (1994) 'Congress Ponders Compensation for Radiation Test Subjects', *Congressional Quarterly Weekly Report*, 52, 1, 21–2.

70. W. Moss and R. Eckhardt (1995) 'The Human Plutonium Injection Experiments', *Los Alamos Science*, 23, 177–223.

71. http://www.hss.energy.gov/healthsafety/ohre/roadmap/achre/summary. html (accessed 15 May 2013).

72. S. Garton, 'Bailey, Harry Richard (1922–1985)', *Australian Dictionary of Biography*, http://adb.anu.edu.au/biography/bailey-harry-richard-12162/ text21793 (accessed 24 November 2012); B. Bromberger and J. Fife-Yeomans (1991) *Deep Sleep: Harry Bailey and the Scandal of Chelmsford* (East Roseville, NSW: Simon and Schuster); J. Newling (1992) 'The Forgotten Children of Chelmsford', *New Idea*, 14 March, 34–7.

73. See W. Sargant (1966) 'Psychiatric Treatment in General Teaching Hospitals: A Plea for a Mechanistic Approach', *British Medical Journal*, 2, 5508, 257–62; also D. Streatfeild (2006) *Brainwash: The Secret History of Mind Control* (London: Hodder & Stoughton).

74. W. Sargant (1957) *Battle for the Mind: A Physiology of Conversion and Brain-Washing* (Garden City, NY: Doubleday).

75. Homosexuality has been pathologized since the late nineteenth century and the *American Psychiatric Association* only removed it from its Diagnostic and Statistical Manual (DSM) in 1973, following gay protests against the view that their gayness was an illness. J. Drescher MD (2012) 'The Removal of Homosexuality from the DSM: Its Impact on Today's Marriage Equality Debate', *Journal of Gay & Lesbian Mental Health*, 16, 2, 124–35.

76. Moreno, *Undue Risk*, p. 251.

77. E. Dyck (2008) *Psychedelic Psychiatry: LSD from Clinic to Campus* (Baltimore, MD: Johns Hopkins University Press); B. Sessa (2005) 'Can Psychedelics have a role in Psychiatry Once Again?' (Editorial), *British Journal of Psychiatry*, 186, 6, 457–8.

78. P. Weindling (2010) *John W. Thompson: Psychiatrist in the Shadow of the Holocaust* (Rochester, NY: University of Rochester Press), p. 50.

79. Weindling, *John W. Thompson*, p. 161.

80. Weindling, *John W. Thompson*, p. 85.

81. 'W. S'. (1967) 'Ewen Cameron, M.D., F.R.C.P.(C.), D.P.M.', *British Medical Journal*, 3, 5568, 803–4.

82. D. Gillmor (1987) *I Swear by Apollo: Dr. Ewen Cameron and the CIA-Brainwashing Experiments* (Montréal: Eden Press), p. 1.

83. D. E. Cameron (1960) 'Production of Differential Amnesia as a Factor in the Treatment of Schizophrenia', *Comprehensive Psychiatry*, 1, 1, 26–34, pp. 26–7.

84. Cameron, 'Production of Differential Amnesia', pp. 26–7. Cameron gives the 'average' number of days of sleep as '15 to 30', with the longest being 65 days for 'some patients' (p. 27).

85. Cameron, 'Production of Differential Amnesia', p. 27.

86. A. Collins (1988) *In the Sleep Room: The Story of the CIA Brainwashing Experiments in Canada* (Toronto: Lester and Orpen Dennys).

87. D. Payne (1986) 'The Dirty Legacy of Brainwashing', *New Scientist*, 112, 1533, 6 November, 28–9.

88. R. A. Cleghorn (1990) 'The McGill Experience of Robert A. Cleghorn, MD: Recollections of D. Ewen Cameron', *Canadian Bulletin of Medical History / Bulletin canadien d'histoire de la medicine*, 7, 53–76, p. 75.

89. Payne, 'The Dirty Legacy of Brainwashing'.

90. B. Bromberger and J. Fife-Yeomans (1991) *Deep Sleep: Harry Bailey and the Scandal of Chelmsford* (East Roseville, NSW: Simon and Schuster), p. 153.

91. Bromberger and Fife-Yeomans, *Deep Sleep*, p. 153.

92. M. Robertson, *An Overview of Psychiatric Ethics*, no year, http://heti.nsw.gov.au/ Resources/View.aspx?pid=5841 (accessed 18 December 2012).

93. J. Healy (2011) *Improving Health Care Safety and Quality: Reluctant Regulators* (Surrey: Ashgate Publishing), p. 31.

94. H. V. Beecher (1959) 'Experimentation in Man', *Journal of the American Medical Association*, 169, 5, 461–78.

95. J. Harkness, S. E. Lederer and D. Wikler (2001) 'Laying Ethical Foundations for Clinical Research', *Bulletin of the World Health Organization*, 79, 4, 365–6.

96. Harkness et al., 'Laying Ethical Foundations for Clinical Research', p. 366.

97. H. K. Beecher (1966) 'Ethics and Clinical Research', *New England Journal of Medicine*, 274, 24, 1354–60, pp. 1354–5.

98. Harkness et al., 'Laying Ethical Foundations for Clinical Research', p. 366.

99. Beecher saw Saul Krugman as contravening the 1964 World Medical Association's Helsinki Code reference to not undertaking actions that would weaken subjects.

100. Beecher, 'Ethics and Clinical Research', p. 372.

101. S. Wilde (2004) 'See One, Do One, Modify One: Prostate Surgery in the 1930s', *Medical History*, 48, 3, 351–66; A. J. London and J. B. Kadane (2002) 'Placebos that Harm: Sham Surgery Controls in Clinical Trials', *Statistical Methods in Medical Research*, 11, 5, 413–27. Thanks are due to Dr Elli Storey for the latter reference.

102. Beecher, 'Ethics and Clinical Research', pp. 1354–5.

103. The studies are identified by David Rothman: see Rothman, *Strangers at the Bedside*, pp. 273–5.

104. Beecher, 'Ethics and Clinical Research', p. 1356.

105. Harkness et al., 'Laying Ethical Foundations for Clinical Research', p. 366; Beecher, 'Ethics and Clinical Research', p. 1360.

106. Louise Lasagna was a junior colleague of Beecher's in the 1950s. A. Gaw (2012) 'Exposing Unethical Human Research: The Transatlantic Correspondence of Beecher and Pappworth', *Annals of Internal Medicine*, 156, 2, 150–5, p. 153.

107. Gaw, 'Exposing Unethical Research'.

108. Hazelgrove, 'The Old Faith and the New Science', p. 111.

109. M. Pappworth (1967) *Human Guinea Pigs: Experimentation on Man* (London: Routledge & Kegan Paul), p. 215.

110. A. Hedgecoe (2009) '"A Form of Practical Machinery": The Origins of Research Ethics Committees in the UK, 1967–1972', *Medical History* 53, 3, 331–50, p. 337.

111. Hedgecoe, '"A Form of Practical Machinery"'.
112. D. J. Rothman and S. M. Rothman (1984) *The Willowbrook Wars*, 1st edn (New York: Harper & Row), pp. 263–5. See the ethical discussion in P. Ramsey (1970) *The Patient as Person: Exploration in Medical Ethics* (New Haven: Yale University Press). Krugman was not the only researcher to feed live excretory bacteria to subjects. Hazelgrove, 'The Old Faith and the New Science', p. 115.
113. Rothman and Rothman, *The Willowbrook Wars*, p. 262. Krugman later found that asymptomatic numbers were much higher. S. Krugman (1986) 'The Willowbrook Hepatitis Studies Revisited: Ethical Aspects', *Reviews of Infectious Diseases*, 8, 1, 157–62, p. 159.
114. Krugman, 'The Willowbrook Hepatitis Studies Revisited', p. 162; Moreno, *Undue Risk*, p. 250.
115. Letters included: S. Goldby (1971) *The Lancet*, 297, 7702, 749; S. Krugman and S. Shapiro (1971) *The Lancet*, 297, 7706, 966–7; E. N. Willey and B. Pasamanick (1971) *The Lancet*, 297, 7708, 1078–9; M. Pappworth, (1971) *The Lancet*, 297, 7710, p. 1181; H. K. Beecher (1971) *The Lancet*, 297, 7710, p. 1181; G. Edsall (1971), *The Lancet*, 298, 7715, 95.
116. Krugman, 'The Willowbrook Hepatitis Studies Revisited', p. 160, Rothman and Rothman, *The Willowbrook Wars,* p. 265.
117. Rothman and Rothman analyse the consent letter sent to mothers of the children in detail. Rothman and Rothman, *The Willowbrook Wars*, pp. 265–6.
118. Rothman and Rothman, *The Willowbrook Wars*, p. 266.
119. Krugman, 'The Willowbrook Hepatitis Studies Revisited', p. 161.
120. Krugman, 'The Willowbrook Hepatitis Studies Revisited'; Rothman and Rothman, *The Willowbrook Wars,* p. 260.
121. W. M. Robinson and B. T. Unrah (2008) 'The Hepatitis Experiments at Willowbrook State School', in E. J. Emanuel et al. (eds), *The Oxford Textbook of Clinical Research Ethics* (Oxford: Oxford University Press), 80–5, p. 83; Rothman and Rothman, *The Willowbrook Wars*, p. 266.
122. See M. G. Wagner and P. Stephenson (1993) 'Infertility and In Vitro Fertilization: Is the Tail Wagging the Dog?' in M. G. Wagner and P. Stephenson (eds) *Tough Choices: In Vitro Fertilization and the Reproductive Technologies* (Philadelphia: Temple University Press), 1–24.
123. Ovarian hyperstimulation syndrome (OHSS), in particular, is a widely occurring and well-documented set of side effects from drugs used in IVF to increase the number of ova. http://www.hfea.gov.uk/docs/ 2011-05-04_SCAAC_-_OHSS_presentation_-_Raj_Mathur.pdf (accessed 15 May 2013). See also R. Arditti, R. D. Klein, and S. Minden (eds) (1984) *Test-tube Women: what future for motherhood?* (London; Boston: Pandora press); R. Rowland (1992) *Living Laboratories: women and reproductive technologies* (Sydney: Sun Books); D. S. Ferber (2007) 'As Sure as Eggs? Responses to an Ethical Question Posed by Abramov, Elchalal and Schenker', *Journal of Clinical Ethics*, 18, 1, 35–48.

124. See G. Nargund and R. Frydman (2007) 'Towards a More Physiological Approach to IVF', *Reproductive BioMedicine Online*, 14, 5, 550–2.
125. S. Coney and P. Bunkle (1987) 'An "Unfortunate Experiment" at National Women's', *Metro Magazine*, June, 47–65; available at http://www.womens-health.org.nz/index.php? page=cartwright; S. Coney (1988) *The Unfortunate Experiment: The Full Story behind the Inquiry into Cervical Cancer* (Auckland, NZ; Ringwood, Vic: Penguin).
126. M. R. E. McCredie, C. Paul, K. J. Sharples, J. Baranyai, G. Medley, D. C. G. Skegg and R. W. Jones (2010) 'Consequences in Women of Participating in a Study of the Natural History of Cervical Intraepithelial Neoplasia 3', *Australian and New Zealand Journal of Obstetrics and Gynaecology*, 50, 363–70. See also C. Paul (1988) 'The New Zealand Cervical Cancer Study: Could it Happen Again?' *British Medical Journal*, 297, 6647, 533–9.
127. McCredie et al., 'Consequences in Women'. See also Paul, 'The New Zealand Cervical Cancer Study'.
128. McCredie et al., 'Consequences in Women', p. 363.
129. McCredie et al., 'Consequences in Women', pp. 363, 366–7.
130. W. A. McIndoe, M. R. McLean, R. W. Jones and P. R. Mullins (1984) 'The Invasive Potential of Carcinoma in situ of the Cervix', *Obstetrics and Gynecology*, 64, 4, 451–8.
131. Coney and Bunkle, 'An "Unfortunate Experiment" at National Women's'.
132. L. Bryder (2009) *A History of the 'Unfortunate Experiment' at National Women's Hospital* (Auckland: Auckland University Press); in responding to critics, see L. Bryder (2009), 'Unfortunate Criticisms', *Listener* [New Zealand], 12–18 September, 220, 3618.
133. Bonah paraphrasing Ludvik Fleck. Bonah, '"Experimental Rage"', p. 206.
134. J. Mitford (1973) 'Cheaper than Chimpanzees' in *Kind and Unusual Punishment: The Prison Business* (New York: Alfred A. Knopf) Ch. 9; V. Packard (1957) *The Hidden Persuaders* (London: Longmans, Green & Co); R. Carson (1962) *Silent Spring* (London: Houghton Mifflin).
135. R. Brynner and T. Stephens (2001) *Dark Remedy: The Impact of Thalidomide and its Revival as a Vital Medicine* (Cambridge, MA: Perseus Publishing), pp. 34–5. P. Knightley et al., as *Sunday Times of London* Insight Team (1979) *Suffer the Children: The Story of Thalidomide* (London: André Deutsch).
136. Beecher, 'Ethics and Clinical Research'.
137. Anon. (2010) 'Why Did Susan Reverby Wait So Long?', http://hubbub.wbur.org/ 2010/10/04/questions-for-susan-reverby (accessed 9 December 2012).
138. P. I. Folb (1977) *The Thalidomide Disaster, and its Impact on Modern Medicine* (Cape Town: University of Cape Town), p. 7.
139. R. A. Morton (1971) 'The Social Responsibility of the Scientist', *Journal of Biosocial Science*, 3, 1, 69–80, p. 73.
140. J. Buckman (1977) 'Brainwashing, LSD, and CIA: Historical and Ethical Perspective', *International Journal of Social Psychiatry*, 23, 1, 8–19, p. 18:

141. Weindling, *Nazi Medicine*, pp. 325–6.
142. J. Bell, J. Whiton and S. Connelly (1998) *Final Report: Evaluation of NIH Implementation of Section 491 of the Public Health Service Act, Mandating a Program of Protection for Research Subjects June 15, 1998*, The Office of Extramural Research, National Institutes of Health, p. 2, http://www.hhs.gov/ohrp/archive/policy/hsp_final_rpt.pdf (accessed 10 December 2012).
143. Council for International Organizations of Medical Sciences (2002) 'International Ethical Guidelines for Biomedical Research Involving Human Subjects', http://www. cioms.ch/publications/guidelines/guidelines_nov_2002_blurb.htm (accessed 20 December 2012).
144. J. E. Idääpään-Heikkilä and S. S. Fluss (2008) 'International Ethical Guidance from the Council of International Organizations of Medical Sciences', in Emanuel et al. (eds) *The Oxford Textbook of Clinical Research Ethics*, pp. 168–73. An overview of the regulatory environment may be found at circare.org, 'a nonprofit national organization of concerned professionals and lay persons who share the common goal of improving safeguards for human research subjects. We oppose the exploitation and deception of human subjects in unethical studies that violate the human rights, welfare, or the best medical interests of the individual subject.' A useful link is its digest of international ethical codes and guidelines at http://www.circare.org/info1.htm.
145. R. Steinbrook, (2002) 'Protecting Research Subjects: The Crisis At Johns Hopkins', *New England Journal of Medicine*, 346, 9, 716–20; J. Savulescu and M. Spriggs (2002) 'The Hexamethonium Asthma Study and the Death of a Normal Volunteer in Research', *Journal of Medical Ethics*, 28, 3–4.
146. R. G. De Vries and C. Forsberg (2002) 'What Do IRBs Look Like? What Kind of Support Do They Receive?', *Accountability in Research: Policies and Quality Assurance*, 9, 3–4, 199–216, p. 213.
147. See articles in *Bioethics*, 24, 6 (July 2010); C. Elliot (2008) 'Guinea-pigging: Healthy Human Subjects for Drug-safety Trials Are in Demand. But Is it a Living?', *New Yorker*, 83, 42 (7 January), 36–41, p. 36; C. Elliott (2005) 'Should Journals Publish Industry-funded Bioethics Articles?', *Lancet*, 366, 9483, 422–24; A. Petryna (2009) *When Experiments Travel: Clinical Trials and the Global Search for Human Subjects* (Princetown: Princetown University Press).
148. See, for example, C. A. Morgan III et al. (2004) 'Accuracy of Eyewitness Memory for Persons Encountered during Exposure to Highly Intense Stress', *International Journal of Law and Psychiatry*, 27, 3, 265–79.
149. Caplan, 'Too Hard to Face', p. 394.
150. Moreno, *Undue Risk*, p. 62.
151. Rothman, *Strangers at the Bedside*.
152. Caplan, 'Too Hard to Face', p. 398.
153. B. Lane (2006) 'Ethics Draft Provokes Anger', *Australian*, 16 August, 35. The electric chair example had been used by the co-inventor of IVF, Robert G.

Edwards in 1974, four years before the first IVF birth. R. G. Edwards (1992) 'Fertilization of Human Eggs in Vitro: A Defense' reprint in K. D. Alpern (ed.), *The Ethics of Reproductive Technology* (New York: Oxford University Press), 71–82.

154. National Health and Medical Research Council (NHMRC), the Australian Research Council (ARC), and the Australian Vice-Chancellors' Committee (AVCC) (2007) *National Statement on Ethical Conduct in Human Research*, http://www.nhmrc.gov.au/publications/ synopses/e72syn.htm (accessed 7 May 2008), p. 3.

155. V. Roelcke and G. Maio (eds) (2004) *Twentieth Century Ethics of Human Subjects Research: Historical Perspectives on Values, Practices, and Regulations* (Stuttgart: Franz Steiner Verlag).

156. Roelcke and Maio, *Twentieth Century Ethics of Human Subjects Research.*

157. Anon. (1998) 'Auschwitz Doctor Has No Regrets', *Courier-Mail* (Brisbane), 29 September, p. 18.

158. Beecher, 'Ethics and Clinical Research'; Coney, *The Unfortunate Experiment.*

159. See P. Weindling (1989) *Health, Race, and German Politics between National Unification and Nazism, 1870–1945* (Cambridge: Cambridge University Press); R. Porter (ed.) (2006) *The Cambridge History of Medicine* (Cambridge: Cambridge University Press).

## Chapter 6

1. C. Elliott and T. Chambers (eds) (2004) *Prozac as a Way of Life* (Charlotte, NC: University of North Carolina Press); for benzodiazepine's history see J. Haafkens (1997) *Rituals of Silence: Long-term Tranquilizer Use by Women in the Netherlands: A Social Case Study* (Amsterdam: Het Spinhuis); E. Shorter (2009) *Before Prozac: The Troubled History of Mood Disorders in Psychiatry* (Oxford: Oxford University Press); A. Tone (2009) *The Age of Anxiety: A History of America's Turbulent Affair with Tranquilizers* (New York: Basic Books).

2. B. L. Neiger (2000) 'The Re-emergence of Thalidomide: Results of a Scientific Conference', *Teratology*, 62, 432–5, p. 433. Another source cites 20–36 days after conception. S. L. Walker et al. (2007) 'The Role of Thalidomide in the Management of Erythema Nodosum Leprosum', *Leprosy Review*, 78, 197–215, p. 208.

3. In 2006, Celgene was at the top of the list of the world's fastest growing technology companies. Anon. (2006) 'Celgene Tops Fastest-Growing List', http://www.allbusiness.com/ professional-scientific/management-consulting-services/4078101-1.html (accessed 8 February 2012).

4. T. Morrison (2011) 'Celgene Delivers Again: Top and Bottom Line Strong in Q2', *Bioworld*, 29 July; T. Clarke (2010) 'Celgene CEO Mulls Succession as Company Expands', *Reuters News*, 9 April, via Factiva.

5. H. Sjöström and R. Nilsson (1972) *Thalidomide and the Power of the Drug*

*Companies* (London: Penguin); G. J. Annas and S. Elias (1999) 'Thalidomide and the Titanic: Reconstructing the Technology Tragedies of the Twentieth Century', *American Journal of Public Health*, 89, 1, 98–101. It is notable that some of the most basic facts pertaining to the drug's history – dates, numbers of cases, even the stage of pregnancy at which the drug has damaging potency – are routinely divergent. This chapter has been screened to eliminate the most egregious errors.

6. Thalidomide has not in general featured as a 'textbook' bioethics subject. A search for 'thalidomide' in the Hastings Center Report (1988–February 2011) yields no articles using the 'citation and abstract' search and nine which refer to it in document text. By comparison, for the same period, a 'citation and abstract' search for 'euthanasia' yields 120 articles; the *Kennedy Institute of Ethics Journal* (1991–February 2011) yielded four articles which refer to thalidomide in a document. Searches conducted February 2011.

7. The sobering epithet is that of historian of thalidomide, Rock Brynner and thalidomide anatomist and embryologist, Trent Stephens, whose co-authored book is at present the best overall account of the lead-up to the drug's reintroduction to the market. R. Brynner and T. Stephens (2001) *Dark Remedy: The Impact of Thalidomide and its Revival as a Vital Medicine* (Cambridge: Perseus Publishing), p. 8. Until the appearance of the Brynner/Stephens book the best account of the drug's early history was the 1979 *Suffer the Children: The Story of Thalidomide*, by the Insight team of the *Sunday Times*. Brynner acknowledges his debt to the latter. P. Knightley et al., as *Sunday Times* Insight Team (1979) *Suffer the Children: The Story of Thalidomide* (London: Deutsch).

8. Brynner provides a longer and very insightful discussion of the mix of naïve optimism and wariness about modern technology that characterized the post-World War II era. Brynner and Stephens, *Dark Remedy*, p. 2.

9. A. Daemmrich (2002) 'A Tale of Two Experts: Thalidomide and Political Engagement in the United States and West Germany', *Social History of Medicine*, 15, 1, 137–58, p. 138.

10. Brynner and Stephens, *Dark Remedy*, p. 186. The German is 'Contergankinder'.

11. S. K. Teo, D. I. Stirling and J. B. Zeldis (2005) 'Thalidomide as a Novel Therapeutic Agent: New Uses for an Old Product', *Drug Discovery Today*, 10, 2, 107–14, p. 107.

12. Brynner and Stephens, *Dark Remedy*, p. 8.

13. Brynner and Stephens, *Dark Remedy*, p. 9.

14. Brynner and Stephens, *Dark Remedy*, p. 8.

15. Daemmrich, 'A Tale of Two Experts', p. 153.

16. Brynner and Stephens, *Dark Remedy*, p. 21.

17. Celgene Corporation, 'THALOMID® (thalidomide) Capsules', (Patient Information Form), Celgene.com website, http://celgene.com.au/download/ThalomidPI.pdf (accessed 1 February 2011).

18. Knightley et al., *Suffer the Children*, pp. 72–8; Daemmrich 'A Tale of Two Experts', p. 153.

19. Daemmrich, 'A Tale of Two Experts'; Knightley et al., *Suffer the Children*, p. 109.

20. Nick McKenzie and Richard Baker (2012) 'The 50-year Global Cover-up', *The Age*, 26 July, http://www.theage.com.au/national/the-50year-global-coverup-20120725-22r5c.html (accessed 1 July 2013).

21. Each believed himself to have been the first.

22. S. G. Stolberg (1998) 'Their Devil's Advocates', *New York Times Magazine*, 25 January, 20–5, p. 23.

23. J. G. Gordon and P. M. Goggin (2003) 'Thalidomide and its Derivatives: Emerging from the Wilderness', *Postgraduate Medical Journal*, 79, 127–32, p. 130.

24. Knightley et al., *Suffer the Children*, p. 121; Stolberg, 'Their Devil's Advocates', p. 23.

25. See also: Teo et al., 'Thalidomide as a Novel Therapeutic Agent', p. 107.

26. Daemmrich ,'A Tale of Two Experts', p. 138.

27. J. Hope (2006) 'Thalidomide Given to Young Cancer Victims', *Daily Mail*, 30 May, p. 24.

28. Knightley et al., *Suffer the Children*, p. 2.

29. National Institutes of Health, DES Research Update 1999: Current Knowledge, Future Directions. NIH (1999) 'National Institutes of Health Workshop. DES Research Update: Current Knowledge and Future Directions', 19–20 July, NIH publ. no. 00-4722.

30. Parents would try to shield their children from public exposure because of reactions that occurred when they took them out. Knightley et al., *Suffer the Children*, p. 118.

31. Stolberg, 'Their Devil's Advocates', p. 23.

32. G. Adams-Spink (2005) 'Thalidomide Gets Musical Treatment', *BBC News*, 18 October, http://news.bbc.co.uk/2/hi/entertainment/4338784.stm (accessed 19 December 2011).

33. P. Folb (1977) *The Thalidomide Disaster, and its Impact on Modern Medicine* (Cape Town: University of Cape Town), p. 6.

34. Anon. (2011) 'Thalidomide Victims Protest 50 Years On', 25 November, *The Local*, http://www.thelocal.de/national/20111125-39121.html (accessed 5 February 2012).

35. Folb, *Thalidomide Disaster*, p. 7.

36. H. Evans (2012) 'Thalidomide's Big Lie Overshadows Corporate Apology', *Reuters*, Online, 12 September.

37. Knightley et al., *Suffer the Children*, p. 46.

38. Knightley et al., *Suffer the Children*, pp. 79–80.

39. Knightley et al., *Suffer the Children*, p. 46.

40. Evans, 'Thalidomide's Big Lie Overshadows Corporate Apology'.

41. Stolberg 'Devil's Advocates', p. 23.

42. Folb, *Thalidomide Disaster*, p. 6.
43. A. Lowe (2011) 'Thalidomide Case Set to Be Heard in Victoria', *The Age*, 19 December (accessed online 8 February 2012); McKenzie and Baker, 'The 50-year Global Cover-up'.
44. A. Jack (2007) 'Aid Pledge to Thalidomide Victims', *MarketWatch*, 20 September 2007. http://www.marketwatch.com/story/aid-pledge-to-thalidomide-victims (accessed 5 February 2012).
45. Evans, 'Thalidomide's Big Lie Overshadows Corporate Apology'.
46. R. Collier (2009) 'Drug Development Cost Estimates Hard to Swallow', *Canadian Medical Association Journal*, 3 February, 180, 3, 279–80. R. B. Walter et al. (2010) 'Shortcomings in the Clinical Evaluation of New Drugs: Acute Myeloid Leukemia as Paradigm', *Blood*, 7 October, 116, 14, 2420–8. R. Speige, 'Thalidomide Gets a Second Chance', National Institutes of Health: Office of Science Education website, http://science-education.nih.gov/Home2.nsf/ Educational+Resources/Resource+Formats/ Online+Resources/+High+School/544E6D04B78B8E9E85256CCD0063E875 (accessed 1 January 2012).
47. Therapeutic Goods Administration (2000) 'Note for Guidance on Good Clinical Practice', Commonwealth Department of Health and Aged Care, http://www.tga.gov.au/pdf/euguide/ ich13595.pdf (accessed 4 January 2012). L. Rägo and B. Santoso, (2008) 'Drug Regulation: History, Present and Future', in C. J. van Boxtel, B. Santoso and I. R. Edwards (eds), *Drug Benefits and Risks: International Textbook of Clinical Pharmacology*, revised 2nd edn (Uppsala: IOS Press and Uppsala Monitoring Centre), pp. 65–77. See also http://www.ilep.org.uk/technical-advice/ilep-technical-bulletins/technical-bulletin-9/ ILEP *Federation of Autonomous Anti-leprosy Associations* (The International Federation of Anti-Leprosy Associations) (accessed 5 January 2013).
48. Folb, *Thalidomide Disaster*, p. 8.
49. Anon. (1984) 'Post-thalidomide Knee-jerk Reaction', *Australian Doctor Weekly*, 21 October, pp. 39–40.
50. P. Lachmann (2011) 'Thalidomide Is Still Casting Dark Shadows 50 Years On', *Daily Telegraph*, 22 November, http://www.telegraph.co.uk/science (accessed 8 February 2012).
51. S. Timmermans and V. Leiter (2000) 'The Redemption of Thalidomide: Standardising the Risk of Birth Defects', *Social Studies of Science*, 30, 1, 41–77, p. 55.
52. F. Teixeira, M. T. Hojyo, R. Arenas, M. E. Vega, R. Cortes, A. Ortiz and L. Dominguez (1994) 'Thalidomide: Can it Continue to Be Used?', *The Lancet*, 344, 8916, 196–7, p. 196; V. Pannikar (2003) 'The Return of Thalidomide: New Uses and Renewed Concerns', *Leprosy Review*, 74, 3, 286–8, p. 287; G. F. M. Pereira (2003) 'On Thalidomide and WHO Policies', *Leprosy Review*, 74, 3, 288–90, p. 289. B. Naafs (2003) 'The Return of Thalidomide: New Uses and Renewed Concerns – Reply', *Leprosy Review*, 74, 3, 294–5.

53. Teixeira et al., 'Thalidomide', p. 196.
54. Stolberg, 'Their Devil's Advocates', p. 23; Brynner and Stephens, *Dark Remedy*, p. 137.
55. S. Timmermans and V. Leiter (2000) 'The Redemption of Thalidomide: Standardising the Risk of Birth Defects', *Social Studies of Science*, 30, 1, 41–77, p. 47.
56. Food and Drug Administration Centre for Drug Evaluation and Research (1996) 'Summary Minutes of the Dermatologic and Ophthalmic Drugs Advisory Committee Meeting #44: Thalidomide Issues', http://www.fda.gov/ohrms/dockets/ac/96/minutes/ 3235m1.pdf (accessed 8 February 2012).
57. Clarke, 'Celgene CEO Mulls Succession'.
58. Celgene (2005–11) 'History', http://www.celgene.com/about-celgene/biopharmaceutical-company-about.aspx (accessed 1 February 2011).
59. Timmermans and Leiter, 'The Redemption of Thalidomide', p. 59; quote from Pannikar, 'The Return of Thalidomide', p. 287.
60. The subheading is used in a report on thalidomide: A. Saphir (1997) 'Jekyll and Hyde: A New License for Thalidomide?', *Journal of the National Cancer Institute*, 89, 20, 1480–1, p. 1481.
61. Stolberg, 'Their Devil's Advocates', p. 24.
62. US Food and Drug Administration (1999) 'Managing the Risks from Medical Product Use: Creating a Risk Management Framework: Appendix F: Examples of Risk Confrontation', http://www.fda.gov/Safety/SafetyofSpecificProducts/ucm180604.htm (accessed 1 January 2012).
63. Timmermans and Leiter, 'The Redemption of Thalidomide', pp. 47–8.
64. Cited in Timmermans and Leiter, 'The Redemption of Thalidomide', p. 59.
65. US Food and Drug Administration, 'Managing the Risks'.
66. Timmermans and Leiter, 'The Redemption of Thalidomide', pp. 48–9.
67. There has been ongoing debate about whether or not any so-called mutagenic effects can be passed across generations through DNA. The balance of evidence points to this not being the case and indeed the process of reintroduction of the drug relies on this. D. Smithells (1998) 'Does Thalidomide Cause Second Generation Birth Defects?', *Drug Safety*, 19, 5, 339–41.
68. Timmermans and Leiter, 'The Redemption of Thalidomide', p. 54.
69. Food and Drug Administration Centre for Drug Evaluation and Research (1996) 'Summary Minutes of the Dermatologic and Ophthalmic Drugs Advisory Committee Meeting #44: Thalidomide Issues', http://www.fda.gov/ohrms/dockets/ac/96/minutes/ 3235m1.pdf (accessed 8 February 2012).
70. Timmermans and Leiter, 'The Redemption of Thalidomide', p. 61.
71. Stolberg, 'Their Devil's Advocates', p. 24.
72. Stolberg, 'Their Devil's Advocates', p. 24.
73. Clarke, 'Celgene CEO Mulls Succession'.
74. A. Ault (1997) 'Thalidomide Comes Close to US approval', *The Lancet*, 350, 9081, p. 873.

75. Timmermans and Leiter, 'The Redemption of Thalidomide', p. 64.

76. Timmermans and Leiter, 'The Redemption of Thalidomide', p. 65.

77. Timmermans and Leiter, 'The Redemption of Thalidomide', p. 63.

78. A. Ault (1998) 'Thalidomide Makes a Return in US Healthcare', *The Lancet*, 352, 25 July, p. 298.

79. This is the argument of Timmermans and Leiter, 'The Redemption of Thalidomide'.

80. Annas and Elias, 'Thalidomide and the Titanic', p. 99.

81. 'The Problem with Thalidomide's New Incarnation', *Nature Biotechnology* (editorial), 16, August 1998, p. 695.

82. See, for example, the Thalidomide Association of Sweden website: http://www.thalidomide.org/web/letter-to-who/ (accessed 1 January 2012).

83. Stolberg, 'Their Devil's Advocates', p. 24.

84. C. E. Rosenberg (2006) 'Anticipated Consequences: Historians, History, and Health Policy', in R. A. Stevens, C. E. Rosenberg and L. R. Burns (eds), *History and Health Policy in the United States: Putting the Past Back In* (New Brunswick, NJ: Rutgers University Press) 13–31, p. 13.

85. Annas and Elias, 'Thalidomide and the Titanic'.

86. The conclusion is that of oncologist, Howard Fine. Saphir, 'Jekyll and Hyde', p. 1481.

87. See, for example, D. D. Edwards (1987) 'Thalidomide: Is There a Silver Lining?', *Science News*, 131, 13, 198; P. Mehta and M. Hussein (2003) 'Thalidomide as Anti-inflammatory Therapy for Multiple Myeloma', *Leukemia* 17, 2237–8. Conditions for which the drug has been considered include: chronic graft versus host disease (in transplant patients), rheumatoid arthritis, uremic pruritus and post-herpetic neuralgia. P. Calderon, M. Anzilotti and R. Phelps (1997) 'Thalidomide in Dermatology. New Indications for an Old Drug', *Journal of Dermatology*, 36, 12, 881–7, p. 881; T. Adler (1994) 'The Return of Thalidomide: A Shunned Compound Makes a Scientific Comeback', *Science News*, 146, 26–7, 424–5, p. 424; S. Squires (1989) '"Drug of Infamy" Makes a Comeback', *Washington Post*, 9 July, via Factiva.

88. T. Morrison (2011) 'Celgene Delivers Again: Top and Bottom Line Strong in Q2', *Bioworld*, 29 July, via Factiva.

89. 'Celgene Corp to Acquire Signal Pharmaceuticals for $196 Million', *The Pharma Letter*, 3 July 2000, http://www.thepharmaletter.com/file/274/celgene-corp-to-acquire-signal-pharmaceuticals-for-196-million.html (accessed 8 February 2012); M. Fraser, (2004) 'It's Back ...', *The Guardian*, 30 March, http://www.guardian.co.uk/society/2004/mar/30/ lifeandhealth. brazil (accessed 8 February 2012).

90. According to one report, 'Revlimid is Celgene's flagship product and key to its future growth. It had $2.5 billion in sales in 2010, making up the majority of Celgene's total revenue of $3.6 billion.' T. Gryta (2011) 'Celgene Discloses Justice Dept Probe into Drug Marketing', *Dow Jones Business News*, 1 March, via Factiva.

91. CQ Transcriptions, 'Celgene Corp at Canaccord Genuity Global Growth Conference – Final', 11 August 2011, *CQ FD Disclosure*, via Factiva.

92. http://www.revlimid.com/ (accessed 10 December 2011). The company's history may be found at: http://www.celgene.com/about-celgene/biopharmaceutical-company-about.aspx (accessed 11 December 2011).

93. M. Johns, D. Hochstedler, K. Lewis and J. Katz (2001) 'The Big Pitch – How Would You Conduct a PR Campaign for the New Thalidomide Drugs?', *PR Week*, 9 July, via Factiva.

94. Morrison, 'Celgene Delivers Again'.

95. J. Bennett (2010) 'Weekday Trader. A Great Bet in Biotech', *Barron's Online*, 13 May, via Factiva.

96. 'Celgene Receives FDA Warning Letter over Thalidomide Promotion', *The Pharma Letter*, 9 May 2000, "http://www.thepharmaletter.com/file/71774/celgenes-adverse-drug-reports-were-late-says-fda.html (accesed 8 Febuary 2012).

97. Gryta, 'Celgene Discloses Justice Dept Probe'.

98. 'Celgene's Adverse Drug Reports Were Late, Says FDA',*The Pharma Lette*r, 30 August 2004,"http://www.thepharmaletter.com/file/71774/celgenes-adverse-drug-reports-were-late-says-fda.html, via Factiva.

99. Gryta, 'Celgene Discloses Justice Dept Probe'.

100. L. O. Gostin (2011) 'The FDA, Preemption, and Public Safety', *Hastings Center Report*, 41, 5, 11–12, p. 11.

101. M. Herper (2011) 'Celgene Stock Falls on Worries about Secondary Cancers', *Forbes*, 5 May, "http://www.forbes.com/sites/matthewherper/2011/05/05/celgene-stock-falls-on-worries-about-secondary-cancers/"http://www.forbes.com/sites/matthewherper/2011/05/05/celgene-stock-falls-on-worries-about-secondary-cancers/ (accessed 8 February 2012). The possibility of increased metastasis from using thalidomide was raised as early as 1996: R. J. Powell (1996) 'New Roles for Thalidomide', *British Medical Journal*, 313, 7054, 377.

102. B. McIsaac and K. Crain (2011) 'Supreme Court of Canada Confirms Patented Medicine Prices Review Board Interpretation of the Term "Sold in any Market in Canada" and Underlines the Consumer Protection Purposes of the Board's Role', *Mondaq*, 24 January, "http://www.mondaq.com/canada/article.asp?articleid=121054"http://www.  mondaq.com/canada/article.asp?articleid=121054 (accessed 8 February 2012).

103. My thanks are due to Dr Jo Robertson for her advice on this section and the provision of online materials. I thank, too, Dr Ben Naafs for kindly providing me with background about these debates. His view as a specialist is that thalidomide is a 'drug of choice' in some forms of multi-drug therapy for ENL. Personal correspondence.

104. Pannikar, 'The Return of Thalidomide', p. 287; Pereira, 'On Thalidomide and WHO Policies', p. 289. Naafs, 'The Return of Thalidomide', pp. 294–5.

105. Powell, 'New Roles for Thalidomide', pp. 377–8.

106. Pannikar, 'The Return of Thalidomide', p. 287.
107. Pannikar, 'The Return of Thalidomide', p. 287.
108. Pereira, 'On Thalidomide and WHO Policies', pp. 288–9.
109. Pannikar's figure is cited from 'The Return of Thalidomide' p. 286; Pereira, 'On Thalidomide and WHO Policies', p. 289.
110. Naafs, 'The Return of Thalidomide', p. 295. See also B. Naafs (2006) 'Treatment of Leprosy: Science or Politics?', *Tropical Medicine and International Health*, 11, 3, 268–78, p. 274.
111. Lockwood and Bryceson, 'The Return of Thalidomide', p. 290; Naafs, 'The Return of Thalidomide', p. 295. Naafs' later article, 'Treatment of Leprosy: Science or Politics?', developed the case for thalidomide in the context of a critique of the WHO's proposed goal of elimination of leprosy, which has proven to be at once controversial, unsuccessful and possibly deleterious to people with Hansen's disease.
112. His preferred treatment choice in this instance is steroids, which his interlocutors note have their own side effects. Naafs, 'The Return of Thalidomide', p. 295.
113. Sinésio Talhari, MD, Leprosy Mailing List, 30 December 2003.
114. Around 30 other drugs have a similar risk profile to thalidomide. Annas and Elias, 'Thalidomide and the Titanic', p. 99.
115. Leprosy Mailing List, 9 November 2005, http://www.aifo.it/english/resources/ online/lml-archives/index.htm.
116. Leprosy Mailing List, 9 November 2005.
117. This message can no longer be traced on the site.
118. S. Krishnamurthi, Leprosy Mailing List, 30 December 2003.
119. Leprosy Mailing List, 30 December 2003.
120. Dr Pannikar retired in 2009 to help his local community.
121. Mention of 'politics' in two articles by B. Naafs seems to suggest something along these lines; however, it is not wholly clear what politics are referred to, if indeed only one issue is at stake. Naafs, 'The Return of Thalidomide', pp. 294–5; Naafs, "Treatment of Leprosy: Science or Politics?', pp. 268–78.
122. Pereira, 'On Thalidomide and WHO Policies', p. 289.
123. D. N. J. Lockwood, S. L. Walker and M. F. R. Waters (2007) 'The Role of Thalidomide in the Management of *erythema nodosum leprosum*', *Leprosy Review*, 78, 3, 197–215, p. 207.
124. One author of the article below, for example, disclosed appropriately that she was a paid adviser to Pharmion during their application to the European Medicines Agency to have thalidomide licensed for use in the treatment of erythema nodosum leprosum. Lockwood et al. 'The Role of Thalidomide', p. 212.
125. Lockwood et al. 'The Role of Thalidomide', p. 198.
126. C. Wiesemann (2006) 'The Contribution of Medical History to Medical Ethics: The Case of Brain Death', in C. Rehmann-Sutter, M. Düwell and D. Mieth (eds) *Bioethics in Cultural Contexts: Reflections on Methods and Finitude* (Dordrecht: Springer), 187–96, p. 194.

# Condensed Bioethics Research Library Classification Scheme, Kennedy Institute of Ethics Library, Georgetown University, Washington DC

**1 Ethics**
1.1 Philosophical Ethics
1.2 Religious Ethics
1.3 Applied and Professional Ethics

**2 Bioethics**
2.1 General
2.2 History of Health Ethics/Bioethics
2.3 Education/Programs
2.4 Commissions/Councils

**3 Philosophy of Biology**
3.1 General
3.2 Evolution and Creation

**4 Philosophies of Medicine and Health**
4.1 Theory and Practice of the Health Professions
4.2 Concept of Health
4.3 Concept of Mental Health
4.4 Quality/Value of Life/Personhood
4.5 Enhancement

**5 Science/Technology and Society**
5.1 General
5.2 Technology/Risk Assessment
5.3 Social Control of Science/Technology
5.4 Nanotechnology

## 13 Population
13.1 General
13.2 Population Growth
13.3 Population Policy

## 14 Reproduction/Reproductive Technologies
14.1 General
14.2 Artificial Insemination and Surrogacy
14.3 Sex Predetermination/Selection
14.4 In Vitro Fertilization and Embryo Transfer
14.5 Cloning
14.6 Cryobanking of Sperm, Ova, or Embryos

## 15 Genetics, Molecular Biology and Microbiology
15.1 General
15.2 Genetic Counseling/Prenatal Diagnosis
15.3 Genetic Screening/Testing
15.4 Gene Therapy/Transfer
15.5 Eugenics
15.6 Behavioral Genetics
15.7 Biohazards of Genetic Research
15.8 Genetic Patents
15.9 Sociobiology
15.10 Genome Mapping
15.11 Genetics and Human Ancestry

## 16 Environmental Quality
16.1 General
16.2 Nuclear Power/Radiation
16.3 Occupational Health

## 17 The Neurosciences and Mental Health Therapies
17.1 General
17.2 Psychotherapy
17.3 Behavior Modification
17.4 Psychopharmacology
17.5 Electrical Stimulation of the Brain
17.6 Psychosurgery
17.7 Involuntary Civil Commitment
17.8 Right of the Institutionalized to Treatment

## 18 Human Experimentation
18.1 General
18.2 Policy Guidelines/Inst. Review Boards
18.3 Informed Consent
18.4 Behavioral Research
18.5 Research on Special Populations
18.6 Social Control of Human Experimentation
18.7 Stem Cell Research

## 19 Artificial and Transplanted Organs/Tissues
19.1 General
19.2 Hearts
19.3 Kidneys
19.4 Blood
19.5 Donation/Procurement of Organs/Tissues
19.6 Allocation of Organs/Tissues

## 20 Death and Dying
20.1 General
20.2 Definition/Determination of Death
20.3 Attitudes Toward Death
20.4 Care of the Dying Patient
20.5 Prolongation of Life and Euthanasia
20.6 Capital Punishment
20.7 Suicide/Assisted Suicide

## 21 International/Political Dimensions of Biology and Medicine
21.1 General
21.2 War
21.3 Chemical and Biological Weapons
21.4 Torture and Genocide
21.5 Prisoners and Detainees
21.6 International Migration of Health Professionals
21.7 Cultural Pluralism

## 22 Animal Welfare
22.1 General
22.2 Animal Experimentation
22.3 Animal Production

# Glossary

**Advance directive:** Document stating the medical treatment preferences of a person in the event that subsequent impairment renders the person unable to express their views on medical treatment; usually associated with granting permission for removal of life support.

**Aktion T4:** Programme named for the address in Berlin (Tiergartenstrasse 4) from which the Nazi government administered a program of mass killing of children and adults with disability, between 1939 and 1941.

**Alienism:** nineteenth-century word for psychiatry.

**Amniocentesis:** test of amniotic fluid during pregnancy to detect chromosomal or genetic conditions affecting a developing foetus.

**Analogy:** a perceived similarity between two things (usually the course of two kinds of events). In bioethics, the use of historical analogy, notably in references to Nazi medicine or historical eugenics, is one mode through which the ethics of innovations are discussed.

**Applied ethics:** branch of academic philosophy, increasingly in evidence since the 1960s, which applies philosophical reasoning to real-world ethical issues.

**ARTs:** assisted reproductive technologies, formerly referred to as NRTs (new reproductive technologies).

**Autonomy:** Independent agency. In bioethics, autonomy is a principle based on the view of Immanuel Kant (1724–1804) that a rational individual will know wrong from right; it is one of the most cited principles underpinning the formulation of clinical and research ethics.

**Belmont Report:** Influential 1979 document commissioned by the United States Department of Health, Education, and Welfare to set out

'Ethical Principles and Guidelines for the Protection of Human Subjects of Research'.

**Bioethics:** Term coined c. 1970 to identify a branch of applied ethics concerned with medicine and the biological sciences; also general term for the fields in which these matters are addressed, such as law, health policy and regulation, clinical practice and the ethical oversight of experimentation.

**Biological determinism:** A view that human beings' behaviour and fate are governed by purely biological mechanisms, to which ideas and emotions are by implication subordinated.

**Bio-politics and bio-power:** terms used by scholars influenced by Michel Foucault (1926–1984), who argued that power is maintained in modern societies through diverse systems of control of the human body and mind among notionally free citizens. Bio-politics overlaps with bioethics, considering for example developments such as Synthetic Biology and experimental ethics. Influential thinkers in the field include Nikolas Rose and Paul Rabinow and its principal journal is BioSocieties.

**Casuistry:** ethical argumentation based on appraisal of all factors deemed relevant to a particular situation. In bioethics, casuistry is distinguished from the major philosophical schools of deontology and consequentialism because its ethical resolutions are reliant on unique empirical knowledge. Historically, it is an approach to ethics associated with the Jesuit order.

**Chromosome:** found within cells, an organized coil of DNA bound around proteins. In humans, each cell has 23 pairs of chromosomes.

**CIA (Central Intelligence Agency):** United States Government agency which deals with national security intelligence operations.

**CIOMS:** Council of International Organizations of Medical Sciences, a UNESCO/WHO body which produces guidelines for governments on the subject of medical research ethics. (www.cioms.ch)

**CIRCARE:** (Citizens for Responsible Care and Research): independent watchdog group, formed in 1996, to monitor research on human subjects.

**Clinician:** a person, usually with some form of medical training, directly involved in the treatment of patients.

**Cloning (embryonic):** The process of using laboratory techniques to create an embryo genetically identical to one of the 'parents'. Cloning of animals has led to live births but the technique has not yet been perfected for human beings. Ethical debate surrounds the use of cloned embryos for research, during which they are destroyed.

**Cold Spring Harbor (Long Island, USA):** location of an eponymous genetics research centre founded in 1904 by zoologist Charles Davenport (1866–1944). Associated with the history of eugenics through its research on family networks, currently a major genetic research centre. (www.csh.edu)

**Cold War:** Period between 1945 and 1989 dominated by global blocs representing communism (centred on the USSR and People's Republic of China) and capitalism (centred on the USA). Significant for bioethics history because of high levels of government funding in relation to research into: the physical effects of radiation; chemical and other non-traditional weapons testing; and the testing of substances and procedures related to mind control and hence intelligence security.

**Communitarianism:** Branch of philosophy which emphasises the importance of the community in reaching normative conclusions.

**Consequentialism:** School of moral philosophy which emphasises that the rightness or wrongness of an action can be judged by the ends it will lead to. Associated with the utilitarian philosophy of Jeremy Bentham (1748–1832) and John Stuart Mill (1806–1873); also referred to as teleological ethics, contrasted with deontological ethics.

**Contingent:** Dependent on circumstance.

**Dalkon Shield:** Intra-uterine contraceptive device (IUD) widely used in the 1970s which became subject to legal class action as a result of 17 deaths and numerous injuries to users.

**Declaration of Helsinki:** World Medical Association 'statement of ethical principles to provide guidance to physicians and other participants in medical research involving human subjects'. First promulgated in 1964 and occasionally updated, the current version is dated 2008.

**Deontology:** In moral philosophy, duty-based theory associated with Immanuel Kant (1724–1804) which maintains that moral duties exist which cannot be deviated from, regardless of circumstances.

**DES (Diethylstilboestrol):** pharmaceutical prescribed in the mid-twentieth century for the prevention of miscarriage; led to the birth of children with malformed genitalia and to a significant number of daughters of women affected by a rare form of cancer, and to other effects on health.

**DNA (deoxyribonucleic acid):** molecule found in chromosomes which transmits genetic information.

**ECT (electro-convulsive therapy):** Referred to colloquially as 'shock treatment', psychiatric intervention entailing delivery of electric currents via the patient's brain. Historically often highly injurious, today used in moderated form for treatment of some forms of mental illness.

**Empiricism:** Philosophical tradition which holds that what can be known is what can be perceived by the senses; generally associated with the British tradition of John Locke (1632–1704), George Berkeley (1685–1753) and David Hume (1711–1776). Empiricism is also historically the starting point of the social sciences, in which the goal is to generate new data as evidence, before making a statement about the nature of a human society.

**Endocrinology:** Study of and medical specialism in the role and operations of hormones in the body.

**Enlightenment (The):** Seventeenth- and eighteenth-century European intellectual movement associated with repudiation of religious worldview and emphasis on the power of human reason.

**Epidemiology:** study of the spread and prevalence of disease.

**Ethical pluralism:** View of ethics as non-universal and based on diverse but often equally valid moral starting points.

**Ethicist:** Specialist in the philosophy of moral conduct.

**Ethics:** Variously: the agreed-upon internal behavioural code of a profession or group; a general term for rules of moral conduct; a branch of academic moral philosophy concerned with moral conduct.

**Eugenics:** Influential late nineteenth- to mid-twentieth-century ideology which grew out of social and scientific activism directed to the control of human heredity; aimed to select and control human reproduction.

**Euthanasia:** From Greek roots meaning 'good' and 'death', mercy killing or killing of a person at their own request, usually as a consequence of the person's suffering, using non-violent methods (such as drugs).

**FDA (Food and Drug Administration):** United States government authority founded in 1927 charged with ensuring quality and safety of food, drugs, medical devices and techniques.

**Feminism:** series of political movements and a political and scholarly perspective with diverse ameliorative social goals based on the view that women have been historically and are in the present day subject to prejudicial social treatment.

**Gamete:** In human beings, a sperm or ovum.

**Gene:** name given by Danish biologist Wilhelm Johannsen (1857–1927) in 1909 to refer to the Mendelian unit of hereditable characteristics. Genes are found in all living cells, are composed of deoxyribonucleic acid, and are located on chromosomes.

**Genetic exceptionalism:** Term (often used pejoratively) to describe a view of genetic techniques and knowledge as requiring coverage in special laws and regulations (e.g. in genetic privacy laws).

**Genetics:** the science of genes.

**Genomics:** study of the genetic makeup of entire organisms (as distinct from the study of single genes).

**Genetic Privacy:** concept developed in light of increasing genetic knowledge which reflects the view that the predictive capacities of genetic technology can change the meaning of traditional forms of privacy (e.g. in relation to prejudicial employment and healthcare policies), and thus require new legislation.

**Germ-line or germinal therapy:** Potential use of IVF and genetic technology to change permanently the genome of an embryo, with follow-through of the change to later generations.

**Germ plasm:** Term coined by August Weismann (1834–1914) which posited the existence of a substance within the body with the capacity to shape hereditary characteristics.

**Gynaecology (also gynecology):** medical specialism focused on female health and specifically the female reproductive system. Usually paired with obstetrics (the medical specialism relating to birth).

**Hastings Center:** first major bioethics centre and think tank, founded in 1969; currently situated at Garrison, New York; home of the influential journals *Hastings Center Report* and *IRB: Ethics & Human Research.*

**Helsinki Declaration:** see Declaration of Helsinki

**Hereditarianism:** idea which promotes the control of human biological heredity as the basis for the creation of good people and the good society.

**HFEA:** Human Fertility and Embryology Authority. Statutory authority established in the United Kingdom in 1991, building on the recommendation of the 1984 *Warnock Report*, to monitor and provide guidelines on the conduct of IVF and related interventions, such as embryo experimentation.

**Historicism:** a view of history that gives pre-eminence to the unique configuration of factors which shape a historical moment or event. In bioethics, a historicist view can be contrasted to the use of historical analogy.

**Historicity:** unique historical characteristics of a particular event.

**History and philosophy of science (HPS):** academic discipline which brings together history of science and philosophy of science. Along with newer fields of sociology of science and science and technology studies (STS), HPS is a discipline which studies medicine and bioethics in their social and historical contexts.

**Human Genome Project:** international publicly funded genetic research collaboration which from 1989 to 2003 mapped the human genome, providing basic genetic knowledge available for further research via data in the public domain.

**Human Genome Diversity Project:** program based at Stanford University's Morrison Institute for Population and Resource Studies which collects and preserves unique genetic cell-lines from diverse human populations worldwide. Distinct from the Human Genome Project the HGDP has been subject to criticism in relation to the ethics of collecting biological samples from populations whose health needs it is not directly serving.

*In vitro*: (Lat.) in glass.

*In utero*: (Lat.) in a woman's uterus.

*In vivo*: (Lat.) in a living being.

**IVF** (*in vitro* fertilization): Fertilization of an ovum by a sperm, carried out in a laboratory environment.

**Kennedy Institute of Ethics:** Major US bioethics research/training centre and library located at Georgetown University, Washington, DC.

**Lebensborn:** Lit. 'wellspring of life'. Nazi 'baby-farming' programme for the creation of children born to eugenically approved women and men who were not married couples.

**Liberal feminism:** branch of feminism which privileges an individual woman's autonomous choice over collectivity of women as a group.

**Liberalism:** eighteenth- and nineteenth-century philosophy, which positioned the individual, as opposed to the state, at the heart of all political decision-making; associated with philosophy of John Stuart Mill (1806–1873)

**Medical autonomy:** Unwritten doctrine of medical profession which, in the context of bioethics, maintains members of the profession are those best able, individually and collectively, to judge individual clinical decisions and the wider profession's ethics.

**Mendelian genetics:** Principles of heredity based on the botanical research of Austrian scientist Gregor Mendel (1822–1884) which established patterns of variation in genetic characteristics as they occurred across multiple generations.

**Metaethics:** branch of philosophical ethics concerned with applying reason to moral issues; influential in mid-twentieth century and later contrasted to fields of applied ethics, such as bioethics.

**Metaphor:** term used to convey a sense of the nature of a thing by reference to another not literally related to it.

**Nanoethics:** Ethics of nanotechnology.

**Negative eugenics:** policy of directing human genetic capacities through the use of restrictive, destructive or prejudicial policies.

**Neoliberalism:** Post 1980s political shift in the democratic world which reduced emphasis on government regulation and service provision in favour of policies privileging individual choice and freedom of economic action.

**Neonate:** a newborn

**Neuroethics:** Field which considers the ethical implications of the neurosciences (which might, for example, assist in the development of undetectable advertising techniques or neurologically targeted bioweapons).

**NTD (neural tube defect):** One of several congenital medical conditions which affect development of a foetus's spine and/or brain *in utero*, such as anencephaly (no brain); hydrocephalus (fluid on the brain); spina bifida (a divided spine).

**Nuremberg Code:** Code issued in 1947 as part of the Nuremberg War Crimes trial verdict in relation to trials of Nazi medical and health workers. The ten-point Code emphasised principally the need for freely given and informed consent to participation as a subject in medical experimentation.

**Obstetrics:** Medical specialism relating to birth, usually paired with **gynaecology,** specialism in women's (particularly reproductive) health.

**Opt-in/opt-out, ethics of:** field of discussion in bioethics as to whether there is a duty to take part in medical procedures or research, e.g., whether organ donation should be expected from suitable donors who have not authorised donation in advance, or whether public health research can be carried out on health data for the use of which patients have not provided consent.

**Organicist metaphor:** Influential nineteenth-century view of the social world as part of a single biological organism. Historically not a metaphor at all, this view was understood as a reality.

**Paternalism:** belief of a person or group that they know what is best for another person or group.

**Pathology:** an illness or the study of illness.

**PGD:** pre-implantation genetic diagnosis; technique used prior to implantation of embryos following IVF and laboratory analysis.

**Pharmacogenetics:** Research leading to the creation of pharmaceutical products tailored to individual genetic profiles.

**Phrenology:** nineteenth-century science which posited that human attributes, moral and physical, could be 'read' through the topography of the skull. Eventually ridiculed for its popular form as the study of bumps on the head, its central tenet that 'the brain is the organ of the mind' remains influential for modern neurosciences and neuropsychology.

**Physician-assisted suicide:** Death following provision by a doctor of the means for a patient to end their own life.

**Porton Down:** UK establishment associated with chemical warfare research.

**Positive eugenics:** A form of eugenic thinking which argues for optimising human genetic capacities without the use of restrictive, destructive or prejudicial policies.

**Presentism:** Assumption that the views held in the present day are always the most advanced. In bioethics, presentism is reflected in the idea that the present is an ethically privileged moment because it contains all previously garnered ethical wisdom.

**Principlism:** pejorative term coined by philosophers K. Danner Clouser and Bernard Gert in to denote reliance on bioethical principles as a means to determine complex ethical scenarios.

**Psychiatry:** Medical study of mental illness.

**Psychology:** non-medical study of behaviour and mentality.

**Psychosurgery:** Use of surgical techniques on the brain (including lobotomy/leucotomy) to alter behaviour. Widely repudiated in the 1970s and made illegal in some jurisdictions, it is still used minimally, for example, in relation to obsessive-compulsive disorders.

**Reprogenetics:** neologism for modern reproductive genetics coined by molecular biologist Lee Silver to reinforce the view that ARTs should not be identified with historical eugenics.

**Roe v Wade (1973):** US Supreme Court decision which positioned abortion as subject to laws of privacy, curbing US states' restrictions on first-trimester terminations.

**Secularism:** Belief that non-religious values are the best foundation of a social order. In particular, a secularist view would hold that church and state should not intersect.

**'Slippery slope' argument:** Claim that one set of social changes bears the seeds of future developments which will inevitably be deleterious.

**Social history of medicine:** Branch of history research which investigates medicine in its social context (as distinct from medical history written from the perspective of the medical profession.)

**Social sciences:** academic disciplines which use data-gathering and hypothesis-testing techniques identified with the natural sciences, in order to study human societies. In bioethics, they contribute empirical evidence intended to give insights to contextualise and thereby improve ethical decision-making.

**Somatic gene therapy:** the use of genes in non-reproductive genetic treatments of living patients. (Distinguished from 'germ-line' therapy.)

**Stem cell:** Cell derived either from a human tissue source (adult stem cells) or from a laboratory-created human embryo (embryonic) with the capacity to be cultured for potential somatic gene therapy.

**Superovulation:** use of fertility drugs to create more than the usual one ovum in a woman's monthly reproductive cycle.

**Surrogacy:** lit. 'substitution'. Practice in reproductive medicine and at law in which a woman (the 'surrogate') gives birth to a child whom she agrees in advance to relinquish to (usually) a couple, who will be registered as the child's legal parents. Can entail reproductive techniques ranging from sperm donation to IVF in which gametes of the male and female 'genetic parents' are used.

**Thalidomide:** laboratory-created pharmaceutical the use of which led to many thousands of severe birth defects, particularly in the 1950s and early 1960s.

**Theology:** the study and interpretation of dicta attributed to a divine entity, usually said to have been revealed in sacred texts; the study of religious belief from within a specific tradition.

**Therapeutic cloning:** Potential use of cloned embryonic stem cells to create genetically identical cell lines for therapeutic use (e.g., to regenerate tissue or other cells) by the patient whose own cells have gone into the creation the embryo.

**Trisomy 21:** chromosomal disorder formerly known as 'mongolism' and later Down Syndrome. Significance in bioethics as the condition was one of a small number of disorders which early in the history of prenatal testing could be detected during pregnancy.

**Tuskegee:** Town in Macon County, Alabama, near to which the US Public Health Service carried out a large study of the progression of untreated syphilis in around 400 affected African-American men, between 1932 and 1972. The men did not consent to the study and many were untreated when effective medicine became available. Regarded as a low point of harmful medical research in the USA and of particular importance to the attitudes of African-American people to research involvement.

**Ultrasound (echography):** use of sonic signals sent into the human body to enable visualisation of the internal organs.

**Utilitarianism:** In philosophy, a school of thought which privileges the 'greatest good theory', associated with Jeremy Bentham (1748–1832) and John Stuart Mill (1806–1873); often referred to as 'consequentialism' and sometimes positioned in contrast to deontology.

***Warnock Report*:** Report named for its author, philosopher Baroness Mary Warnock, who chaired a UK committee from 1982 to 1984, to investigate terms under which ARTs and embryo experimentation might be carried out. The report formed the basis of the *Human Fertilisation and Embryology Act* (1990), which created the Human Fertilisation and Embryology Authority (1991-present).

**Willowbrook State School:** Institution on Staten Island, New York, for children with intellectual impairment (closed in 1987); in bioethics, known as the site of a controversial series of hepatitis experiments conducted by Dr Saul Krugman (1911–1995) between the mid-1950s and early 1970s.

**Zygote:** early fertilised human ovum, prior to the commencement of cell division.

# Index

*Note*: page references in *italics* are to subjects in the endnotes.

226